THE SILENT HOLOCAUST

Recent Titles in
Contributions to the Study of World History

The Silent Holocaust
ROMANIA AND ITS JEWS

I. C. BUTNARU

FOREWORD BY

Elie Wiesel

CONTRIBUTIONS TO THE STUDY OF WORLD HISTORY,
NUMBER 31

Greenwood Press
NEW YORK • WESTPORT, CONNECTICUT • LONDON

Library of Congress Cataloging-in-Publication Data

Butnaru, I. C.
 The silent Holocaust : Romania and its Jews / I.C. Butnaru ;
foreword by Elie Wiesel.
 p. cm. — (Contributions to the study of world history, ISSN
0885-9159 ; no. 31)
 Includes bibliographical references and index.
 ISBN 0–313–27985–3 (alk. paper)
 1. Holocaust, Jewish (1939–1945)—Romania. 2. Jews—Romania—
Persecutions. 3. Antisemitism—Romania. 4. Romania—Ethnic
relations. I. Title. II. Series.
DS135.R7B78 1992
940.53'18'09498—dc20   91–21181

British Library Cataloguing in Publication Data is available.

An earlier version of this book was printed in Israel in the Romanian language, under
the title *Holocaustul Uitat*

Library of Congress Catalog Card Number: 91–21181
ISBN: 0–313–27985–3
ISSN 0885–9159

First published in 1992

Greenwood Press, 88 Post Road West, Westport, CT 06881
An imprint of Greenwood Publishing Group, Inc.

Printed in the United States of America

The paper used in this book complies with the
Permanent Paper Standard issued by the National
Information Standards Organization (Z39.48–1984).

10 9 8 7 6 5 4 3 2 1

Copyright acknowledgment

The photographs and map were selected from the collection of the Center for
Romanian Jewry at Hebrew University in Jerusalem; Yad Vashem; *The Black Book* by
Matatias Carp, vols. 1–3; and other sources.

To my parents, Marc and Anna Butnaru

If someone is attributing all the misfortunes of his country, or part of them, to the presence of the Jews in his community, and he is suggesting to remedy this state of affairs by depriving the Jews of their rights or removing them from certain economic and social positions or banishing them from the country, or exterminating all of them, one can say that his opinions are anti-Semitic.

Jean-Paul Sartre, *Réflexions sur la question juive*

Contents

Photo essay follows chapter 3

Foreword

The writer who has agreed to preface this disturbing reminder is a son of the Jewish people. He was born in Romania. The Carpathian mountains filled my childhood with fear and excitement; in their shadow I dreamed of adventure. Their presence can still be felt in most of my work. Though Yiddish was my mother tongue and "Lashon kodesh" the language of my prayers, Romanian was the vehicle I used to penetrate the outside world. I sang its songs, tried to memorize its grammar and saw in its vocabulary, as in all others, an enchanted window to culture and civilization.

Thus it is with a true sense of nostalgic melancholy that I look back at my childhood in Romania. Naturally, it used to be disrupted by occasional incidents. Jewish children were not spared by antisemites. The word "Zhidan" (Kike)—that sounded like a curse—was not limited to the fanatic mobs; it was shouted in the street, whispered in the train, heard in the street, in city-parks, in government offices and in school courtyards, too. Christian children followed the example of their elders and insulted and attacked Jewish children. And I wasn't even surprised. I felt: that's how things are, that's how they have been for centuries; why should they stop now.

They didn't. Still, Jews fared better in Romania than in what later became Hungary. Hungary's Fascist government handed over its Jews to Eichmann; Romania's didn't. But it did send many of them to Transnistria where they lived and died in terror and isolation.

How can a Jew, a Romanian-born Jew think of that period and not feel overcome by sadness?

And by anger?

The man who led the Romanian government then is now celebrated as a Romanian heroic figure in some circles here. The Senate has stood up and observed a moment of silence to honor his memory. And no one raised his voice in protest. What puzzles and pains us even more is the realization that this is only an indication of the situation in general. We read antisemitic articles in publications, of anti-Jewish statements by known personalities or obscure persons, we hear of an atmosphere of threat and peril surrounding the remnant of the Jewish community in Romania. Taken from cheap and vulgar antisemitic pamphlets of the thirties and early forties, offensive, obscene, false and absurd accusations are being levelled at Jews, accusing them of being responsible for all that is wrong under the sun. Some are vicious and ugly and stupid to boot: do the antisemites in your midst really hope to convince any decent person that Jews established concentration camps and organized a genocide in Romania—or anywhere else? Their lies constitute an insult to human intelligence!

I confess I do not understand: have these antisemites no shame? How dare they, fifty years after the massacre in Iasi, summon yesteryear's evil demons and awaken them to renewed lust for hatred, persecution and humiliation? Don't they know what antisemitism means to its victims? Articles that were printed in "Romania Mare" constitute an open appeal to murder, slaughter and pogroms. Don't the editors and publishers know what such propaganda can do? The harm it does to the Romanian people as such? Haven't they learned an essential lesson from history, both ancient and contemporary, namely that hatred also destroys the hater and harms those who do nothing to stop and disarm him? Hate is contagious: it is a cancerous cell that devours one cell after the other, one group after the other, and ends up by invading the whole organism. Those who hate Jews will later hate others, those who hate Jews will eventually hate everybody, and will unavoidably end up hating themselves.

There is no evil more dangerous to a society than hate. It distorts the image man has of himself and of his place in history; it makes the person morally ill just as others are mentally ill. Values are undermined by hate. Ideas lose their loftiness and ideals their humanity. The other is seen by the hater as an intruder, not as an ally, a friend or a brother. The other arouses suspicion, envy, jealousy, bitterness, instead of sympathy and compassion. Hate negates solidarity. It turns truth into falsehood, beauty into ugliness. There is, there can be no beauty in hate. Hate is the enemy of beauty as it is of truth. Hate is the enemy of whatever lifts up the human condition and is the ally of whatever drags it down to the basest and vilest instincts of man. But the hater is also his own enemy:

hate destroys the hater as well as the hated. Antisemitism imperils the Jews but also poses a threat to those who condone it.

Romania's position today in the international community is visibly not the best. Not in the political spheres, and surely not in the intellectual ones. Whether justified or not, there is distrust toward what is happening now in Romania. All I, a Romanian-born Jew who lives and teaches in the United States, a Jew who loves Israel with his heart and soul, can say is that whatever is happening to the Romanian Jewish community is being observed in the major capitals of the planet. Every civilized government is watching Bucharest with sorrow, anguish and outrage. Unless its leaders put an immediate end to this vicious, ugly and perilous antisemitic press-campaign, unless they place the fanatic hate-mongers outside the accepted norms of society, Romania runs the risk of being isolated and condemned by the international community as few others have been. On the other hand, they could vanquish all distrust abroad by mobilizing their creative energies to denounce and rend harmless the racist, antisemitic hate-mongers in their midst.

The best and noblest way of achieving this is to remain faithful to memory. I hope Romanians will open its gates. And allow yourselves to be penetrated by its dazzling truth: it has remained concealed too long. What do Romanian textbooks say about prewar antisemitism? What do they say about Antonescu? What do they say about the ghetto of Moghilev? What do they say about the murderous pogroms in Bucharest and Iasi? Remember: when memory is muted, truth is the victim. When the past is silenced, the future is jeopardized. When history is falsified, humanity is impoverished.

Remember the past and Romanians will benefit from its lessons.

Remember the harm fanaticism could do—and did—and they will discover the infinite possibilities of tolerance, understanding and intellectual honesty.

The author of this preface defines himself as a son of an ancient people whose quest for justice is as old as its memory. And since he was born in Romania, he uses this occasion to plead with Romanians: help him speak of the moral geography of his childhood, somewhere in the Carpathians, with fondness.

Not with shame.

Elie Wiesel

Preface

The customs officer handed over to me a greenish plastic card, and smilingly said, "Welcome! You are now a permanent resident. Good luck!" Suddenly I felt lost in the crowd at Kennedy Airport, but somebody who guided us kindly showed the direction. In this way, I started one of the most incredible journeys of my life: to discover America.

I wrote in one of my books that the discovery of America was mistakenly credited to Christopher Columbus. He discovered just a certain territory. During the centuries, those who followed him, arriving on these shores, were bound to "discover," for themselves, their "own" America.

One of my discoveries occurred when I faced the shelves of books at Boston University Library for the first time. I discovered my own identity, and that I belonged to a human community which had disappeared almost entirely from my native country, Romania!

After World War II, life changed in this corner of Europe, too. Happiness depended upon the whims of new leaders, and everyone tried to find a niche for himself in this universe where words carried more weight than deeds. The silence, forgetfulness, and especially the lack of any information regarding the Holocaust period in Romania perverted the way of thinking. People detached themselves little by little from the old tree of Judaism which had helped them to survive during harsh times.

I was one of them. I do not confess this with a guilty feeling, because I did not know then that what I did was wrong. I never denied my roots, and I did not consider that Jewishness, in those specific circumstances, was a major problem of my generation. When the reality became more clear, the options were definite: to emigrate, or to stay and live on my knees!

I started to find out about the proportions of this silent and mostly unknown drama during my "journey" to discover America. Doing thorough research in the libraries, I first discovered myself: who I am, what my responsibilities are as a human being and as a writer. The world of the Holocaust in Europe stood in front of my eyes housed in hundreds of books, but something was missing: I couldn't find anything comprehensive about the Holocaust in Romania. Later on, I started to read scattered articles, studies and chapters about Romania published during those years in newspapers and magazines. At the beginning I read with great curiosity; after that with anger, bitterness, and bewilderment.

One question bothered me profoundly: How was it possible? I lived through the epoch, I was a part of it, but I knew almost nothing about it! It is well stated that the Holocaust was not an "accident" of history, but a consequence of it; the Holocaust was not a certain "happening"; it was premeditated, prepared, and carried out with abnegation and devotion.

We commonly associate the term "Holocaust" with Nuremberg and Kristallnacht, Hitler and Himmler, Eichmann and Mengele, the ghettos of Warsaw and Vilna, Auschwitz and Treblinka. Appearing as they do in countless books, plays, and films, these symbols of hatred penetrate our consciousness, memory, and history. Like Pearl Harbor, they live on in infamy.

But our memory of the Holocaust is selective, and our knowledge scant, especially in the case of Romania. Who has ever heard of Corneliu Zelea Codreanu or A. C. Cuza, Ion Antonescu or Mihai Antonescu, the Iron Guard Rebellion or the death trains of Iasi, the ghetto in Cernauti or the lagars (concentration camps) in Transnistria, Dr. W. Filderman or Chief Rabbi Dr. Alexandru Safran? The meager attention given to the destruction of Romanian Jewry is perplexing, considering the magnitude and malignity of that event.

In 1939, on the eve of World War II, the Jewish population of Greater Romania was almost eight hundred thousand, the third largest concentration of Jews in all of Europe. By 1944, an estimated three hundred fifty thousand remained. Most of those who disappeared had, in fact, been murdered. Some other tens of thousands of Ukrainian Jews died at the hands of Romanians in Odessa and throughout the whole Transnistrian area. In the quest for a "final solution" of the Jewish problem, Romania proved to be Hitler's most enthusiastic ally.

As the tide of war turned against the Germans, so did the fascist Romanian military dictator, Ion Antonescu. He reversed his decision to allow Adolf Eichmann to transport the remaining Romanian Jews to the more efficient extermination camps in Poland. Romania would later break its pact with Germany and join the Allies. Ever since, Romania has portrayed itself as a nation that rescued Jews and as a victim of

German fascism. This revisionist view has gone virtually unchallenged in Romania.

The events related to the Holocaust in Romania have not been unnoticed. Some people, due to their profession, happened to be in the right place at the right time. They became witnesses, and then chroniclers, sharing awful testimonies with their readers.

Robert St. John, an American journalist, was in Bucharest during the years 1940–1941. In four interesting chapters of his book *Foreign Correspondent*, published in 1957, he described the situation in Romania during this time. The last chapter is dedicated to the Legionary Rebellion. In those days and nights of dread and sorrow, he was caught between the fights on the streets, recording the events faithfully. When the shooting stopped and crime retreated in his lair, Robert St. John wrote: "That January morning in Bucharest . . . I made a silent promise that as long as I live I would devote at least part of my time and energy toward trying to atone to the Jews of the world who survived, for the sins committed on the edge of Bucharest, Romania, by men who knew better, for they had been born Christians, as I had been, and at least exposed to the Christian precepts of humility, gentility and non-violence. The worst part of it was that they had done it with prayers on their lips, and crosses and crucifixes in their hands or hanging around their necks."[1] After many years the American journalist had the urge not just to share with his readers what he witnessed, but to keep his testimony printed for the years to come.

Regarding such events carried out on different geographical meridians, two significant facts reveal not just a specific mentality, but a categorical position of Romanian officialdom regarding the Holocaust in Romania. In the June 19, 1986 issue of the newspaper *Scînteia Tineretului* (Youth Spark), Petre Ivancu published a poem titled "Song," dedicated to "The Fatherland." In an incomprehensible way he brought back in memory, with a perverted satisfaction and satanic hatred, the events when the Jews were gathered at the Bucharest abattoir, killed, and their bodies hung on hooks on the walls. Robert St. John wrote: "For sixteen years I have been trying to forget some of the little snapshots my mind took that day. But some things [one] never forgets. Perhaps it is well, even if it does interfere with sleep."[2]

The "poet," a young man when he wrote and published his "poem," was not even born when these tragic events occurred. He did not have any way of finding out the truth because nobody had written about it. Someone taught him (and many, many others) the story of hatred, and the poet was a good student. His poem was truly an incitement to pogrom, and this was, in fact, the purpose: this poem was published in the same year and month the survivors commemorated the pogroms of forty-five years earlier in Romania.

This was the way in which the newspaper commemorated and reported to the new generation of Romanian youth this abominable crime. In the same year, 1986, M. Pelin wrote an article titled "The Approximations of a Phrenetic Reporter." Criticizing Curzio Malaparte's work *Kaput*, Pelin stated his opinions with so-called objectivity, displaying in fact yet another face of the same rabid anti-Semitism. This article was without any doubt ordered by those in charge of the ideology of the Communist party's high command. This explains how Pelin had the opportunity to use the secret files of the dreadful Security (Siguranta) Police who were in charge of tailing the foreign correspondents in Romania during the war.

Following a specific byzantine way of interpreting and reporting the facts, Pelin in fact used Malaparte's book as a pretext to go beyond the written text, and to deny as "approximative" too, the relevant testimonies regarding the pogrom in Iasi. Contesting the trustworthy statements made by Malaparte, the Romanian journalist concluded, "It is proved that for the massacre in Iasi the Germans from the Todt Organization and SS who were then present in Iasi are responsible."[3]

Pelin tried hard to demonstrate that the high-ranking military assigned to Iasi and sentenced after the war as war criminals were, in fact, not guilty. In the same way, denigrating the veracity of Malaparte's assessments, he showed his "doubts" about the likelihood that General von Schobert, the commander of the Eleventh German Army in the region, had participated at the inauguration ceremony of a brothel for soldiers in Balti (Bessarabia). He had total amnesia about the "girls" from this "establishment"; all of them were Jewish girls from Romania, who after twenty days, being worn out and useless, were shot on the banks of the river Dniester and replaced by new ones.

It is not my intention thoroughly to analyze this article, which profaned the memory of so many victims, but to underline how Nicolae Ceauşescu's Romania "honoured" the Holocaust at its forty-fifth commemoration.

Poetry and literature, newspapers and magazines are inoculated with a new and virulent brand of anti-Semitism. These sentiments are openly expressed, loudly and sometimes quietly, politely, even subtle, but neverthless pernicious and powerful. All of the above are not new and unexpected. The old roots of Romanian anti-Semitism are still alive and vigorous, regardless of who is holding the reign of power. What is surprising however, is the violence with which it is expressed, the malignity of these ideas and the vocal or silent approval of a large spectrum of the Romanian society.

Taking advantage of democracy and liberty, hate starts to use the power of political forums, being spread by representatives of the people elected in free elections. In April 1991 the Romanian Parliament observed a moment of silence to commemorate solemnly the 45th anniversary of the execution of Ion Antonescu as a war criminal. "The homage was the most formal action taken to rekindle nationalist and anti-Semitic propaganda. No one opposed the parliamentary motion honoring Antonescu offered by an obscure member of the Assembly. Only a handful of deputies representing the ethnic Hungarian minority refused to join the tribute."[4]

During the whole period of time, before and after these commemorations, one can say that the majority of the media supported the motion and gave it a large representation in the pages of newspapers and magazines.

This book makes no accusations, no claims, only notations. It is a modest call to meditation, an urge towards understanding certain facts and events that unfolded over a large historical area. The permanency and, therefore, the continuity of the Jewish population in the Moldavian and Wallachian territories, and later in that of Romania, are presented with the intent of demonstrating that the Jews, as a people, have existed for centuries within this geographical perimeter, that they identified themselves with the life and aspirations of the native population to the extent that they were allowed.

The historical eras and the political and social implications that affected the life of the Jewish population in Romania are presented accurately. Anti-Semitism in Romania was not a product of the people, but of the leaders and the so-called intellectual elite. It was spread among the masses and adopted by them after lengthy education and propaganda.

Every author considers himself the exponent of the absolute truth, of the integral truth. The reader, with respect to this book, will be able to appreciate and compare. All those who broached the topic and tried to describe the era did so out of a desire not to let time and oblivion hide the facts. The intent, therefore is good and praiseworthy, to the degree to which their presentation is honest and objective.

One problem remains unsolved: naming the countless people who were killed, mocked at, robbed, humiliated. What could the selection criteria have been? The pain that gnawed at the flesh and soul belonged to everyone and everyone felt it individually. The blood that dripped, drop by drop, from the abused body was that of the slain, and nobody else's. Who has the right to ignore one individual while praising another? For the same reason, the author could not name all the killers, robbers, and oppressors, the multitude who, from political forums, schools, and universities, from pulpits, newspaper columns, streets, and wherever possible, raised hate to the rank of doctrine, while sanctioning crime as a heroic act. There are many of those, too, very many!

An impossible task!

Someday, maybe, there will be people with means and resources greater than those of the author of these pages who will bring to light, in detail, the entire procession of shadows which claim with dignity the modest right to be mentioned, as were the legions of those who despotically sent them into a world from which there is no return.

Eastern Europe has crumbled! A wind called "Freedom" dismantled the Berlin Wall, and everyone breathed a sigh of relief. People turned toward one another and hugged. They lived intensely in the present, but nobody could forget the past.

From the floor of the East German Parliament the new President apologized to the Jews for the sufferings brought to them by the Germans. A majestic monument to honour the victims of the Holocaust is to be erected in Berlin on the site of Hitler's bunker; in Warsaw, beside the actual Holocaust Memorial, another one will be built on the site of the former ghetto; in Budapest, in front of a great crowd, with the participation of the President and the Prime Minister, a monument dedicated to the Holocaust was inaugurated honouring the Jews from Northern Transylvania killed at Auschwitz.

In Romania such events did not occur. The Holocaust is still a "forbidden" topic. Thanks to the "new democracy" people can now freely light candles in memory of Corneliu Zelea Codreanu; others are working hard to rewrite history, depicting Ion Antonescu as a national hero.

Trying to be in step with other European countries, a memorial was dedicated to the Holocaust in Romania. "The facts widely known elsewere, were never acknowledged here: that a great number of Jewish men, women, and children were killed in pogroms of a brutality that sometimes shocked even the Germans, in pogroms carried out by the Romanian military and the police. Or, the Jews were worked, starved or frozen to death in concentration camps established and run by Romanians."[5]

The ceremony was attended by distinguished guests from abroad. Although the event had the blessing of the top brass of the government, they were absent from the inauguration. This memorial is undoubtedly a step forward on the road of repenting for some, and to helping others to look the truth straight in the face; but the place where it is erected is surprisingly odd. Everywhere in the world these kinds of memorials stand in public places, where everybody has the opportunity to see them and to pay tribute to the memory of the oppressed.

In Bucharest the memorial is hidden, and obviously protected behind the iron gates and fences of the Coral Temple. In Romania even a stone honoring so many victims cannot be found, not even at least a plaque on which somebody could read that this is a place where Jews have been hunted and brutally killed. It is a sense of silent, frozen time! It is like hearing old echoes called out to a new generation from a past which is not able to die.

It was felt plainly in Iasi during the commemoration of the massacre from June 1941. In the old and beautiful National Theatre from the Capital of Moldavia the survivors of the Holocaust from Iasi, Romanian representatives and foreign guests gathered to commemorate the event. But the shadow of the swastika was raised again! When professor Elie Wiesel delivered his speech, a well dressed, middle-aged woman started to shout: "Lies! It's a lie! The Jews didn't die (at Iasi). We won't allow Romanians to be insulted by foreigners in their own country."[6]

The obstinacy, the stubbornness with which the reality is rejected was shown once again in Iasi, 50 years since the pogrom where 8,000 Jews were killed.

But a voice of reason was heard calmly and powerfully. In an Address sent to the Romanian people on the occasion of the commemoration of the pogrom in Iasi and the inauguration of the memorial dedicated to the victims of the Holocaust at the Coral Temple in Bucharest, King Mihai I said:

Speaking in the name of my family, and I hope in the name of all Romanians I want to express again my regrets and profound sorrow for the sufferings imposed on our brothers and sisters thereupon of God, Romanian citizens of Jewish descent who perished during this conflagration. Although it is true that the majority of the Jews and gypsies who lived under Romanian administration during World War II were not deported to the extermination camps in fascist Germany, it is also true that many of them were deported to concentration camps where they died of hunger, lack of care, and persecutions. We could not forget the discrimination which was thrown upon our citizens of Jewish origin, in this awful period of time, the pogroms in some cities, and the destruction en masse of the Jewish community in Northern Transylvania. They will be forever our countrymen, our brothers and sisters, and in this solemn day I urge you: RE-MEMBER THEM![7]

It was, and still is, a paradox: the Romanian people had and have many commendable qualities, but during their entire history they have had to pay dearly for the sins and stupidities of the few.

Romanian fascism with its whole train of misdeeds, has not yet been brought before the judgment of history or the nation.

"The Ceauşescus are gone but their dirty secrets are scarcely known to the Romanian people. Their ex-Communist leaders only murmur disapproval as Antonescu's memory is feted; journalists who once touted

Ceausescu swell a chauvinist clamor for an ethnically pure Romania. Only the truth can liberate Romania from its totalitarian past. The task of telling it has scarcely begun."[8]

In Romania there are still alive about fifteen to twenty thousand Jews, most of them over sixty-five years of age. The question is, What happened to those almost eight-hundred-thousand Jews who lived in Romania fifty years ago?

Living in the United States, I "discovered" the answer.

I. C. Butnaru

Acknowledgments

When you have committed yourself to the difficult task of writing a truthful and objective account of events; when, in order to do this, you must search through old books and research public and private archives; when you are living with the thrill of finding new information and updating old; when your steps bring you at last to the point when you are about to fulfill your goal; you sooner or later realize that it does not matter how long you have worked or how deep your dedication has been because none of it could have been carried out without the stimulus, and especially the sweet feeling of responsibility, shared with others in the struggle.

To those wonderful people who are close to my heart, I dedicate these lines:

A deep feeling of gratitude for the leadership of the United States Holocaust Memorial Council in Washington whose staff helped me to translate the book. It was the first step in the journey toward publication.

Special gratitude and appreciation to The Skirball Foundation, The Edmond De Rothschild Foundation, and Lemberg Foundation for their kind understanding in helping this book to reach the readers.

My thanks to Dr. Brewster Chamberlin, Director of the Archives at the United States Holocaust Museum in Washington for his support during the long process.

Of great help in illuminating the book are the photographs received from Yad Vashem in Jerusalem, as well as those received from Matatias Carp and Marius Mircu books.

Thanks to Dr. Valentina Dogmarova of the Center for Research of Romanian Jewry at the Hebrew University in Jerusalem for all the documents and information sent to me, and for her understanding of my work.

My gratitude to Rhoda Bilansky, supervisor of the Interloan Department at Boston University, for the precious help she provided with great dedication throughout the entire period of research—providing me with all the books and material that could not be found in the Boston University Mugar Library. I want to add my thanks to all those people from Boston University's Mugar Library who, with modesty and great efficiency, helped me when I needed information, directions, and reference books.

In the complicated process of finalizing this work, I appreciated the attention given me by Dr. Howard Gottlieb, Director of Special Collections at Boston University's Mugar Library, and his help toward finding the proper way to complete the book.

My special thanks and gratitude go to Dr. Robert I. Sperber, Special Assistant to the President of Boston University. With his calm patience, and outstanding support, he assisted me through the many ups and downs related to completion of the book. I am deeply indebted to him for his confidence in me, and it was and still is a great privilege for me to enjoy his friendship and boundless kindness. His assistant, Ms. Sue Nauss, good-hearted and efficient, was always there when needed, and spared no effort when asked.

In the same way I have to express my thanks to Ms. Martha L. Hauptman, assistant to Professor Elie Wiesel, for her understanding and support in promoting the book.

The friendship showed to me by author, journalist and literary critic Sylvia Rothchild, her sincere interest in my work, and the discussions we had, opened doors for me and helped me to better understand America's literary life. She was, and still is, my teacher who has calmly but firmly guided me in eliminating any number of stylistic blunders (any remaining ones are of course my own). I want to assure her of my gratitude and respectful affection.

I must give great credit to Ms. Renee Spodheim, my literary agent, for the trust she has shown and for her perseverance in finding the right person for my manuscript.

Special thanks to Nita Romer, production editor of my book. I consider myself fortunate, being blessed to have near me a person so kind, with so rare an insight and professionalism. With calm, perseverance, and steadfastness she guided me throughout all the traps of the English language to the finalization of this book.

My warm thanks to Dr. James T. Sabin, Executive Vice President of Greenwood Publishing Group for promoting this book. His interest is much more than merely the significance of publishing; he has helped to open a window to the world so that a story about long-ago happenings, which are still alive in the memories of so many, can be told.

Last, but far from least, I wish to thank my wife, Jeanine, for her stimulus, patience, and confidence over many years. Without her support I would not have been able to travel this long and bumpy road. She has a special place in my heart.

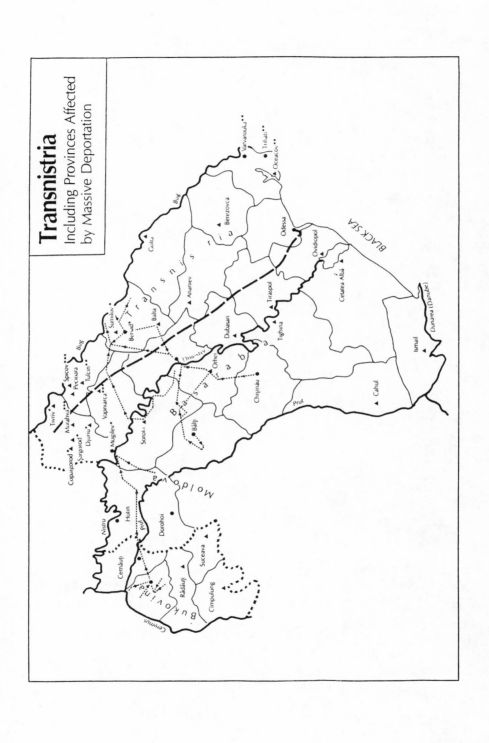

Transnistria

Including Provinces Affected
by Massive Deportation

BLACK SEA

1

A Romanian Problem:
The Jewish Problem

1

Anti-Semitism, as a form of social expression, has always existed in the life of Romanian society, being directed—in various forms and using a variety of means—against isolated individuals or, periodically, against the entire mass of the Jewish population. Anti-Semitism in Romania cannot be regarded as an imported product, brought from abroad and adapted to local realities. Its forms and expression became specific, contributing to the international anti-Semitic movement a characteristic recklessness and singular violence. Anti-Semitism in Romania was neither a transient manifestation of an isolated passion or resentment nor a momentary madness.

The origins of so many pogroms, as well as the crimes, robberies, and sufferings perpetrated, must be sought in the distant past. Especially from the beginning of the nineteenth century, the masses were prepared from early childhood to take to the streets, ready to participate in anti-Semitic disturbances. These "spontaneous" demonstrations were planned and premeditated, always by those who had an interest in diverting the attention of the masses from the real problems they faced.

In Romania, anti-Semitism, was used, successfully most of the time, to harm not only the economic structure of the Jewish communities but also their psychic formation. The object was to destroy their moral cohesion, forcing them to give up their long struggle for the rights they considered natural and legitimate, and to leave the places where they lived and which had flourished in their presence.

The endemic frustrations of the Romanian people—poverty; lack of culture; a high rate of mortality due to lack of basic medical care; dreadful exploitation of the peasantry by the great landowners or their agents; the desperate situation of the Romanian middle class, which appeared late in the national history of the country, swayed by all the winds and storms of political demagogues who promised everything and gave nothing; a youth frustrated by the poor conditions in which it grew up and was educated, looking uncertainly to the future; a serious economic situation during the nineteenth century, an entire historical era—were attributed, deliberately and permanently, to the existence of the Jewish population on Romanian land.

The Jewish population became a *problem* the moment the upper class of Romanian society was fully aware of its inability to solve the serious social problems brought on by the political evolution of Romania in those years. The Romanian aristocracy could neither accept a change in the peasants' condition, since this would have been against its own interests, nor allow the rise and development of the Romanian middle class, since this potentially threatened its class privileges.

This situation allowed the Jews who lived in the Danubian Principalities, especially during the nineteenth century, to develop their economic activity in trade and finance, thus becoming an important factor in the social life of the country.

They represented, under those conditions, a social group with no political rights and no acknowledged or accepted representation. Caught between the great currents and dissatisfactions that disturbed the masses, they were held responsible for everything that was wrong with the structure of society in those days; most of the time, they paid dearly for this characterization. The limited acts of despoiling the Jews of their worldly possessions and civil rights or removing them from certain economic or social sectors were no longer considered adequate. What was felt to be imperative, and promoted from all forums as a unique and unfailing solution, was to root out of Romania, using all means, this population, which was considered parasitic, and about which no adjective was sufficiently insulting to place it in its proper place in Romanian society.

2

With the conquest of Dacia by the Romans and the settling of legions and colonists in this area, the appearance of Jews in cities and at military installations is confirmed by the discovery of tombstones bearing Hebrew inscriptions. Archeological activity in Romania led to the discovery of sixteen funeral inscriptions revering *Deus Aeternus* and *Adonai Aeternus*.

The Greek colonies on the coast of Pontus Euxinus, before their conquest by the Romans, had maintained direct trade ties with the kingdom of Judea, while Jewish merchants and craftsmen plied their trade in the towns mentioned above. In fact, there are inscriptions with Greek characters confirming the existence of Jews in those parts, starting with the fifth century B.C.[1] Decebal, the hero-king of the Dacians, bestowed special privileges on the Jews of Talmaci, although they had the right to settle wherever they wished to on Dacian land.

Consequently, the presence of large numbers of Jews on the land of Dacia Felix may be directly tied to the existence of Roman colonists and legions. This fact must be regarded in the broader context of the structure of these legions, which, marching to conquer the world, enlisted soldiers or freed slaves from the countries that fell under Roman domination. Within the legions brought to Dacia were Gauls, Iberians, Greeks, Jews, and others. A decree issued in the year 397 by the Roman emperor gave the Jewish Dacians protection, which also extended to their synagogues.

The situation is confirmed by the tombstones bearing Hebrew characters. On some stone blocks were found chiseled the names Taemas and Bar Simeon,[2] centurions of Jewish descent, in command of companies of Roman legionnaires. These were professional soldiers who joined the Roman armies after they had conquered Judea in 73 B.C. Similar tombstones were discovered in the area of Salona (Solin), a city on the Dalmatian coast in Yugoslavia, and in Hungary, in the old town of Aquincum, where the city of Budapest was later built. These brief notes are sufficient to establish a basis for acknowledging the early existence of the Jews in the land that was to be called Romania. At the beginning of the fourteenth and fifteenth centuries the Jews settled in Moldavia, coming from Poland, Russia, Germany, and the Hanseatic cities following the bloody pogroms that always seemed to ignite in these communities. In the case of Wallachia, they came from the south of the Balkan peninsula, following their exodus from Spain.

Others were urged by the voievods of the country and its boyars to immigrate and settle down in a variety of places, in order to establish small towns and cities and especially to lay the foundation of commercial activity, which the population acutely lacked. The Jews made their presence known from the oldest times, at first through their economic activity, and later through their political and cultural activity.

Generally, those who settled in these places were poor people who earned a meager living through very hard work; among them were shoemakers, tailors, tinsmiths, blacksmiths, and dyers. There were also people of higher education: physicians, professors, or jurists. They lived, as they did in their countries of origin, in restricted neighborhoods in the cities and towns where they settled; in fact, these were true ghettoes, although they were never surrounded in these places by walls.

Living in isolation and adhering to rigid religious practices; categorically refusing to accept proselytes into a religion it considered exclusive: constantly alert to prevent intermarriages, which could bring scorn upon the entire family and ultimately destroy it; fiercely insisting on keeping its identity by wearing clothes different from those of others; speaking a language and practicing different customs; celebrating holidays that were not understood; and most of all, particularly in the beginning, communicating with difficulty in the language of the land, the Jews in Moldavia and Wallachia lived, throughout their historical presence in these principalities, an existence filled with a profound feeling of insecurity and uncertainty.

They felt their existence to be transient in areas where they never knew if or for how long they could establish roots; they experienced short, infrequent periods of tranquility, security, and prosperity. Interesting, in this respect, are the statements made by deputy George Missail who, although of Judaic extraction, was known for his anti-Semitism. In a speech made before the Romanian Parliament on March 27, 1879, opposing a bill granting civil rights to the Jews, he was forced to admit certain facts:

Gentlemen, let us see what history says: The first positive, certain, clear mention of the Romanians' contact with Judaism, [says] Mr. Hajdau, [was] in the so-called province of Aurelian (Dacia). We find the valuable narrative of Rabbi Benjamin of Tudela, who visited the borders of Macedonia before the year 1170, and left the following strange passage: "Beyond the Sperchis River lies Wallachia, whose inhabitants settled in the mountains and call themselves Vlahi. In swiftness they resemble the deer, darting into Greece to plunder and steal. Nobody dares to confront them. They do not abide by Christian laws, as they give their children Hebrew names and consider all Hebrews brothers, which determines some to credit them with an Israelite origin. When they get hold of a Jew, they strip him but do not kill him, because they are accustomed to slaying the Greeks."[3]

The observations made by Benjamin de Tudela may be viewed seriously if one is aware that this territory was occupied in the eighth century by Khazar troops from the south of Crimea, who were of Judaic religion. This might explain the famous Spanish traveler's notes, which were used by B. P. Hajdau in spite of his well-known anti-Semitic feelings.

Although there is little information regarding the existence of Jews in those places, Benjamin de Tudela and other passing travelers or merchants noted the presence of Jews settled there.

The presence of Jews in the Danubian Principalities became evident not only by their number, but also by the different roles and social positions they held. In this respect, Dr. Isaac Beg's account of his trip to Voievod Stefan's court in Moldavia is significant.[4] This physician from the court of the Persian Shah was sent by his monarch to the Moldavian ruler to prepare an alliance between the two voievods against their common enemy, the Sultan of Turkey, Mahomed the Second. Qualified dignitaries at the royal courts of Moldavia and Wallachia sometimes were Jews who knew foreign languages, as well as those in high professions, physicians, jurists, and merchants.

At the court of the same Moldavian, Stefan the Great, lived an Isaac Benjamin Shor, from Iasi. He spent his life at the court of this voievod, first as a steward, later as an overseer. He continued to hold this title under the reign of Voievod Bogdan (1504–1517).

Taking a number of facts into account, we must consider the decree issued in 1579 by Petru Schiopul, the voievod of Moldavia. This ruling was meant to expel the Jews from Moldavia, under the pretext that they jeopardized Christian trade.

The relationship Petru Schiopul maintained with the Jews, despite the aforementioned decree, is also discussed by Nicolae Iorga in *Documents Pertaining to Petru Schiopul and Mihai Viteazul*, published in the Collection of the Romanian Academy XI (pp. 87–88):

In the name of God, we studied the books with Petru Voda and found that we were granted the sum of five hundred and thirty-two thousand seven hundred aspri on this signing my name: Moshe, the son of Eliezer, deceased.[5]

It appears that the attitude of Petru Schiopul towards the Jews had radically changed during the second part of his reign. He was assisted in regaining the throne of Moldavia by the Jewish physician Benveniste, a close friend of Solomon Ashkenazi, the influential diplomat from the court of the Sultan in Constantinople.

In Wallachia, at the court of Alexandru Mircea (1567–1577), the position of personal secretary was held by the Jew Isaiah ben Joseph, a very educated and talented man who had a strong influence on the ruler with respect to his attitude towards the Jews. Due to a court intrigue, he was exiled in 1573.

Notes of this sort appear with greater frequency, emphasizing not only relations between distinguished persons and the rulers of the country, but also persons who succeeded in science, the study of the Talmud, and mathematics. We should mention at this point a work by Moise Mita published in Basel, Switzerland, in 1628, *Noveloth Hohma*. It is the biography of the great mathematician and philosopher Dr. Iosif Solomon Del Medigo of Candia (Crete). The author, who was a former student and disciple of this great scholar, writes:

Rabbi Joseph S. Del Medigo, the illustrious and phenomenal scholar, was born on 6/16 July, 1591 (28th of Sivan 5351). At the age of twenty-seven he left Constantinople for Poland. Journeying through Wallachia, he stopped in the city of Iasi, where he found the learned saint Rabbi Solomon Ben Arayo (or

Arowi), a distinguished physician who had been studying the kabbala for over forty years, and had written various works. Del Medigo resided there for eleven years (1618–1629), studied science and became a profound Kabbalist. Thereafter, he traveled to Poland and settled in Litau where he became physician of Prince Radziwill.[6]

It seems evident that Jews not only settled in important cities such as Iasi and Bucharest, but also in most of the towns in the Danubian Principalities, establishing businesses in these areas.

We also find Jews in Braila, Pitesti, and Calafat. Beginning in the fourteenth century, there were thriving Jewish communities in Botosani, Suceava, and Siret. The development of commerce and specialized skills, along with the founding of towns enroute to Poland, Bessarabia, Transylvania, or south to the ports on the Danube, led many to settle down in these areas.

At the same time, Jewish dignitaries of great prestige at the court of the Sultan in Constantinople established close diplomatic ties with the royal courts in Moldavia and Wallachia. Thus, Joseph Nasi (1524–1579) and Solomon Ashkenazi (1520–1602) remained in constant contact with the Wallachian and Moldavian voievods.

At this time, the acceptance of Jews because of their specialized skills and development of trade was not a problem. They actively participated in the organization of financial operations and even granted loans to the royal courts. Some of them possessed the mandate to collect state revenues from various public revenue managers, *gelepis*, and customs administrators such as those in Galati. What must be emphasized is that many of the deeds and documents drawn up by Jews in accordance with the country's administrators were drafted in the Hebrew language. Closer scrutiny of these documents also shows the literary quality of the language used, the style of the documents, as well as their penmanship. Undoubtedly, they were drawn up not by ordinary people, but by learned men who had studied many years and who had completed a thorough course of study.

Nevertheless, it is significant that in 1640 the Church Codes in Moldavia and Wallachia stipulated clearly that the Jews be considered heretics, thus banning all Christians from having any relations with them. The variable situation of the Jews continued, with alternating intensity, until April 5, 1710, when the Jews of Piatra Neamt were charged with murder. The accusation, apparently the first to be made in that region, must be tied to similar events that took place in other European countries. The Jews of Piatra Neamt were accused of murdering a Christian girl in order to use her blood in the preparation of unleavened bread (matzoh). The body of the child was found in the synagogue yard. During the first few hours after the discovery of the body, a number of Jews were slain by the incited mob and their homes were robbed, and the representatives of the Jewish community were arrested and tortured. Only after the direct intervention of the voievod were spirits calmed a little and the arrested Jews set free.

In connection with this accusation, which began to be made for various reasons (for example, in the city of Roman in 1714), a significant incident occurred in 1726 in Iasi, the capital of Moldavia.

The Jews that lived in Onitcani, Bessarabia, were accused by the local Christians of having murdered a child whose blood was then used for making unleavened bread for Passover. The charge was taken to the voievod of the country, Mihail Voda Racovita. This voievod, according to *The Anonymous Chronicle of Moldavia 1662–1733*, which was translated into German by Alexandru Amiras, was a man greedy for money, seeking to deprive the people by any means for his personal gain. He used to borrow money from the boyars and Jewish bankers, which he never returned. Every one of these creditors lived in fear, knowing that the voievod owed them money and that he could have them killed at any time.

In this particular case, the voievod ordered the establishment of an unusual court. In *The History of Religious Tolerance*, B. P. Hasdeu writes (p. 86):

A majestic Sanhedrin was set up, consisting of Christians, Moslems, Talmudists; the accused were questioned and even the Israelites pronounced the verdict, telling the voievod: "for their deed, they should pay accordingly."[7]

The story is ambiguous, leaving room for several interpretations. It does not appear, after careful examination, that the Jews who participated in this judicial court would have acknowledged the guilt of the accused; on the contrary, their contention was that they (the accused) should be punished if they were indeed guilty as charged!

We consider as authentic the writings of the old chronicler Neculce (1662–1742) in his Letopiset (Chronicle):

So they caught a few Jews and threw them in jail. They did try them as Jews, in haste to get it over with; they kept them in jail thinking how to take lots of money from them.[8]

Thus the purpose of these accusations, and this masquerade of a trial was to extort large sums of money from the Jewish population. For this purpose, the voievod wrote to Constantinople, and the Jews there collected the amount solicited. This was then sent by special courier, a representative of the Vizier, to obtain the freedom of the accused Jews.

3

Throughout the years, the situation of the Jews in Wallachia and Moldavia underwent many changes that were closely tied to and determined by the relations of the Danubian Principalities with the neighboring Great Powers which, periodically, claimed the right to rule them.

The terms that determined their stature varied from one era to another, from one reign to another. These classifications not only gave an administrative identity to these Jews, but also established the conditions and their responsibilities. Thus, there were *Evrei Pamanteni* (Native Jews),[9] those who were born and raised in the country. Many of these were naturalized by special charters or muniments and became "Charter Jews." A sample of the prerogatives bestowed upon these Jews is found in Article 8 of the Tirgu Ivesti Muniment (in Tecuci County, 1856): "For the Jewish people, the landlord should provide them with a place of education (synagogue), bath, and cemetery, rent-free, to the construction of which the landlord shall contribute."[10] These special provisions, which demonstrated that the Jews were solicited to come to the region in order to help establish small towns, governed the organization of trade and crafts. Under such circumstances, sixty-three small towns were founded in Moldavia, as well as other larger towns, such as Focsani, in 1780.

The Native Jews or *Raiali*, as well as the Charter Jews, who were considered citizens of the country, enjoyed a series of special privileges, one of which was to keep the registrar documents in agreement with state authority, to control the movements of the Jewish population with the help of the town's authority, and to assist in establishing state and town dues. As to the regulating of Jewish interests, these were to be subject to local dispositions. It is noteworthy that these Jewish communities had the right to possess and use their very own seal, bearing the emblem of the country and the following inscription: "Trusteeship of the Jewish Community."

Another group of Jews were the so-called *Suditi* (*it Suddito*), meaning subjects of a foreign power. This name, or rather category, has been very controversial. An explanation is needed, as the following pages will show that the right of the Jews to citizenship, and the consequences of being denied it or being given only partial citizenship, led to violence and to violent anti-Semitic demonstrations.

Considered the bread basket of products, the Danubian Provinces were obliged to sell their agricultural goods to the Turkish administration at nominal prices. Due to these preferential and totally discriminatory tariffs, the supply commissars, under the authority of Turkish officials, traveled throughout the country, monopolizing the products they found convenient. This situation led to a complete standstill of agricultural production. Either the peasants farmed the land just enough to make a living or raised very few cattle. Industry was nonexistent and trade very limited.

The only chance to survive was to be a subject of a foreign state. It was a way to protect estates against the Turkish administration's arbitrary actions. Confronted by this situation, many Romanians, Jewish and of other nationalities, solicited citizenship from foreign consular offices. Beginning at the end of the Eighteenth Century until 1879, Romanian Independence, the Russian and Austrian diplomatic representatives ran real competitions to grant these rights in order to consolidate their influence in the Romanian Principalities.

This special situation was why certain foreign citizens, who in fact were not alien to the country, appeared. Due to intolerable living conditions under Turkish administration, they had to resort to these subterfuges, continuing to live in the same country, in the places where they were born and raised. They were subjects of foreign states to whom they owed nothing and with whom they had no ties whatsoever.

The Church Codes of 1746 and 1780 amplified the provisions of those of the year 1640, stipulating explicit restrictions for the Jews. Among other things, they did not have the right to bear witness in court. This privilege was granted only to Jewish physicians.

In addition to this, two books were printed in Iasi in 1771, and later in 1803: *The Golden Order* and *Confronting the Jews*, which also contributed to the atmosphere of animosity towards the Jews.

The ever-increasing economic development attracted the attention of more and more Christians who became interested in various trades and crafts. The Greeks, Bulgarians, and Armenians, in particular, considered the Jewish presence a competition they wanted to rid themselves of by any means.

The merchants from Wallachia, in particular, enjoyed access to various foreign banks, such as those in Constantinople, while the Moldavian traders found credit available to them in Polish or German banks. These connections led to substantial economic exchanges; at the same time, competition among them increased.

As the lives of the Jews worsened in the Danubian Principalities, the Sultan of Constantinople decided to send Bezalel Cohen to Iasi in 1719 to act as Haham Bashi, the Chief Rabbi. He reigned as the religious leader for the entire Jewish community in Moldavia and had the prerogative of sending an emissary to Bucharest. In addition to his religious obligations, he was also responsible for a host of other administrative duties, such as applying and collecting taxes from the Jewish population and resolving litigations among the Jews.

With all his vast assignments, the Haham Bashi did not enjoy much authority within the Jewish community in Moldavia, because the latter was under the powerful influence of the rabbis and tzadiks from Poland or Russia.

Neverthless, for over one hundred years, the Haham Bashi in Moldavia and Wallachia played an important role not only in organizing the life of the Jewish community, but also in representing them in the superior courts of the country. The Guild of the Jews was also founded along with the Haham Bashi institution, as were the guilds of the Bulgarians, Greeks, Armenians, and other groups.

The existence of this important authority led to the need for better organization of the Jewish population.

4

A further accusation of ritual murder was brought up on May, 9 1801, this time in Bucharest. The inquiry made by Vel Aga, the police prefect, and the report submitted by him to Voievod Alexandru Moruzzi referred to the activity of three persons: Gheorghe Condorogiu, Stoian Sirbu Tabacu, and one Gheorghita. The three spread rumors among those living in the area of Niculescu Inn that the Jews had murdered two Christian children at the inn. The rumors stirred up great excitement among the people. Jews were beaten and killed. Their homes were robbed and then set on fire. Documents indicate that during this time, 128 Jews were killed in Bucharest. The three instigators acknowledged their guilt for having incited the population and were sentenced to hard labor for life.

An interesting note in regard to a time riddled with various forms of anti-Semitic manifestations is the decree dated April 16, 1806, signed by Voievod Ypsilanti and addressed to the country's Metropolitan, which solicited the latter's support in combatting the hostile attitude of the Christian population against the Jews:

Some of the citizens of Bucharest nurtured an unfounded idea that the Jewish people had willfully killed Christians to extract the blood of the victims, causing many villainous acts and disturbances amongst the people. They use this excuse for personal gain through robberies and plundering by inciting against the Jews whose own laws do not allow such things [in addition to the fact that the] inquiries turned up no guilty [Jews].[11]

Life for the Jews in the Danubian Principalities became particularly hazardous in 1821.

At this time an uprising led by Tudor Vladimirescu took place in Oltenia and Wallachia. The Greeks in Russia, led by Ypsilanti, a general of Greek extraction who was serving in the Russian forces, also rebelled against Turkey, hoping to liberate Greece from the Sultan's yoke.

The insurrection of the Greeks was unsuccessful and did not enjoy the support of the Romanian population, which was absolutely necessary for this daring action. The Romanians, although for centuries under Turkish suzerainty, considered the Greeks their oppressors. Tudor Vladimirescu, whose uprising had a purely national and social character, did not respond to Ypsilanti's appeal. Following a great deal of intrigue and a series of betrayals, Vladimirescu was killed, and the Romanian uprising was suppressed.

In Galati, the Greek population incited the Romanians to such an extent that when the Greek troops entered the city the Jewish quarters were robbed and four synagogues were set afire. It is worth mentioning that in this town of old anti-Semitic traditions there were other similar manifestations in 1842, 1846, and 1856.

Terrified of the oncoming Greek troops, the wealthy Jews crossed the Carpathians and took refuge in Brasov or other Transylvanian towns. Others sought refuge inside monasteries and churches. Due to these conditions, trade ceased completely. Horses and fodder were requisitioned from the Jews for the Greek army. The merchants had to submit the necessary cloth, while the Jewish tailors made uniforms for the troops and the officers.

When the Turkish army entered Bucharest on March 7, 1822, to restore order, the troops killed sixty Jews, after which, as usual, plundering began.

Following these events, Russia and Turkey decided to give centralized power to Romanian voievods. Thus, Grigore Ghica was in power in Wallachia and Ioan S. Sturza in Moldavia. This change in the administration of the state's affairs was considered all for the better in the life of Romanian society. The international events, especially the Treaty of Adrianople in 1829, had an immediate and substantial effect on the country's economy.

One outcome of the Treaty of Adrianople was that the Danubian Principalities became Russian protectorates, although Turkey's suzerainty continued. Following the agreement between The Great Powers, Count Paul (Pavel) Kiseleff became acting governor, a high dignitary, able diplomat, but nevertheless a Russian who possessed a specific mentality (toward Jews).

Paul Kiseleff drafted and imposed a type of Magna Carta upon the principalities under his protectorate, known as the Organic Statute (or Organic Regulations). The code of laws, meant as a substitute for the Constitution, was modeled after Russian laws and "was considered as a type of straightjacket which impeded the freedom of the Romanian people."[12]

The Organic Statute contained, among other things, provisions of a retrograde character towards the Jewish population, by inscribing at Paragraph IV, Annex X, regarding natives: "limiting political rights only to those of Orthodox rite, or to those who adopted this faith (meaning, at first conversion)."[13]

These rights were practiced without restriction by all natives of the country. The Organic Statute extended the provision to include all people of "Orthodox rite" regardless of place of birth and denied the Jews the right of citizenship, although, as was shown previously, they had won these rights long ago.

The new law code abolished the notion of Native Jew, Hrisovelit, which included them in a notion which had no objective connection with the reality of the Jews' existence in these parts. The term "Jewish Nation" included all of the Jews living in the Danubian Principalities. On one hand, it arbitrarily separated the Jews and the Romanian people, and on the other hand, it abusively repealed, with the stroke of a pen, rights which the Jews had enjoyed for centuries. Under the new laws, the Jews could not settle in villages, lease land, or build factories in cities.

The conditions imposed by the new legislation gradually limited the activity of the Haham Bashi institution, while its very existence became questionable. The judicial and administrative problems of the Jews had to be solved in court and not under the auspices of the Haham Bashi, as they had been until then. Due to the new ruling, the only rights of the Haham Bashi were to exercise its duties as chief of cult of the Jewish community. In 1834, a decree of the Voievod's Council abolished this institution, which had functioned for over a hundred years. The Jews were allowed to elect a rabbi for the organization and guidance of religious life, after the nominee was approved by the voievod of the country. As a consequence of these measures, the Jewish guild was dissolved in 1838.

5

In the year 1848, the Romanian people, under the leadership of a brilliant galaxy of intellectuals trained by the school of the great and generous ideas of the French Revolution, began to recover the consciousness of its national rights. "The entire populace who had suffered formed a single body, became brothers and marched hand in hand, aspiring for a beautiful future."[14]

The 1848 revolution created new and wonderful horizons for the Jewish population of the Danubian Principalities. The Proclamation of Islaz on June 11, 1848, stipulated clearly in Article 21: "The Emancipation of the Israelites and the political rights of all fellow countrymen of other faiths."[15] And further on: "To all citizens in general! Priests, boyars, soldiers, merchants, craftsmen of all standing, of all nations, of all faiths, the Homeland is ours and yours."[16] This proclamation may be considered a true Magna Carta of Romanian humanity!

These beautiful words were put into practice. Leading personalities of the Jewish community who had actively supported the Revolution of 1848 were nominated to the City Council of Bucharest. Among them were A. Hillel, B. Manoach, D. Bally, and others.

In view of securing democratic freedom, national independence, and social justice, the leaders of the Revolution of 1848 appealed to the Jewish population of the principalities for participation. This population, through its educated representatives, from the very beginning supported the preparation and launching of the revolution. A significant role was played by a number of Jews, including painters Constantin Daniel Rosenthal and Barbu Iscovescu and banker Manoach. These are a few examples that illustrate the attachment of the Jewish population to the struggle fought by the enlightened representatives of the Romanian people in order to achieve century-old ideals.

A painting entitled *Romania*, showing a woman with characteristic features clad in a beautiful folk costume, draped in the red, yellow, and blue flag bears the signature of Constantin Daniel Rosenthal and is preserved as a treasure at the National Museum in Bucharest.

The painter brought a great contribution to the cause of the Revolution of 1848. He was sent to Transylvania for propaganda reasons among the Romanians. He was later arrested, tortured, and died in prison in Budapest.

Maria Rosetti, a great Romanian personality and one of the leaders of the Revolution, published a letter in 1878 in the magazine "Mama si Copilul" (Mother and Child), remembering Daniel Rosenthal. Later on, this article was published in the newspapaer "Adevarul" (The Truth) on May 12, 1923. "I have fond remembrance as a woman and a Romanian citizen. It is that of one of the best and the most loyal people that God created after His image. He died for Romania, for its liberties; he died for his Romanian friends. Because he did not accept any compromise he died, tortured as a martyr. Whoever you are, you have to weep. As member of mankind, you lost a friend and Romania lost a loyal son. This friend, this son, this martyr of Romania is an Israelite, his name was Daniel Rosenthal" (*Hatzionut* 18 April 1991, p. 21).

It is no doubt that Maria Rosetti wrote and published this article commemorating 30 years from the revolution of 1848, and at the same time remembering those Romanians who in that period of time saved no efforts to cancel the provisions of the Peace Conference from Berlin which stated the obligation of the Romanian government to grant citizenship to the Jews from Romania.

The ideals of the Revolution of 1848 were repressed due to the betrayal of certain opportunist elements and the brutal intervention of Russian troops, which again occupied the Danubian Principalities and gave power to Barbu Stirbei in Wallachia and Grigore Ghica in Moldavia. The idea of granting civil rights to the Jews remained an unfulfilled desideratum.

International events throughout history always had a decisive influence on the fate of the Danubian Principalities, due to their geographical position and the role they were able to play. At the end of the Crimean War in 1856 and at the signing of the Treaty of Paris in 1858, it was determined that three districts in Southern Bessarabia be retroceded to Romania. The measure was dictated due to the need of the European countries to stem Russian expansionism to the south.

The renewed presence of Moldavia at the mouth of the Danube gave new importance to the Romanian Principalities in the European concert. As a consequence of this extremely important act, this treaty offered the Romanians the possibility to decide upon an age-old dream, the unification of the principalities.

Both pro-union and anti-union parties solicited the support of the Jews. Both promised the Jews full civil rights. In 1857 and 1858, posters and proclamations on this theme were published. The problem appeared important because it was clearly stipulated in the Treaty of Paris, with regard to the Danubian Principalities, that all inhabitants, regardless of religion, were to enjoy civil and religious rights as well as the right to own property and trade. Only foreign citizens did not have these rights.

Due to the provisions of the Organic Statute, which considered the Jews a separate, alien nation, the rights that they had had for centuries were annulled, and they were excluded from this provision.

The Jewish population protested strongly against this abuse by issuing a memorandum (as requested) in French. One copy was submitted to the Paris Conference, another to the highest authority in the state at that time, Caimacan Theodor Bals. The latter wrote on the document the following resolution: "We recommend that the Council consider this at the proper time. July 15, 1856. Theodor Bals."[17]

The tragedy of this situation was that the draconic provisions of the Organic Statute with regard to the Jewish question could not be changed. It remained in effect and was included later in the 1866 and 1878 constitutions.

The new leader of the country, Voievod Alexandru Ioan Cuza, a Moldavian by origin, had progressive views. A member of the 1848 generation, he was familiar with the situation of the Jews and tried to improve their status.

In 1864 Cuza decided to begin drafting a new constitution which would stipulate a universal right to vote and other rights and provisions of special importance. At the same time, he wanted to win the financial support of the Jews and the Armenians, in exchange for granting civil rights.

It seemed that the voievod was quite modest in his requests, especially since the economic situation of the country was particularly dubious. In view of this, the sum of 40,000 ducats was solicited from the Jews and Armenians. The delegates of the two communities held a meeting to formulate a plan to satisfy the request, but no consensus was reached. For the Armenians, the entire sum was paid by a rich Armenian. However, the Jews could not reach a decision among themselves.

Aware that granting civil and political rights to the Jews was closely related to the problem of assimilating themselves with the rest of the population, Cuza tried to accomplish these goals through the educational system. The Law of Education, a truly revolutionary measure, permitted Jewish children to go to public schools. According to an 1865 circular of the Ministry of Public Education:

This way, the religious communities will not be subject to great expense in building separate denominational schools; besides, the Israeli youth that grew up with the Romanian youth would become more nationalistic and eliminate prejudices, which they often regulated and which today oppose many aspirations, albeit justified, of the Jews.[18]

In addition to educational reform, Jews gained the right to occupy higher ranks in the army. The first commissioned officer was Naiman Hecht, who thereafter attained, the rank of lieutenant colonel. Adolf Buchner was appointed financial inspector, by decree, in 1863. These acts were enforced under the reign of Alexandru Ioan Cuza. They were not only civilized and democratic, but they also served to resolve any problems encountered in a humane fashion.

With regard to extending political rights to Romanians "of faiths other than Christian," the government of Voievod Cuza attempted in all honesty and good will to solve this problem as well.

Thus, the Civil Code of 1864, enforced in 1865, contained provisions by which Jews had the right to citizenship in accordance with the provisions of the 1858 Treaty of Paris.

The interest of our nation is to unite the people, not to divide them. Europe aided and defended us without inquiring about our religion. . . . We want Europe to do justice for Romania, and Romania to do justice for all of its people without discrimination.[19]

Following these provisions, the Council of State drafted a Statute for the Administration of the Mosaic Cult. This statute, with all its imperfections, provided a series of standards and directives concerning the administration of Jewish communities, including their rights and obligations. It represented a decisive step in the modernization of the lives of Jews in Romania.

6

The arrival in 1866 of the new prince, Carol of Hohenzollern-Sigmaringen, began a new era in the life of the Jews in Romania. Acting as the representative of the most reactionary and oligarchic circles in the leadership of Romania, Carol adapted his own anti-Semitic beliefs and resentments to those of the political leaders who helped him secure the throne.

In order to legitimize the anti-Jewish measures to be included in the new Constitution, ironically derived from the liberal and profoundly democratic Belgian Constitution, anti-Semitic demonstrations were organized in Bucharest on an unequaled scale in the very first year of Carol's reign. The participants were school children and university students, assisted by highly professional thugs, faithful supporters of the politicians.

The unleashed masses plundered the entire Jewish district, and a splendid building, the recently inaugurated Coral Temple, was set afire. This political maneuver was organized with the intent of forcing Parliament to vote for measures against Jewish rights to citizenship.

Article VII of the Constitution, denying Jews citizenship, was passed. The humane and democratic program of the 1848 generation was forgotten. The anti-Semitic attitude of the Romanian authorities as well as support given by the masses to violent and discriminatory actions provoked the indignation of international political circles.

This situation convinced the renowned French politician Adolphe Crémieux to go to Bucharest. He spoke before the Romanian Parliament and demanded civil rights for the Jews. His visit gave the Romanian press an opportunity to launch a campaign of insults and slander against him. Obscene and clearly anti-Semitic cartoons portrayed him in various ridiculous attitudes.

In the first years of Carol's reign, social, political, and economic conditions in the country were in a critical state. There were no highways that could meet the standards for organized transportation of goods within the country and beyond its frontiers; the country had an unstable monetary exchange and a domestic market that could not absorb the products. The ruling classes, the great landowners, enjoyed the same privileges bestowed in the Organic Statute, and practiced the same feudal relationship with the peasantry. The generous ideas on which the land reform of 1864 was based, were totally compromised.

The Romanian lower middle class was almost nonexistent, the representatives of this class being Greeks, Bulgarians, Jews, Armenians, and others. The peasantry, the most powerful mass of the people, continued to live in squalor and cultural backwardness. Economically, it depended on the contracts or agreements it had with the landowners or with the people who rented the land from their masters.

Politically, the change in the leadership of the country was undoubtedly an important step towards the creation of a modern Romania. Conditions for the country's economic development, in spite of all the difficulties with which it was confronted, appeared to be favorable. The ports on the Danube began to be modernized, while new roads and railways guaranteed an increasingly more efficient transportation system for the public and also for the import and export of goods on the Danube and the Black Sea. The European Commission continued to keep the Danube navigable; meanwhile, an open policy was formulated for the European countries which allowed many foreign investors to create industrial and commercial companies.

In order to keep pace with this economic upsurge, the landowners intensified agricultural output and concentrated specifically on raising cattle. This led to excess demand for manpower, while liberalization and stimulation of private initiative became a top political priority of the state.

The development of trade, especially foreign trade, the transformation of small artisan workshops into large manufacturing shops or even into major industries, along with the appearance of industrial organizations using modern technology and substantially increasing production of consumer goods, led gradually to the appearance of an expanding urban middle class made up of Romanian elements.

From the very beginning, the phenomenon had direct political, social, and economic implications. On the one hand, it influenced relations between the new class and the upper class, that is, the landowners, who found new and easy markets for their products; on the other hand, it influenced the latter's relations with the existing lower middle class, which consisted of Greeks, Armenians, and Jews, who became wary of the eagerness with which newcomers made their way into the society of that time.

The members of this class were no longer content with low-level positions. Their goal was to attain high-level positions, to make a fortune, rub shoulders with dignitaries, and establish social relationships in a world which otherwise repudiated them, although it accepted them because of the economic power they represented.

Thus, we find these *ciocoi* (upstarts) on the boards of directors of various companies in commerce, industry, finance, and estate management, making their way, with elbows and fists if necessary, soliciting, claiming, and imposing their presence with the supreme and only argument: I am Romanian! If this could not easily be demonstrated due to their ethnicity (be it Greek, Bulgarian, Armenian, etc.), their argument had to be more decisively stated: I am a Christian!

Tension continued to grow, while anti-Semitism, abandoning its religious framework, manifested itself virulently from an economic standpoint. Inflammatory slogans such as "The Jews are bleeding our country" and "The Jews are drinking the people's blood" not only incited the masses but also made the masses determined to expel the Jews from their professions and from the country. Thus, the new class, the *ciocoi*, could then take over the Jews' positions.

After much anti-Semitic unrest during the voting for the new Constitution and also at the time of the introduction of the notorious Article VII, which denied the Jews the right to become citizens of the country, Ion Bratianu became the leader of the government. Although he belonged to the generation of 1848, he was the first Romanian political leader who, as head of government, pursued the strict application of various anti-Semitic laws initiated by him or by his predecessors.

Jews who did not earn a certain level of income were considered vagabonds; this, by virtue of some older provisions in the Organic Statute that were still in force, gave the local authorities the right to establish a Jew's social condition. The enforcement of the regulations depended on wealth, which required, for some time, that the person not leave town. At this point, the Commission Against Vagrancy of December 12, 1850, was reactivated. As a first step, Jews were banished from villages. Peddler trading, a means for providing food for many Jewish families, was prohibited.

As a consequence, Romania was visited in the summer of 1867 by Sir Moses Montefiore from England, who wanted to see for himself, without intermediaries, the true situation of the Jews. In his meeting with Prince Carol, Sir Moses emphasized the unjust conditions of the Jewish population; his intervention bore no results.

Legislation against the Jews continued. In 1873, a bill was passed prohibiting Jews from selling alcoholic beverages in the villages. This led to the closing of some inns which, besides selling these beverages, supplied the villagers with other goods and manufactured products. The consequence was large-scale economic stagnation in the villages.

The political events of 1877 favored Romania. When Russia declared war on Turkey, Romania allowed Russian troops to pass through its territory, which led to genuine economic prosperity since Romanian contractors supplied the Russian armies.

When Prince Carol asked the Russians to allow the Romanian army to participate in the fight against the Turks, he was flatly turned down. However, later developments of the war and an unsuccessful attack on the fortification at Plevna forced the Russians to solicit Romania's assistance.

Prince Carol ordered the Romanian army to cross the Danube. It was a particularly favorable moment for the fulfillment of the Romanians' golden dream: independence from the secular suzerainty of the Turks.

Jews eligible for enlistment also took part in the battles of this war of liberation. Those enlisted were greatly supported by the entire Jewish population. Mobile hospitals were organized, and packages of food and clothing were gathered for the troops at the Danube River's crossing points at Turnu Magurele, Giurgiu, and Zimnecea, with the participation of Jewish physicians and nurses. A significant fact should be mentioned: during the final attack on the Grivita fortification executed exclusively by Romanian troops, Valter Maracineanu died as a hero. At his side was his aide, Warrant Officer Ehrlich from Bacau.

The Jews contributed fully to the victory of the Romanian armies in the war for the independence of the country during 1877–1878. At the Berlin Peace Conference, which followed Turkey's defeat in the Russo-Turkish War, Romania won its independence. Jews were granted civil rights *sine qua non*.

Other decisions made by the Berlin Congress established that Russia regain the three districts in Southern Bessarabia which had been ceded to Romania after the Crimean War in 1856. Russia was again at the mouth of the Danube.

The restitution to Russia of the three districts in Southern Bessarabia was a heavy blow to the Romanians. They considered themselves betrayed by the action of their ally, Russia. Victorious in a war in which Romania had shed a great deal of blood, Russia, instead of rectifying the arbitrary act of stealing Bessarabia in 1812, demanded and obtained from the European Powers the south of Bessarabia, thereby achieving control of navigation on the Danube. In compensation, Romania obtained a part of Dobrogea with access to the Black Sea through Constanta. This decision, Russia's representative, Prince Gorceacov, remarked cynically, was in fact a gesture of generosity on the part of Russia.

The Romanian and Russian delegations agreed on one point: in their protest against the provisions of the treaty granting civil rights to the Jews.

On the domestic front, widespread anti-Semitic demonstrations began to be organized, which diverted popular attention from the true discontent of the people and especially from the latest loss of Romanian territory, which provoked an avalanche of protest. Demonstrators took to the streets and asked the government not to accept the provisions of the Berlin Congress that granted rights to the Jews.

The anti-Semitic movements were meant to demonstrate to the European public that it was the *people* who did not accept the provisions. However, Parliament convened for the necessary changes to the notorious Article VII of the 1866 Constitution. In the Message of the Throne addressed to the special session of Parliament, Prince Carol said that the Jews had an evil influence on the Romanian peasants and on economic life in general.

In this atmosphere, the debates were emotional. Deputies spoke either for the strict application of the treaty's provisions or took an unyielding position totally rejecting the idea that the Jews be considered citizens with equal rights.

Ion Bratianu managed to convince Parliament that Article XLIV of the Berlin Treaty stipulated Jews' rights to citizenship in Romania, but did not clearly show that those rights should be fully honored. Consequently, Parliament modified Article VII by adding that "aliens who are not citizens of another state may—depending on each individual case— be approved by the Parliament." On that occasion, Romanian citizenship was granted to 883 Jews who directly participated in the war of 1877– 1878.

Thereafter, the problem of citizenship for Jews in Romania became a permanent pretext for new and frenzied anti-Semitic attacks. Statistics are significant: in 1880, citizenship was granted to six Jews; in 1883, to two; and from 1886 to 1900, to only eighteen.

Processing and formalities were so slow and clumsy that many who requested citizenship died before receiving it. Between 1879 and 1914, approximately two thousand Jews became citizens following this procedure.

At that time, Pop Martian and Petre Aurelian, economists from Nationalist Transylvanian schools, and the historian Xenopol, descendent of a family of converted Jews, began to consider ways to attract foreign capital and to use it in the creation of modern industrial and commercial companies. Meanwhile, even they demanded the expulsion of those aliens who had laid the foundation of their economic enterprises.

To this end, a law was passed on May 24, 1887, requiring foreign entrepreneurs after five years of activity, to employ a staff that was two-thirds Romanian. This meant training them and guaranteeing them a position upon completion of training.

The problem of removing Jews from those areas of economic activity where Christian elements appeared in ever large numbers took a different direction. Anti-Semitic hatred was no longer directed only against those employed in commerce and industry, but against the entire Jewish population. The Jewish population was considered to be a threat to competition; as aliens, they should be removed from society, thus placing them outside the protection of the law.

In those years, a new element appeared in the firmament of Romanian society (alongside the interested boyars and *ciocois* in commerce and industry): the tenant (arendas).

The Christian tenants, as opposed to their Jewish competitors, not only had the right to rent the land, but also the right to own agricultural areas personally. So, frequently, the owner of a smaller estate rented yet another estate to increase his income. Thus, he always was searching for a way to acquire more wealth by purchasing more property whenever possible. Under these circumstances, the only expected buyers were Christian tenants. Banned from owning land, the Jews could only lease it for a period not longer than five years. Many of these tenants, particularly those in Northern Moldavia, benefited from credits extended to them by Austrian banks. This way, they were able to pay the owners what they asked and become serious competitors to the other tenants.

This state of affairs led to sharp tensions among them. The Christian tenants, using local administrative officers, priests, teachers, notaries public, and mayors, as well as clerks from the administrative offices of the respective estates, tried to incite the masses of peasants against the Jewish tenants. This led to tragedies and grave consequences to the life of an entire national Jewish community.

In the village of Brusturoasa, in the Bacau district, a genuine revolt lasting five days broke out on August 15, 1885, during which the Jews were beaten, robbed, and driven out. The true causes of the tragedy were never discussed. No one was compensated for losses suffered. No one was brought to account for the things that were done against a collectivity of about one hundred thirty people.

In an article published on September 6, 1885, in the newspaper *Romanul* (The Romanian), Rabbi Moses Gaster wrote:

What surprised me most of all was the unprecedented fact that the peasant villagers rose against the Jews and expelled them from the village. I am sure that no Jew in Romania will hesitate to protest against the slanderous affirmation of some journalists that the Jews complained against the Romanian people; I emphasize this. On the contrary, I found a plenitude of peaceful and friendly cohabitation among the Jews and peasants. I fear that the venom of hate and intolerance will infiltrate the innocent heart of the people, through the procedure adopted to alter the facts, and present them in a way far from the truth. A bad example always finds imitators, and I hear the peasants around here would indeed like to imitate it; this must be prevented.[20]

The generous ideas of the nineteenth century flashed like bolts of lightning in Romania's firmament, disappearing as quickly as they struck! In that century, the country went from total subjugation by neighboring powers, which disputed their supremacy, to independence.

In 1803 there were 30,000 Jewish heads of families in the Danubian Principalities. In 1899 the Jewish population had risen to 266,652 people.

The status of the Jews' existence remained unchanged. Hooligan demonstrations had become cyclical, with various outbursts of violence. Deeply anti-Semitic legislation reflected total contempt towards a population which had demonstrated its contribution to the development of the country.

Viewed as a recalcitrant and unapproachable element, isolated through tradition, culture, and customs from the rest of the population, rejected when they tried to approach, the Jews suffered abuse especially because they would not assimilate. This concept led to various interpretations, developing in time into an accusatory characteristic which was added to a long list of epithets, insults, and definitions cast against this population.

The most important factor determining the isolation of the Jewish population from the rest of the Christian population was the reactionary politics of the leading circles on matters of education.

The 1893 law banning Jewish children from attending state schools stipulated: "Elementary education is compulsory and free for Romanians.... Aliens will pay a tax determined by regulations. Should the number of students be in excess of available places, preference shall be given to Romanian children."[21]

These laws of a blatantly racial character had grave consequences for later generations, which made school a place where anti-Semitic feelings were passionately displayed. In Piatra Neamt a teacher had his students write a dictation: "Jews are like leeches, they suck wherever they settle; Jews have come in masses and robbed like ravens at the sight of corpses."[22] Later, all categories of schools, high schools, and particularly universities became hotbeds of hate and anti-Semitic propaganda.

A chain reaction ensued, and feelings of frustration and isolation deepened. The assimilation of the Jewish population to the point of losing its national identity, as desired by Romanian reactionary circles, did not materialize because of the discriminatory measures imposed by governing circles.

In addition to this sentiment, the Jews were guilty by *law* and sentenced *ex officio*. Years of drought with disastrous results for the country's economy also plagued the Jewish population. Under the circumstances, many among the impoverished mass of the Jewish population, lacking material resources to weather this difficult period, restricted by laws and regulations that suffocated its existence, and vulnerable to the anti-Semitic movement, which had grown to alarming proportions, decided to emigrate.

The emigration of Jews from Romania then and thereafter did not stem from any adventurous spirit of the larger populace or out of desire to settle among strangers. They left Romania because they could no longer endure their living conditions, being considered aliens and treated as enemies.

At the end of May, last year (1898), a flow of emigrants from Romania crossed the Carpathians, traveling to Austria and port cities. Europe's first impression was that of stupefaction.[23]

The Zionist groups of Jews, made up mostly of youths, made for Eretz Yisrael. Entire families emigrated to the United States, England, and other countries.

A mute, silent, and dramatic outflow began in 1879, varying in intensity but remaining constant since then. Statistics fluctuate, but estimates run at around seventy thousand persons from 1878 until about 1915.

Paradoxically, this wave of emigration, desired and advocated in all forums, provoked a new and furious wave of anti-Semitism: "Why are the Jews leaving?"

This situation unleashed a genuine procession of protests in the European press, which was impressed by these unhappy people who had left their native places on foot, facing indescribable hardships and deprivations.

The Romanian newspapers, particularly those that were government controlled, deplored the exodus and regretted the departure of this population, about which they began writing in an unusual manner, emphasizing the qualities of these people, their abilities, their active and organizational spirit, and so on.

Those who remained in the country, those who rejected the idea of emigration as something alien to their way of thinking, and those who returned from the borders, persuaded by government emissaries to return to the places they left where small merchants and tradesmen had disappeared, tried to readjust their lives to the new conditions.

In 1900 Romania stepped on the brink of a new century under the most promising of omens, although its social, political, and economic problems appeared difficult and hard to solve. To bring about a normal situation, Parliament voted for an austerity program, which soon showed some timid results.

Irrespective of this serious economic situation, or maybe due to it, new steps were taken against the Jews. One of them, designed to give priority to the Romanian element, was the so-called Law of Guilds, passed in May 1902. This law banned Jews from practicing their professions. Although they were valued for their crafts, the law made it impossible for them to succeed at them. "It is impossible to find fault with the Jewish craftsman. He deserves... respect. Temperate, orderly, a tireless worker, he can rarely be criticized."[24]

This law was severely criticized abroad, and some countries even took a stand against it. In September 1902, the United States protested to the Romanian government, showing that on account of this law, which cut off all possibility of their making a living, masses of Jewish craftsmen were determined to immigrate to America. The American note reminded the Romanian government that the latter had alluded to the provisions of the Berlin Treaty regarding civil rights for the Jews.

Along with this law of a definite anti-Semitic character, the foreign press condemned the practice in Romania of obligating Jews to take an oath in conformity with the well-known formula from the Middle Ages, *More Judaico*, a discrimatory ceremony. In addition, there was the action of the Jews living in Romania, led by Rabbi Jacob Niemirower. Thanks to him, the authorities called off this defamatory practice in 1904.

Following this serious economic crisis, the landowners paid the peasants reduced wages for work in their fields to keep up with the competitive prices in the European market when it became invaded by American grain products.

Small landowners preferred to sell their estates and invest in industry. The Hungarian competition in cattle trading dealt a serious blow to the cattle trade in Romania. The increasingly important credits granted by Austrian banks to tenants in Northern Moldavia, especially to Jews, posed a serious obstacle for Christian competitors.

Wanting to increase the profit margins on the rent from their land, the landowners incited tenants against one another as well as the leaders of the village communities. By taking advantage of the competition among them, their aim was to make the best profit.

A series of articles, books, and studies appeared that attempted to demonstrate the noxious role played by Jews in Romanian society, particularly after the Message of the Throne read by Carol I in 1879 regarding the Jews. It is significant that propaganda material of an anti-Semitic character began to be published in foreign languages and in circulation materials that were totally unusual in that period. Without any doubt, these works were ordered, printed, and disseminated abroad by the Romanian ruling class for well-defined purposes. Such was *La Roumanie et les Juifs*, signed "Verax" and published in English in 20,000 copies. With the use of historical sources which gave it a subjective interpretation, it proposed to demonstrate that the Jews were never wanted in Romania. The author of this book wrote:

Romania, therefore, should avoid withdrawing from the wise measures adopted since 1878 until our times [1903]; they represent for Romania a condition for its national existence. The Jews must be resigned to the idea that they are and will be aliens in Romania, a country to which they were not invited but nevertheless arrived against the wish of the Romanians. They shall not be granted political rights except by way of individual naturalization and to a degree that the Romanians will deem necessary. . . . Should these conditions seem too harsh, they should try to emigrate, an efficient remedy for their sufferings. The country as well as the Jews will benefit by this. . . . The succeeding governments in Romania, whatever party to which they may belong, will see that the Jews enjoy the protection of the current laws, and will prevent and severely punish any brutality committed. But, in choosing between the vital interests of the Romanian nation and the advantages of the Jews, . . . they shall not hesitate.[25]

These words constituted in the future a genuine political program for A. C. Cuza. The latter deviated from Verax's viewpoint when he promised the Jews "protection under the law against brutality."

Educated in the French and German schools of anti-Semitism at the end of the nineteenth century, A. C. Cuza began his political involvement as an atheist and a socialist. Albanian by origin, an opportunist in public oration, and a careerist, he joined the nationalist populist camp with dedication, hostile to economic liberalism and, especially, to the most elementary notions of democracy. He hated the parliamentary regime, but used it nevertheless as a forum from which he spattered for decades his hate and scorn against a population he never loved, and from whose existence he drew many benefits.

Appointed professor of political economy in 1901 at the university in Iasi, on the basis of a thesis that later proved to have been plagiarized, he used his professorial position to preach the doctrine with which he infected the spirit of generations of Romanians.

In 1895, Cuza founded the International Anti-Semitic Alliance with Nicolae Iorga and Jean de Biez. His later writings reflected the character and the level of his concerns. In 1908 he published a book entitled *Nationality in Art* and in 1910 *The Reduction of the Christian Population and the Increase in the Number of Kikes*. In 1906 he began to write for the *Neamul Romanesc* (The Romanian Nation), published by Iorga.

Born in Botosani of Greek parents, Nicolae Iorga, an intellectual of encyclopedic training and a prestigious scholar and writer whose works encompass a wide range of studies, affirmed himself as a first-class cultural authority with an overwhelming influence on Romanian modern thinking.

With regard to coexisting nationalities which "by accident of geography or history" lived on Romanian soil, he considered that they must be *admitted* as inhabitants among Romanians. He not only accepted their presence, but also preached respect for their culture, language, and traditions, under condition *sine qua non* that they accept in turn the supremacy of the Romanian element and its predominant role.

Iorga set out from the idea that the nationalities living on Romanian territory brought their contribution to the development of the Romanian state, but he did not give them the right to interfere in questions of state or in the most elementary activity which could lead to a dominant position for the minority element. Later, especially after World War I, Iorga accepted the Hungarians and Germans as national minorities, yet flatly denied this status to the Jews and others.

Iorga did not consider the repressive measures against minorities as absolutely necessary, although his platform, regardless of the forms he preached, remained unchanged: "Romania for Romanians, and only for Romanians!" This slogan was later used by other groups and extremist political parties, and although Iorga had directed the slogan against all nationalities, in the last instance it was exercised exclusively against the Jews.

Iorga never denied that he was anti-Semitic. He stated it clearly, categorically, and unequivocally, and demonstrated this by all his actions and involvement. Without a doubt, as the years passed, his anti-Semitism took attenuated forms of expression. At the beginning of the twentieth century, though, he regarded the Jews as parasites who should be treated as such.

This was the area in which these two controversial personalities, A. C. Cuza and Nicolae Iorga, found a common platform to launch their campaign of hate and incitement against the Jews for several decades. Their methods differed, but their goals were the same!

Cuza advocated a pure Romanian spirit, a culture to be exercised only by "true born" Romanians, while Iorga professed the idea that Jews, once they were excluded from the economic circuit and the other free professions and replaced in all these areas by Romanians (in other words, causing the disappearance of the "Jewish problem"), could be admitted or tolerated on Romanian soil. The fact that some Jews had abandoned, according to Iorga, the old commercial and artisan professions and entered professions previously reserved for Romanians only was considered by Iorga an offense which he fiercely repudiated.

Like his predecessors, Mihai Eminescu, Ion Bratianu, and others, Iorga deplored the fact that the Romanians concentrated on the state-protected professions, leaving economic positions vacant for strangers. Cuza professed the idea that the Jews, purely and simply, must be excluded through administrative measures from these areas; Iorga wondered who would replace them.

Iorga insisted that "his nationalism derived from nationalistic-economic considerations, not from religious or metaphysical considerations or from an appreciation that the Jews are people of an inferior level."[26] Like his predecessors, he firmly maintained the idea that Jews could not be assimilated into the mass of the Romanian people.

The emigration of the Jews, caused by the conditions mentioned above, was considered by Iorga as a personal offense, prompting him to write fiery articles. "Zionism, after Iorga, became a provocation since, by this means, a national minority dared have political influence over Romanian public opinion."[27]

All these theories, propounded in writings or speeches, resulted from powerful political, social, and economic currents under discussion in Romania in the early 1900s. Publications appeared that argued the same topics, with direct repercussions upon the thinking of generations to come.

7

The event that shook Romanian society down to its very foundation was the peasants' revolt. The uprising broke out on February 8, 1907, in Botosani County, in Northern Moldavia. And although the flames of that peasant movement were unusually strong, it is important to mention that it was concentrated, even if only for several weeks, in that region alone.

The violence began in Flamanzi village, the property of Prince D. M. Sturdza, a rich landlord who owned 16,774 hectares of arable land, forests, orchards, and pasture. Just like all the other rich landowners, Sturdza had leased the land to the highest bidder, Mochi Fischer.

The very fact that the uprising broke out on an estate leased to a Jew was amply debated by the press and gave new forms to anti-Semitic demagoguery. First-rank personalities, politicians, journalists, and writers published a series of inflammatory articles, urging the population to take drastic measures against the Jews.

The peasants requested that their taxes be reduced and that they be given the right to lease the land through the village communities (*obsti*) that had been organized in order to help the peasants avoid the double exploitation of the boyar and of the leaseholder. They did not want to destroy the social system, nor did they want to seize the land in order to get rid of a social class, the landowners.

Considering the situation, it was difficult to imagine that the uprising could have broken out without support from the small landowners, the rich peasants, the schoolteachers, and the clergy. They were all interested in obtaining the land at an advantageous price since they could not get parcels of land through leases because of the existing leaseholders, who had large amounts of capital.

In his outstanding work, David Mitrani makes an interesting remark that sheds new light on the beginning of the uprising:

It is difficult to assess to what extent the peasants played a role at the beginning of the revolt; there are certain military and administrative reports attesting to the fact that in the small town of Bivolari, in Iasi district, hoodlums from other places came and incited the masses. Rather than rallying with them, the local peasants and peasants from neighboring villages gave the Jews shelter when they were attacked. But regardless of . . . where the riot started or . . . the reasons that led to the violence, as soon as the villagers took up arms, the peasants had a heavy score to settle with their oppressors.[28]

When the uprising spread all over the country to other estates leased by Christians or under the direct supervision of their owners, the army intervened. At the beginning, the great landowners were frightened by the violence that accompanied the uprising as it spread all over the country. They asked the government to call the Austrian army in order to set things straight. The Romanian army put things in order: 11,000 peasants were savagely killed! No one will ever know the number of those beaten, tortured, or mutilated.

The wave of anti-Semitism manifested during the uprising, and especially during its aftermath, was evidently orchestrated by the government with the help of the press, which had old anti-Semitic traditions.

During those years, and especially due to some personalities prominent in Romanian political and cultural spheres, anti-Semitism acquired different dimensions, expanding beyond the rudimentary forms of religious anti-Semitism to embrace expelling Jews from economic competition as well as official anti-Semitism practiced through laws and regulations.

Anti-Semitism became a form of mass education, and the decades during which this doctrine was disseminated made this poisonous feeling part and parcel of the moral and intellectual structure of a great part of Romanian society.

When the Romanians entered fields where they came into contact with Jews, competition did not unfold quantitatively and qualitatively. The Jews were the competitors. They *took* the positions that the Romanians wanted, and since the Romanians considered that those positions were theirs, the Jews had to be replaced by all means!

The tragic events of 1907 were forgotten or, at best, people tried to ignore them. For the Jews, this was extremely difficult: during those bloody events, 2,280 Jews and their families had suffered savagery at the hands of the revolting peasants.

In 1908, Nicolae Iorga and A. C. Cuza founded the first political party in Romania with an anti-Semitic platform, using the swastika as its symbol. Romanian anti-Semitism sought forms of political organization, and the masses were ready to obey and follow. The platform of this party had been worked out long ago by generations of people who had been taught that the Jew was the enemy, so fighting against the Jew was natural and normal.

During that period, a great number of Romanians who lived in Ardeal, Bucovina, and Banat immigrated to America and Australia. The situation was unparalleled. The Romanians in those provinces left as part of a massive emigration of minorities living in the Austro-Hungarian Empire. Undoubtedly, one of the reasons for the emigration was the discriminatory conditions that they had to live under.

The Jews in Romania after the 1907 uprising fled not only as a result of economic conditions, but as a result of anti-Semitism. The beginning of the twentieth century witnessed a real exodus of the Jewish population. Many small merchants, craftsmen, poor Jews, and young people with no prospects who could not aspire to an education or learn a trade decided to leave.

Between 1900 and 1914, 15,000 Jews left Romania on foot, wandering from town to town and living at community expense; in their constant and peaceful drift, tough and proud, these masses rallied other people wishing to change their lives.

These circumstances required the organization of institutions aimed at protecting the rights of Jews in Romania and at carrying out the fight, at whatever cost, to denounce and stop anti-Semitism.

After an abortive attempt in 1903, the Union of Native Jews (Uniunea Evreilor Paminteni) was founded in 1910; this organization's main objective was to carry out intense activity in the cultural field and to explain the danger of anti-Semitism to the Romanian masses. It fought for the emancipation of the Jews. The organization functioned mostly in Romania until 1948, when it was dissolved by the Communist regime.

A great contribution towards the above-mentioned objective was made by the intense activity of the Jewish press. Constantly, with unflinching tenacity, the press fought for the civil rights of Jews, denouncing anti-Semitic obscurantism. During that period, a number of Jewish newspapers, as well as other publications, appeared in various Romanian towns; all of them advocated civil rights and debated local problems. For the first time these newspapers published articles with news about the life and activity of Jews in other countries; the Jews in Romania thus came into contact with facts and events that were extremely interesting to them.

In the late nineteenth and early twentieth century, intense activity took place in Romania aimed at the establishment and organization of the Jewish community. A number of congresses of Jewish Communities were convened: in 1896 in Galati, in 1902 in Iasi, and in 1905 in Focsani. Unfortunately, these congresses did not yield concrete results, since there was no clear point of view on the role and aim of the Jewish community.

Those who were interested in organizing new anti-Semitic demonstrations did not miss the opportunity; they declared that these communities were "a state within the state" whose aim was to establish the supremacy of the Jews over the Romanians.

Later on, due to the activity of such personalities as Rabbis Niemirower and Nacht, the government granted the Jewish communities autonomy, thus forbidding local authorities to interfere in the affairs of the communities. This proved to be a real victory against those who were fighting for assimilation and who tried to prevail in Jewish life.

The Balkan War erupted in 1912. Jews participated, just as they had participated in the war for independence of 1877–1878.

The events of 1914 disclosed that Romania had been involved in secret alliances with Germany and Austria ever since 1883. Given the military circumstances and after a period of neutrality that brought unusual prosperity to the country, Romania decided to enter the war on the side of the Allies.

Jews took part in all of the battles from the beginning of the 1916–1918 war, intensely contributing to the creation of Greater Romania (*Romania Mare*).

2

"Romania for Romanians and Only for Romanians!"*

1

After World War I, due to the massive increase of the country's territory and population, according to the 1930 census, Jews numbered 756,930, or 4.2 percent of the country's entire population.

In 1867, the Jews from Transylvania, who had lived for centuries in the Austro-Hungarian Empire, obtained full political rights, which they enjoyed completely. Participating in the life of the state in all areas of activity, they spoke mainly in Hungarian. In Northern Transylvania, with a strong influence of the Hasidim and of Orthodox Jews, they spoke both Hungarian and Yiddish. The Christian population in Transylvania, especially the Romanians, did not experience any anti-Semitic feelings vis-à-vis the Jews, like the Romanians in the Old Kingdom. They treated the Jews in the same way that they treated the Hungarians, and the adverse feelings matched those felt against the Hungarians.

The largest Jewish population in Transylvania centered mainly in the economic sector, although a great number were involved in agriculture and in small crafts. The Jews worked predominantly in trade as well as in industry. When Transylvania became part of Romania, this sector was fully developed, flourishing with established traditions.

The Jews of Banat, who lived under Austro-Hungarian rule, had the same traditions as Jews in Transylvania. Those in the southern part of Banat had close economic and family ties with the Jews of Serbia.

In Bucovina, culture, language, and traditions were all German, es-

*Nicolae Iorga

pecially in Cernauti. In the other cities, according to particular national influences, Russian and Polish culture emerged, becoming apparent in relations with the other inhabitants as well. One could say that the Jews of Bucovina enjoyed a higher cultural standard than those in the other provinces. The influence of German culture could be found in all areas of social life, leaving a strong mark on the attitudes and conceptions of life of the Jewish population.

The Jews played an important part in the local economy, in trade, industry, and the banking system. The Jewish intellectuals of Bucovina played a remarkable role and eventually exerted great influence on the life of the Jewish people in Romania. Relations between the Jews of Bucovina and the other nationalities, such as Ukrainians, Russians, Poles, and Germans, were generally good, although anti-Semitic feelings existed in Poland and Russia and often broke out into violence. As time passed, the Jews of Bucovina developed good terms with the Romanian population, without anti-Semitic outbursts. Such outbursts surfaced later on with unusual violence.

The Jews of Bessarabia led a different life. Under Russian rule they had suffered discrimination in everyday life. Living under the permanent threat of pogroms, robberies, and arson, they had vivid memories of the pogrom in Chisinau in 1903. They lived in restricted zones without civil rights, and therefore organized their lives within their own community. Economic activity was closely connected with that of Jews from across the Dniester (Nistru). When Bessarabia was incorporated into the Old Kingdom, these economic relations disappeared and almost all the Jews living there became paupers. The local market had meager resources for absorbing goods produced by industrial firms or by small workshops, and the population lacked the material means to buy the goods offered by the small merchants.

The spoken language was Yiddish. The young people, the intellectuals, and people with professional backgrounds in all areas of activity spoke Russian. The education they received was influenced by nineteenth-century ideas and literature; the same process was experienced by Christian intellectuals. Both in Bessarabia and in the Old Kingdom, the Jews suffered due to permanent and violent anti-Semitic outbursts. The urban and rural population had strong anti-Semitic feelings. However, after 1917 Bessarabia was no longer part of the Russian Empire, and the Jews there obtained equal rights with the rest of the population, comprised of Romanians, Ukrainians, Bulgarians, and Tartars, with whom they had never had good relations.

The Jews in Moldavia were equally heterogeneous, oscillating between assimilation and traditionalism, speaking Yiddish and Romanian, trying to reconcile their existence with the resentments, the laws, and the adverse rulings that always threatened them.

In Muntenia, Oltenia, and Dobrogea, the Jews formed a small part of this population with strong assimilationist tendencies, speaking mainly Romanian and taking after the Romanian population. They considered this a means of "improving" their social status in a world that had proved so often to be against them.

2

For the entire Jewish population of Greater Romania, the years of struggle to obtain their civil rights occurred after World War I. Following the separate peace treaty signed with Germany at Buftea in 1918, the Germans asked the representatives of the Romanian government to include in the treaty an obligation binding Romania to grant Jews their civil rights.

This produced intense debates in the Romanian Parliament; in the draft bill it was written:

This population [i.e., the Jews] that together with us, participated in all the hardships and joys of the country and have accomplished their duty for the homeland, is to be given equal rights in public life.[1]

The notorious anti-Semite A. C. Cuza delivered a two-day speech on July 17–18, 1918, in which he slung mud at the entire Jewish population, especially those who fought on the Romanian fronts, with mean insinuations and false accusations.[2] Since he considered his speech a "contribution" to the war against the Jews in Romania, Cuza published it in a volume entitled *Jidanii în Război* (The Kikes in the War). This issue had become extremely acute after the drafting of the Versailles Treaty and the Statute of the Minorities.

After the capitulation of Germany, Ionel Bratianu understood that he could not go to the Peace Conference in Paris without resolving this problem in some way. This was the sole cause for acceptance of the decree on December 28, 1918, which announced the right to citizenship for all Jews in Romania, using the same system as that of the 1879 Constitution. At this time, citizenship was granted by local authorities upon the request of the Jews.

Although the government warned the Jews that they would face severe repercussions if they did not go to local authorities to request citizenship individually, the Jews ignored this warning, which was meant to divert the attention of international forums from the real situation.

In May 1919, when the Romanian delegation, headed by Ionel Bratianu, went to the Peace Conference in Paris, the great French politician Georges Clémenceau reminded Bratianu that Romania had not fulfilled its obligation to grant Jews their civil rights, according to the Berlin Treaty of 1878.

Although the Romanian government considered the Jewish problem to be an internal Romanian problem, the Great Powers decided to include again in the peace treaty the obligation of the Romanian government to grant Jews their rights.

In order to counterbalance the measures that the Great Powers were about to take with respect to this matter, Ionel Bratianu phoned the text of a law to Bucharest. This was to take the form of a decree, in which it was stipulated that citizenship would be granted by simply submitting a declaration of intentions at the local law courts. A certificate would be issued stating that the Jews had been granted political rights.

However, the Paris Peace Conference did not buy this subterfuge and included in the peace treaty the legitimate right of the Jews to enjoy equal rights with the entire population of Romania. Bratianu resigned as a sign of protest. The Great Powers gave an ultimatum, and a new government was formed in Bucharest. Alexandru Vaida-Voievod was charged with signing the peace treaty.

After lengthy debates, and owing to public pressure from the Union of Romanian Jews, in spite of fierce opposition from different political parties and groups with obvious anti-Semitic traits, on March 23, 1923, Parliament granted citizenship to all Jews living in Greater Romanian territory.

However, after only two months a series of instructions as issued concerning the actual implementation of the constitutional provisions, worded in such a manner as to prevent the implementation of the law. Although Romania had signed the accord in St. Germain regarding the Statute of the Minorities, agreeing in principle to grant them equal rights, Jews were completely barred access to public service jobs, the army, higher courts, university positions, and so on.

Jews were expelled from public schools after 1893 and were forced to study in special schools organized by the Jewish communities. The graduation certificates issued by these schools were not honored by higher education institutions; consequently Jews were barred access to university studies. In order to be accepted to institutes of higher education, Jews had to take an extremely difficult examination, almost impossible to pass, and were also obliged to pay a high fee that by far surpassed their material means.

In 1925, the examination was no longer required as long as classes in the Jewish schools were taught in Romanian. However, the Jewish school system continued to function, especially in the recently reintegrated provinces. This school system produced a remarkable group of Jewish intellectuals who became prominent in their professions.

These intense activities were initiated and carried out by the Union of Romanian Jews. In 1919, Dr. W. Filderman recommended to the Jews that they vote for those political parties that they thought would best represent them. This attitude was severely criticized, since the voice of Jews could not be heard from political platforms.

In 1926, the first five Jews, representing Bucovina, Transylvania, and Bessarabia, were elected to Parliament. In 1928, four Jews were re-elected, and they sounded very strong from the parliamentary platform, although they had to face the fierce opposition of the representatives of the anti-Semitic parties.

In the same year, Parliament passed a bill on freedom of religion, stressing that Judaism was one of eight historic religions in Romania and that the Jewish communities enjoyed legal status. In 1933, the Chief Rabbi, Dr. Niemirower, was nominated Senator. The Jewish party, founded in 1930, was represented in 1931 and 1932 by five members in Parliament.

These changes reflecting the status of Jews in Romania and their traditional organizations represented achievements aimed at the orientation of the entire population. Shortly, they proved to be a formality. They took place against the will of an important part of the Romanian people and the ruling class. They stemmed from external pressures manifested at various levels of social life.

One thing was apparent: the profound anti-Semitism in Romanian society. An example, by no means singular, explains the situation vividly: in the beautiful and picturesque Cismigiu Park in Bucharest one could see a poster reading, "No dogs and Kikes!" The presence of Jews on the pathways of the park was unauthorized, and the audacity of those who ignored the warning was severely punished with bloody beatings.[3]

Social anti-Semitism, subtle in form and perverse in its manifestations, was not different from religious anti-Semitism or the violent and tough exclusivity of economic anti-Semitism. It generated the discriminatory predispositions of administrative anti-Semitism and created the climate for racial anti-Semitism, a form of hooliganism that brutally surged under the knowing supervision of those who were supposed to defend and enforce the law on the equality of national minorities living in Romania.[4]

Lucien Wolf, the secretary of the Joint Committee of the Board of Deputies of British Jews and Anglo-Jewish Associations, sent a memorandum to Nicolae Titulescu, who was then Romania's Minister in London. That document was significant not only because of its contents but also because it illustrated the virulent aspect of the anti-Semitic movement led and supported by successive governments ruling Romania. After making references to past interventions of the Romanian official regarding this problem, the memorandum stated:

Unfortunately nothing seems to have been done in order to implement the promises that were previously made. On the contrary, in the past six months various groups increased their efforts against the Jews, while being applauded and encouraged by well-known politicians, professors, and important personalities. This enabled a leader of the anti-Semitic movement to ask Parliament that the foreign Jews be expelled, that the Jews born in Romania be banned, and their properties confiscated, that the Treaty of the Minorities (signed by Romania on December 19, 1919) be annulated, and the articles in the country's Constitution providing civil rights to the Jews be suspended. These declarations were not rejected by the audience and, even more, they were hailed by the governmental majority. The country was filled with literature mocking the Jews, inciting hatred against them, asking for an abolishment of Judaism, and banning of the publication of the holy books. Christian students were deliberately incited at the universities, urging them to act violently against the Jewish students. As a result, today, a young Jew would rarely dare enter the university campus. These crimes remained unpunished and generated outrageous unrest in Bucharest, Chisinau, Focsani, Ploiesti, Cluj, etc. . . . Nobody was punished for the above mentioned disorders, although it is known who was responsible for the unrest: the leaders!"[5]

This memorandum, together with others that previously had been submitted (and followed by still others), was given a polite response, but the situation continued.

3

Not far from the small railway station in Husi, on a modest house with a large veranda, there was a swastika. At the beginning of the twentieth century a Ruthenian (from Carpato-Russian) lived there. He was an obscure German-language teacher at a junior high school and later at the Alexandru Ioan Cuza High School. His name was Ion (Ivan or Jan?) Zelinski. He came to Husi in 1898 from Bucovina; he married Elisabeth Brunner, descendent of a Protestant family from Munich, and settled in the northern province of the country, which was under Hapsburg rule at that time.

Their first child, born in Husi on September 13, 1899, was called Corneliu. In 1901, the family changed its name from Zelinski to Codreanu.[6]

Ion Zelea Codreanu dressed in the national costume, wearing during winter a warm coat and hood, in summer a black hat with a wide brim; he carried with him a club that shone due to its frequent use. This character had become well known for the originality of his outfit, and especially for the ostentatious way in which he attested to his "Romanian" roots in the small provincial town in Moldavia.

In 1910, when the anti-Semitic National Democratic party was founded under the leadership of A. C. Cuza and Nicolae Iorga, the German-language teacher from Husi joined them and became a fervent and devoted collaborator. His entire existence and his family's life testified to wild and merciless anti-Semitism. Corneliu Zelea Codreanu's brothers had the same first names as famous persons in Romanian history: Catalin, Horia, Decebal, Ion; the brothers, together with two sisters, lived in an atmosphere of extreme nationalism and anti-Semitism.

When World War I broke out, Corneliu was not yet of age and was sent to a military school. He was rather disappointed that the war ended before he could become an officer and fight. In 1919, together with a few friends, he founded in the Dobrina Forest, near Husi, the organization Fratiile de Cruce (Brotherhood of the Cross), whose aim was to fight against the Bolsheviks and the Jews.

Corneliu Zelea Codreanu left for Iasi to attend law school, where he found a comfortable place under the protective guidance of A. C. Cuza, one of his father's old friends.

In the postwar years Iasi was a troubled city, filled with soldiers coming back from war, dissatisfied workers, and confused peasants. Codreanu, together with electrician Constantin Pancu and some other faithful friends, founded the organization Garda Constiintei Nationale (The Guard of National Consciousness). As with the Fratiile de Cruce, he gave the newly founded organization a romantic setting meant to inspire new members, make them overcome their fears, and execute orders exactly. As its main objective, the organization fought against Communists and Jews.

Using Nicolae Iorga's useful slogan, "Romania for Romanians, and only for Romanians," Codreanu followed the directions given by the worker Constantin Pancu, diluting the nationalist anti-Semitic rhetoric with a number of working-class demands, using slogans such as "rights for workers" and "the workers are entitled to bread and dignity." He also suggested "national workers' unions" and fought against political parties, so that workers could gain their rights within the nation and not against it.[7]

Codreanu, a man of pleasant personality, strong-willed and with a high energy level, was accepted as the unique leader of the Romanian youth from the very beginning of his public involvement. Although he did not achieve anything remarkable on the intellectual level, he knew how to create a myth of invincibility, and was accepted and revered by all of his followers.

Indeed, A. C. Cuza himself assigned to Codreanu the task of organizing the students' activity in Iasi. Codreanu brilliantly carried out his job in keeping with the views of his mentor.

The students' demonstrations of 1922 organized by Cuza's political movement asked the government to approve the implementation of the principle of *numerus clausus* (closed quota), thus barring young Jews from higher education.

Posters mocking Jews and depicting them in abject poses incited hatred and contempt for the Jews, a public activity that was carried out overtly without fear of punishment; they were incitements to murder.[8]

4

The Constitution contained a provision granting Jews the right to citizenship, which led to massive student demonstrations in Bucharest, Iasi, Cluj, and Cernauti during the entire 1922 academic year.

In 1923, A. C. Cuza founded a new party, the Liga Apararei Nationale Crestine (League of the Christian National Defense [LANC]), that used the swastika as a symbol.[9] Cuza assigned the task of organizing it all over the country to Codreanu on behalf of the new party.

Considering violence the only means of forcing the government into taking measures conceived by LANC, in March 1923, Corneliu Zelea Codreanu, together with a group of followers, traveled at midnight to the poor district of Iasi, populated by Jews, and started molesting people and vandalizing property. Codreanu inspired and organized that "heroic" deed; he was arrested and shortly thereafter released from prison.

Realizing that all the attempts made to force the liberal government to take measures against the Jews proved useless, Codreanu decided to undertake the actions he considered fit on his own.

The government denied his request, and because the Jews had "bought" a number of politicians, Corneliu Zelea Codreanu, together with Ion Mota and six other members of the Cuzist party, decided to purify national life by assassinating a number of important Jewish personalities, rabbis, and writers, as well as Christian politicians.

The plot was betrayed by a member of the group, and the other followers were arrested. In court, Codreanu gave a detailed description of the plot and its objectives, mentioning that they had only to set a date.

Before the jury could deliver the verdict, Ion Mota shot the traitor dead in the courtroom. The court handed down a verdict of acquittal for the entire group. Shortly thereafter, Ion Mota was also released from prison and acquitted! The decision led to demonstrations in Iasi to celebrate the victory.

After the trial, Codreanu gathered the members of the brotherhood as well as a new group of young people, peasants, and students, and decided to build a student center on the banks of the Prut, in Ungheni, exclusively for members of this movement.

The police superintendent in Iasi, Manciu, did not favor the project. Policemen were sent to arrest those involved in the project to build the center. Those arrested were beaten at the police station, and it was only due to A. C. Cuza's intervention along with that of prominent members of his party that they were released from prison.

Frustrated by these events, Corneliu Zelea Codreanu decided to take the law into his own hands. On October 24, 1924, he shot Manciu, the police superintendent in Iasi. The arrest of Codreanu after this deliberate crime triggered mass demonstrations in Iasi by his sympathizers. The authorities understood that they could not bring him to trial there due to his immense popularity; they decided, therefore, to have the trial in Focsani, another town with an anti-Semitic tradition.

During the trial, a large number of students and young people from all over the country went to Focsani. Political rallies were held to influence the jury. Three hundred houses were burned down; stores and synagogues were set on fire and vandalized under the indifferent eyes of the local authorities.

As a consequence, the government decided to move the trial to Turnu Severin, a town with no significant Jewish population but with an old nationalistic tradition. The event brought about a euphoric atmosphere in the city. Young school children were taken to the prison to visit Corneliu Zelea Codreanu, and young people from all over the country demonstrated in the streets. The authorities decided to hold the trial in the local theater.

It is also important to mention that Manciu's widow could not find a prosecutor.

After deliberating for five minutes, the jury found the defendant not guilty. When they returned to the courtroom, the members of the jury were wearing small swastikas in their buttonholes!

Turnu Severin witnessed delirious moments. On his way to Iasi, Codreanu was greeted at railway stations by peasants who came to cheer for him; whenever the train stopped, masses were held, priests gave their blessing, and flowers paved the streets.

This rage of anti-Semitism was accompanied by an intensive press campaign aimed at disparaging and rejecting the participation of Jews in the war to achieve Greater Romania. According to statistical data provided by the Ministry of Interior Affairs in 1916, of the 7,897,311 citizens of Romania, 230,000, or 2.9 percent, were Jews. Of the 35,000 Jewish soldiers who participated in the war, 933, or 4.06 percent of the drafted Jews, died. Seven hundred forty soldiers were wounded and 449 were taken prisoner. One should also mention that 825 Jewish soldiers received medals, 661 of them for acts of bravery on the front line and 164 for their contribution behind the lines; 775 were Romanian medals, and 50 were foreign medals. It should also be mentioned that other Jews who had been on the medal list were turned down just because they were Jews.

Significant in this respect is the Notice (*Publicatiunea*) issued by the Interim Commission of the City of Piatra Neamt, which reads as follows:

Anticipating the Festivities that are going to take place in Bucharest on May 17, 1923, we have decided the following: at 11:59 on that day, when the coffin bearing the remains of the unknown soldier is to be buried at twelve o'clock exactly, for two minutes, activity all over Romania will stop; cars, pedestrians, and trains will stop wherever they are; factories and plants will interrupt their activity as a sign of appreciation for the legions of heroes who gave their lives for a sacred cause. The citizens of the city are asked to participate in this festivity and to bring flowers and candles. The procession will start at 9:00 A.M. from the Piata Mare.

At this time, the honor diplomas will be distributed. The diplomas will be given to the families of the heroes and we therefore ask the families be present at the Christian and Jewish cemetery.[10]

The Notice carried the names of the seventy heroes from Piatra Neamt; twenty-six of them were Jews.

Mention should be made of the fact that during World War I the Jews were the only minority living on Romanian soil that fought alongside the Romanian troops. Since the war was waged against the Central Powers, there were in the Romanian army no Hungarians, Bulgarians, or Turks, who as residents of Romania were citizens with equal rights. Because of the wartime situation they could not participate in the war as troops in the Romanian army. The Jews, on being discharged and returning home, had to put up with all the harsh forms of anti-Semitism, which in the meantime had reached unprecedented proportions because of a consistent campaign of defamation and disparagement.

5

In this increasingly tense atmosphere of incitement to hatred, a tragic event took place at Cernauti. A group of more than twenty young Jews between the ages of seventeen and eighteen were arrested on the charge of having plotted to attack the professors who were conducting the registration at the university. The authorities in the Romanian higher education system apparently were against invoking a *numerus clausus* rule for the Jewish students. A stratagem was then employed that would in fact give them the right to apply this discriminatory practice. They just stopped issuing registration forms to students belonging to the minority groups, in order to make registration more and more difficult.

In the fall of 1925, at the entrance examinations for the university at Cernauti, all the Romanians passed the test, 30 percent of the Germans and Ukrainians passed, and 15 percent of the Jews passed. When the results of the examinations were made public, some students belonging to these minority groups appealed to the examination boards, asking them to show the papers they had submitted. The examiners rejected the request and complained to the authorities that they had been threatened by the Jews. As a protest against this obviously unjust act, the minority students organized a demonstration against the examiners.

The entire anti-Semitic press in Romania began an inflammatory campaign, representing what had occurred in Cernauti as an attack by the Jews on Christian professors, demanding that the government take draconian measures against the students, and presenting the entire case as a Jewish conspiracy directed against the nation.

The Minister of the Interior, Octavian Goga, then gave strict orders, and the group of students was arrested. Moreover, M. Petrovici, the Minister of Education, speaking about the disorders at Cernauti, stated that he was convinced that the students could not have passed the examinations, without mentioning the necessity of new examinations before another commission.

On November 10, 1926, the group of Jewish students was put on trial at Cernauti in an atmosphere of great tension. After a harsh exchange between the lawyers for the respective parties, the trial was postponed for a few days. On the day of the trial, when the entire court stood up in accordance with custom, a young man pulled a pistol out of his pocket, aimed, and fired. One of the accused, David Falik, was hit in the abdomen and fell in a pool of blood. The criminal was arrested immediately and frankly stated that his name was N. Totu and that he was a pupil at the Boarding High School in Iasi. Asked why he had fired the gun, he said that he had been impressed by what Professor Diaconescu had written regarding the demonstration organized by the Jewish students. And so he had decided to come to Cernauti, to "revenge the cause of Romania"!

The wounded student died a few days later. In the *Glasul Bucovinei* (Voice of Bucovina), Professor M. Nistor, the former minister for Bucovina, wrote:

Student Totu, who killed Falik, had been fed the teachings of Cuza, which have been spread by Professor Zelea Codreanu, that is, that the Jews must be chased out of Romania, that they must be killed, that the Jews are not human beings, and so on, and on. These teachings rapidly find a response in [the] hot minds of the young people, and there are circumstances in which a man aims and fires on another without thinking that he is ruining his own life by bringing so much pain to others.[11]

These voices of reason, unfortunately, were very few! On November 18, 1926, five students' associations in Cernauti met to discuss the case of the student Totu. They all reached the unanimous conclusion that the so-called criminal represented the Romanian sense of national pride, and consequently they decided to undertake firm action to free the "hero."

A few days before the case went to trial, similar demonstrations were organized by members of the Cuzist party who had been sent there with the purpose of "strengthening" local elements. Special editions of anti-Semitic papers were circulated free to the population. Several women brought Totu a handsome folk costume, which he wore when he came before the full court.

When he was asked by a member of the jury if he had fired with the intention to kill, the accused answered candidly: "Of course! I fired with the firm intention to kill!"[12] A policeman declared as a witness that since he was in the courtroom when the young Jews were being tried, he had heard the shot, and because he was close to the accused, Totu had said to him, "Take the revolver. I have had my pleasure!"[13]

After the prosecutor rested his case, the defense was opened by a member of Parliament, the lawyer Paul Iliescu, who declared:

David Falik died from Totu's bullets, and so will all the dirty beasts and enemies of the country die. Gentlemen of the jury, you should hang icons of this boy on the walls of your houses. You must pray to God that he grant health and long life to the boy-martyr, who is the honor of our nation. Totu is a martyr and a hero. Gentlemen of the jury, he must be set free, and you must not deliberate any longer than is necessary to dip your pen in the ink.[14]

After the plea by the defense, A. C. Cuza took the floor and addressed the jury with these words: "Our beloved boy Totu,"[15] and read a telegram that had come from the university in Bucharest, signed by Professor Paulescu, who asked his friends to tell the jury that "Totu does not deserve to be condemned, but rather to be canonized for all time to come."[16]

After ten minutes, the jury returned from their deliberation room, bringing in the verdict not guilty. Loud cheers shook the walls of the courtroom. Nicolae Totu, adorned with national tricolor ribbons and surrounded by flags, was carried on the shoulders of Cuza's disciples in a triumphal march through the whole city.[17]

After the Students' Congress held in Iasi on December 2, 1926, with the participation of 5,000 students under the chairmanship of A. C. Cuza, who was then a member of the International Anti-Semitic Bureau, it was decided to request application not only of the *numerus clausus* rule in the universities, but also of the *numerus nullus*, that is, the total exclusion of Jews from higher education.

These forms of "cultural" anti-Semitism were determined by the special conditions under which the Jewish intelligentsia exercised their professions in Romania. The contribution of the Jews to Romanian culture was not accepted as being of any value, despite its existence in all fields of activity. Using all forms of propaganda, cultural anti-Semitism indignantly rejected the Jews' contribution to the nation's culture, actually representing it as a foreign culture, damaging to the national spirit.

The successes of Jewish intellectuals stirred violent feelings of envy and inferiority, which could not be accepted under any circumstances. In contrast with the various forms of economic anti-Semitism, where the results translated into sales volume, that is, into immediate profit realized by the respective Jewish or Christian merchant, in the cultural field value could be achieved only through the esteem granted by others. Most of the time people could not contest the Jews' contribution, even against their will. The value of a student, lawyer, doctor, engineer, professor, or scientist could not be arbitrarily denied. The results were public, for all to see.

With the application of *numerus nullus* or *numerus clausus*, it was a question not only of excluding them from the field of culture in general, but of barring others, those who were young and eager to learn, from becoming intellectuals and hence potential adversaries.

Numerus clausus and *numerus nullus*, although they were a subject of agitation in the field of culture, were in the final analysis morbid forms of political anti-Semitism. The consequences of applying these desired measures had strong political implications, and to bar the Jews from any higher education was in fact to prevent them from enjoying the corresponding social status.

Given the living conditions of the mass of the Jewish population of Romania, especially in the first decade after World War I—mostly pauperized, with small craftsmen having no work, and small merchants having no credit and no customers—the young people had no chance to earn a living practicing the professions of their parents. They saw higher education as the only possibility of changing their social status and consequently their standard of living.

At the University of Bucharest Jewish students continued to be beaten or barred from going into their classes; if they succeeded in getting in, they were thrown out of the windows or down the stairs. The Medical School, the Law School, the Polytechnic, and the theological seminaries were among the centers of the strongest anti-Semitic agitation.

At the University of Iasi, Professor Rascanu was attacked by anti-Semitic students while he was giving a lecture. To maintain order in the lecture hall, the professor pulled a revolver from his pocket and fired it into the air in order to intimidate the students.

Following this incident, a group of professors from the university drew up a memorandum and sent it to the king. This fact should be given special emphasis, because this public position of Christian intellectuals in defending Romanian higher education against reprehensible acts of hooliganism was the first of its kind.

Your Majesty, for a long period of time, the normal activity of our university has been disrupted by a number of students, who are trying by agitation, strikes, and acts of violence to solve public problems that are not in the interests of education and cannot be solved by the university.... This inconsiderateness is evidence of an anarchic spirit and a total lack of training which gives the impression that the professors and students belong to two enemy camps.... Those who advocate ... agitation believe that the university exists only to give them diplomas and open their way to public jobs; and that professors are obliged to give them passing grades in the examinations, without paying any attention to their knowledge and extent of preparation.... The immediate consequence is that the time needed and so important for study is wasted in sterile agitation, and the Romanian element is moving into society and into the struggle for existence unprepared and in a disturbing state of ignorance.

What is more, your Majesty, solving this problem depends to a great extent on your attitude.... By the position you hold, Your Majesty, you are authorized to intervene with higher authority so that the important steps for maintaining order will be taken ... and through the position you hold personally in our public life, you can enlighten and influence public opinion in such a way that it will no longer grant moral and material support to agitators who are striking at our country and culture.[18]

This memorandum was signed by thirty-five persons prominent in the cultural life of Iasi, men who distinguished themselves in the years to follow by their principled democratic attitudes. The memorandum enjoyed wide publicity and serious support. However, the only action taken by M. Petrovici, the Minister of Education, was his decision on the memorandum: "It was carefully examined and deemed to be timely!"[19]

Added to all of this was the attitude of various representatives of the Church. On the occasion of the inauguration of the new building of the Academy of Advanced Studies in Commerce and Industry in Bucharest, in which the Patriarch, Dr. Miron Cristea, participated, he declared in speaking about the "nationalization" of Romanian commerce that this could be achieved only "when every craftsman and merchant in this country brings his candles to the same church that we do."

Despite this exacerbation of anti-Semitism at the national level, the relations between Corneliu Zelea Codreanu and his mentor, A. C. Cuza, began to deteriorate. The young disciple wanted to surpass his master! He thought that the methods of the old anti-Semite no longer fit his views. Codreanu wanted a more disciplined political organization, where orders would be strictly carried out. His departure from LANC was decisive for the future evolution of these two political groups, which later became adversaries.

On June 24, 1927, Codreanu issued his so-called Order No. 1 establishing the Legion of the Archangel Michael. The members of this organization took the name of Legionaries. Their uniform consisted of green shirts, over which they wore crossed Sam Browne belts, and black trousers tucked into high boots. Their salute was "Long live the Legion and its Captain!" It was accompanied by a gesture with the right hand first placed over the heart and then raised up, imitating the Roman salute.

The membership of this organization, which pretended that it was not a political party, encompassed great masses of young people, intellectuals, peasants, and a large part of the workers. On August 15, 1927, the publication *Pamintul Stramosesc* (The Ancestral Land), owned by Archpriest Mota, became the official paper of the new group and started its propagandistic activity.

Subjected to strict discipline, to a program of sustained work and marches intended to harden their physical condition, these young people joined the movement under the leadership of Corneliu Zelea Codreanu with enthusiasm and sincerity. They thought they could regenerate the country, and they really wanted to do so. Anti-Semitism was in fact the only platform that united them all.

With a view to broadening activities on a national level, the Legion organized a conference in Oradea on December 9, 1927; this was in fact the first direct and public contact by this organization with the newly annexed province. The Jews in the city viewed with concern this congress, the organization and conduct of which benefited from the direct support of the Under-Secretary of the Interior, the well-known Gh. (Guta) Tatarescu, who later was a Liberal prime minister under Carol II and then Minister of Foreign Affairs under the Communist regime. This personage obtained free trains, support funds, and so on, for the Legionaries, and in particular gave them assurances that he would not punish them for any of the demonstrations they engaged in.

During the congress in Oradea, five synagogues were set on fire, and the sacred Torahs were burned in the public squares. The news about the disturbances spread and brought in new adherents. Eight houses of prayer were burned in Cluj. On their way back from Oradea, groups of Legionaries stopped the train at Huedin, and later at Tirgu Ocna and Iasi, where they devoted themselves to veritable orgies of arson and pillaging of Jewish properties.

The impact of the old hardened anti-Semitism of the Old Kingdom on the Jewish population of Transylvania was strong and had the spreading power of an epidemic. What happened in the town of Borsa on July 4, 1930, confirms this. The town, with an old Jewish population, was simply set afire. Anti-Semitic propaganda asserted that the Jews had set fire to the town in order to create a hostile atmosphere for the Legionary movement! In connection with these tragic events, Mayer Ebner, a Jewish deputy, made the following declaration from the rostrum of the Chamber of Deputies:

The judicial authorities accept the idea that the masses are above the laws and that the Jews are outside their protection. A great part of the brutalities that have been committed have remained unpunished. Jewish students are maltreated and those who are guilty are not punished. The windows of Jewish houses are broken; peaceful travelers are thrown out of moving trains, and not one of the attackers has been sentenced. Since all these states of affairs remain unpunished, the idea has arisen and become very popular that everyone can do what he wants against the Jewish population. It is very regrettable that the government stands by with its arms crossed in the presence of all that is systematically instigated against the Jewish minority.[20]

6

In the years after World War I, Romania's economy underwent the same fluctuations suffered by the entire world economy. In addition, the peasantry, on receiving land after the war through a large-scale land distribution program, was actually unable to cultivate intensively the farms obtained, because they lacked the capital necessary to buy cattle, farm equipment, and choice seeds.

While the peasant had to pay extremely high prices to buy a farm tool or cloth for his shirt, as these were either imported, produced in the country by industries belonging to foreigners, or made with imported raw materials, his crops had to be sold in the marketplace at ridiculous prices. Grain, a vital product of the nation's economy, could not be exported at competitive international prices, because there was little demand for Romanian cereals. This state of affairs was made worse by years with low agricultural production and the excessive interest small farmers had to pay to the banks that had lent them money when they began cultivating the parcels of land received through the distribution program.

The economic ruin and pauperization of the Romanian peasants took a rapid course and led to profound dissatisfaction. Increasingly upset, the masses were ready to join any movement or political organization that could convince them that they were the only ones that had a miraculous solution to the country's problems.

The rising birthrate in the villages meant smaller and smaller farm holdings, leading some of the children in peasant families to seek work elsewhere. Some of them sought higher education, but because of high fees and lack of means of support, most of them were forced to break off their studies. A large percentage of the young people who were frustrated by the impossibility of attending classes that would assure them a higher standard of living, but who did not want to return losers to the villages they had left, made up a large "clientele" for political parties that succeeded each other in the government of Romania in the postwar years. Any job in the state administration assured a modest income, and the person who held out the promise of earning a living gained a faithful political supporter and a reliable backer in future elections.

Meanwhile, government employees were not paid for months and led a precarious existence on loans which they did not know when or how they could pay back. This social stratum, together with the intelligentsia of all categories, became impoverished and were known as "beggars in black clothes." They fell into the same category as the peasants and became in their turn a perfect political clientele.

The Jewish population was severely hurt by this economic situation. The small merchants and craftsmen in the cities and towns found their markets more and more limited, because their potential clients, the peasants and small government clerks, no longer had any purchasing power or any possibility of paying off credits extended them. Usually the peasants would get such credits from the merchants and craftsmen for a period of one year, that is, from one crop harvest to the next. Because of the drop in grain prices, the peasants could not pay their debts to those with whom they had traditional relationships.

This led to the inability of the small merchants, in turn, to pay off their debts to the great wholesalers who supplied them with goods, and to the inability of the small craftsmen to pay those who supplied raw materials. This resulted in a chain reaction. Bankruptcies became daily occurrences, and, as they escalated, affected banks and large industrial and commercial establishments.

For the Jewish young people, the possibility of attending courses at university or advanced schools grew more and more limited. Continuous harassment, maltreatment, forced expulsions from classes, and a discriminatory attitude reduced their chance to learn. Living in miserable conditions in student dormitories supported by small amounts of money from the Jewish communities because access to student dormitories occupied by Romanians was completely forbidden to them, and without the means to pay the fees, these young people timorously viewed their future with uneasiness and mistrust.

Young people whose parents had some means, left to study abroad because of the conditions in the universities in their own country. When they finished their preparation, they would return home to practice their professions. The idea of leaving the country for good was totally strange to them at that time.

Under these circumstanes, out of the desire for a better future, some young Jews, the intellectuals who could not practice their professions and found their future especially uncertain in a society which on so many occasions had shown hatred and contempt, became determined to seek a new direction. Some thought that socialist ideals might give an answer to their pressing needs for a free, dignified life, as well as for building an existence free from fear and terror. The mass of the young Jews fought for Zionist ideals. Leaving for Eretz Yisrael offered a solution for the moment as well as ample prospects for the future. Not only was a place being created where Jews could live, but also a Fatherland they could consider their own, while the country where they had been born and had lived with such deep roots in its soil considered them foreigners and enemies.

7

The Legionary movement carried on its activity in the provinces that had been annexed, and especially in Bessarabia, where the poverty was severe. The population was dissatisfied with the new administration, and the old traditions of anti-Semitism could be successfully revived.

In Bucovina, where the social and national mosaic could be channeled at any time into an explosive situation; in Transylvania, a poor region inhabited by the "Moti" population and totally neglected by the offices of the governmental administration; and Northern Moldavia, where the Jewish population was densest, the Legionary propaganda had taken deep root.

Although Ion Mihalache, the Minister of the Interior, had dissolved the Archangel Michael Legionary organization in 1931, Corneliu Zelea Codreanu put his own name on the movement, calling it the Zelea Codreanu Group. In the by-elections that took place in Piatra Neamt in July 1931 both Corneliu Zelea Codreanu and his father, Ion Zelea Codreanu, won, with 11,176 votes, against the Liberal candidates, who received only 7,124 votes. This constituted an important and decisive step in consolidating his movement politically.

In 1932 five other Legionary deputies received 73,135 votes and took their seats in Parliament. Because of the violent actions organized by the Legionaries at the time of the elections, the Iorga-Argentoianu government dissolved the Iron Guard party, which had recently been formed.

Iuliu Maniu, the well-known politician, bitterly declared in 1932:

Today the nation has been deprived of its constitutional rights; we are on the verge of bankruptcy, both politically and economically; we see how anarchy is dominating the spirits of the people and hatred is marching through the provinces; and in the chaos of this moral disintegration, one finds it harder and harder to hear the voice of the national conscience.[21]

After 1932, the Legionaries changed their tactics. They addressed all Romanians in order to attract them, especially in the regions where the Jewish population was not so numerous, and therefore the "classic" anti-Semitic slogans could not be of particular interest.

There were more than seventeen publications with a Legionary slant, to which an increasing number of prestigious and talented journalists and writers contributed. They brought the Legionary theories into the homes of the Romanians. With patience and subtlety, they continuously penetrated the consciousness of people of all ages, but the young in particular.

In addition to the usual anti-Semitic and anti-Communist slogans, which were not lacking in Legionary phraseology and propaganda, a number of theories obviously fascist in nature were becoming the basis of Legionary ideology, under the guidance of Mihai Manolescu, and giving it greater credibility.

The group known as the Organization of Young Fighters Against Judeo-Communism, which had been founded as early as 1930, continued its political and especially its terrorist activities within the Iron Guard party organization.

King Carol's return from France was a long awaited moment during that period characterized by political agitation and profound uncertainty regarding the country's future. When his plane landed in Transylvania, all of the people blessed the king. He was the embodiment of hope and trust for a people deprived of hope and trust.

One of the conditions set by Iuliu Maniu for King Carol, when the problem of accepting him as king was raised, was that he must not bring back his Jewish mistress, Magda Wolf-Lupescu. Carol broke his promise. The presence of this Jewish woman in the royal entourage was used for years by anti-Semitic propagandists as an example of the "Jewish plot against the nation." As a matter of fact, Magda Wolf was born from a mixed marriage. Her father was a Jew and her mother was a Catholic of Austrian origin.

Sympathizing with the fascist movements, and especially with Mussolini's movement, Carol II wanted to dissolve the political parties or destroy their political importance. Profoundly corrupt, unscrupulous, superficially educated, perverse, and depraved, he was an opportunist. At first he approached the Legionary movement, seeking to use it as a springboard to satisfying his own interests and political ambitions.

One can say without exaggeration that Carol II was the most corrupt crowned head in 20th century Europe. No other king abused to such an extent the sincere faith and love with which the people surrounded him.... Another principal factor in the sins of this country, terror and violence, was the response the Legionaries gave to Carol's corruption, and this unfortunate country found itself caught between these forces.[22]

Confronted with this attitude, which he could not accept, Iuliu Maniu resigned, and the relations between these two men remained frozen forever. The resignation suited Carol II's plans perfectly, since he wanted to have around him subservient men with bowed backs and individuals with no personality. Parties that were called to power and prime ministers who appeared overnight succeeded each other in governing the country in a veritable merry-go-round. So-called political coalitions and ad-hoc electoral combinations with no ideological consistency followed each other, making the people dizzy with their demagogic promises.

This atmosphere suited the extremist movements perfectly; they could carry out their activities without hindrance. When the democratic press violently condemned the massacres, pillaging, and arson at the city of Borsa initiated by the Legionaries and carried out by the local population, a Legionary came into the office of a prestigious Jewish journalist who had taken a strong stand against such agitation, and shot him without any hesitation. Fortunately the bullet did not hit the mark. He fired again, but the revolver jammed, and the journalist escaped with his life. Codreanu asked candidly, "What was illegal about trying to put a hole in the head of this snake with a Kike rattle?"[23]

As a result of this attack, Corneliu Zelea Codreanu was arrested, but, as usual, set free. He made good use of his time in jail to make contact with a number of Macedonians who had been arrested for an attack on the Ministry of Agriculture. These Macedonians and others became reliable activists in the Legionary movement and gave it more vitality and fighting spirit.

In May 1933 Emil Siancu, a Legionary, shot Mauriciu Fischer, the owner of a forest; as a gesture of appreciation Corneliu Zelea Codreanu promoted him in the ranks of the Legion.

Carol's reconciliation with the Liberal party and the decision to bring I. G. Duca to power and to call new elections coincided with a new wave of repression against the Legionaries. The entire police force was mobilized to stop the Legionaries from entering the elections that were to take place. On December 10, 1933, the Legionary party was again dissolved and about eighteen thousand Legionaries arrested. In the course of this action, eight Legionaries were killed, and General Gheorghe-Granicerul Cantacuzino warned Duca that "he had signed his death sentence."[24]

The Liberal party won a landslide victory in these elections where the

Legionaries could not participate. Although he had staged the entire operation, I. G. Duca could not enjoy the fruits of his success. On the night of December 29, 1933, he was shot on the platform of the railroad station at Sinaia by a group of Legionaries known as the Nicadori.

A vast police dragnet was spread to catch and arrest Corneliu Zelea Codreanu, but he could not be found. Some said that he had demanded that Max Auschnit, the well-known Jewish industrialist and friend of the king, hide him, and threatened him with death. Fearing that the threat would be put into effect, Auschnit hid him in the house of a relative of Magda Lupescu, the royal mistress. In connection with this bizarre situation, Horia Sima says in his *History of the Legionary Movement* that Codreanu sought refuge in the house of a brother-in-law of Magda Lupescu, but that he left it when he realized exactly with whom it was that he had sought shelter.

Codreanu was accused of organizing the assassination and tried, but the panel of judges, sympathetic to the Legionaries, acquitted him. The assassins of I. G. Duca were condemned to life imprisonment.

During those years the economic state of the country continued to deteriorate. Massive workers' strikes took place. The strike at the Grivita railroad workshops was put down with unequaled violence. A series of trials followed this action, and well-known Communist leaders were sent to prison for long terms. The fact that many of them were Jews provided lots of grist for the anti-Semitic propaganda mill, and the dictionary was enriched by the term "Judeo-Communism."

Under these circumstances, the people, disillusioned by the political parties and the royal coterie, turned more and more towards the Legionaries, who themselves constituted a response to the problems plaguing their lives. The ranks of people profoundly discontented with the social realities in the country were joined by the priests, officers (especially the young ones), and, above all, the students.

At the same time, the LANC, A. C. Cuza's old political party, had to reorganize its activity after the new fascist pattern that had gained such a powerful ascendancy over the masses. The fusion of this party with the one belonging to Octavian Goga, the anti-Semitic poet, gave a new orientation to the entire movement. In the elections of 1933 the new party gained eighteen seats in the Chamber of Deputies.

The Goga-Cuzists began to use the props long tested by the Legionaries: blue shirts (instead of green), the same black trousers, the same Browne belts, the same pistols, the same marches, the same banners fluttering in the wind. The flag-bearers were called "lancers," the swastika was seen everywhere, and anti-Semitism raged over the length and breadth of the country.

It is significant that at this time the rivalry between the Legionaries and Cuzists grew and took on the aspect of real competition; each one disputed the purity of the other's ideas; each accused the other of having "sold out to the Kikes."

If the older generation of Romanians sided with A. C. Cuza, the younger generation, regardless of its social class, drew nearer to the Legionaries. It must be pointed out that 1936 was a year of powerful advance by the Legionary movement and of obvious tolerance by the authorities who continued to hope for possible collaboration with it.

The workers, the small craft workers, and in general a wide stratum of wage earners of all kinds were not represented by a party through all those years. The Communist party did not have any adherence from the masses, and its contact with them was made with difficulty and under great danger, since the party had been banned in 1924. While a coalition between the workers and the peasants, organized by the Communists, won 73,716 votes in the elections of 1931 and sent five deputies to Parliament, a large majority of these voters were recruited among the Hungarian workers in Transylvania and the Banat. Romanian voters were few, because in general Communist ideas received a poor hearing and little interest from the Romanian masses, especially in those years. The Social-Democratic party, of small importance, had a more intellectual nature, and even so it stood to the right of the international socialist movement.

The establishment of the so-called Legionary Workers' Corps was an unusual event in the history of the Legionary movement. Appreciating the fact that greater and greater numbers of workers were enrolling in the movement, Corneliu Zelea Codreanu decided to organize a new group, for which he reserved a special place, in parallel with the students' organization and the Brothers of the Cross.

Gheorghe Clime was named commandant of this corps; he was a former Cuzist who had become extremely active in the Legionary movement. Under his leadership the workers' organization increased massively in size, and the so-called *cuiburi* ("nests") of Legionaries began to be organized and activated in the large enterprises in Bucharest and the provinces.

An event with important implications for the history of this movement took place on December 10, 1936. On the occasion of the Romanian students' national holiday, workers were present and took part, as guests, in the speakers' panel of honor. "Beginning on that date, these two Corps fraternized and thus began the common struggle of the students and the workers. They [the workers] were always the ones who made up the shock troops of the movements."[25]

At this time a number of new organizations of the fascist type appeared in the political life of the country. While they were very far from having the popularity enjoyed by the Legionaries and the anti-Semitic past of the Cuzists, they revealed the state of mind prevailing in the country. The drift of the right wing towards militant fascist ideas did not constitute a problem, in view of the shift in the general orientation of the people, starting from the idea that in Romania democratic ideals were far from having any traditional roots, and those who had tried to introduce any changes in the name of those ideas had met with total failure.

There is no doubt that in such an atmosphere, to assume the fascist ideology, regardless of nuances or aims, was considered to be the only way out of the impasse at which the country found itself.

In order to counteract the ever-increasing influence of the Legionaries and create for himself a powerful new image among the youth, Carol II founded the Straja Tarii (Guard of the Nation), a youth organization. It should be noted that among the commanders in this organization were members of the Legionary movement who carried out their duties perfectly, under the new conditions.

The visit to Hitler made by A. C. Cuza and Octavian Goga in 1935 marked an important moment in the life of this coalition. Hitler was much more interested in having a "traditionalist" anti-Semitic party lead a country in the Danube basin than a radical party whose turbulent members might compromise German interests in the region. The meeting was cordial, and the old anti-Semite could tell Hitler many things from his own experience, when his host was still an unknown painter in Vienna.

The close relations between these fascist leaders and Hitler and his government, and the large sums of money received to organize a solid propaganda campaign,[26] caused Fabricius, the German Minister in Bucharest, to send a telegram to his superiors in Berlin on January 3, 1938, in which, speaking about the designation of Octavian Goga as President of the Council of Ministers, he noted that Goga had stated that

he [Goga] is convinced that Germany will be pleased with his government. He wants to abstain from granting any support to the Iron Guard, so that one rightist party in Romania will not be given support to oppose another rightist party.[27]

For example, as early as 1928 Corneliu Zelea Codreanu had written to Hermann Esser, Hitler's friend and collaborator, that he intended to come to Berlin "in order to talk with him about questions of interest to the movement, not forgetting to ask that telescopes for weapons and cartridges be sent to him urgently."[28]

Later, when Hitler came to power, it was noted at a meeting which took place in a department of Section IV-a of the Reich's Foreign Ministry with the participation of Alfred Rosenberg, Rudolf Hess, and Heinrich Himmler, that allocation had been made of "the sum of 750,000 gold marks for Romanian internal problems and the Iron Guard organization."[29]

Similar relations continued all the time Legion activities were under
the leadership of Corneliu Zelea Codreanu and they were greatly intensified and amplified when the leadership of the organization was taken
over by other Legionary leaders, and by Horia Sima in particular.

The presence of the Legionaries began to be felt more and more in
other fields of activity. The so-called Legionary Commercial Battalion
began to organize stores, restaurants, and Legionary workshops, wishing
to demonstrate that they were capable of doing business of that sort and
especially that they could replace Jews in various sectors of the economy.

It was not at all surprising to see a university professor serving the
customers at these restaurants, and a girl who was cleaning the table
might be a young philosophy student.

The forms taken by this commerce became more and more varied,
and life became more and more uncertain under the pressure of the
events taking place in the streets and in the sight of all. The newspaper
kiosks that distributed the democratic papers were destroyed and
burned; newspaper vendors were beaten and the papers confiscated.
Books by Jewish writers and highly prestigious Romanians began to be
piled high on the streets for burning. On all the fences and walls of
Bucharest posters printed by *Universul* published the names of Jewish
writers and journalists who used pseudonyms, citing their Jewish names,
in an effort to prove that the nation's press and education had been
"sold to the Kikes."

Meanwhile the Cuzist and Legionary dailies were being printed in
larger and larger editions, and the so-called nationalist dailies, *Curentul*
(The Current), *Universul*, and others, were demanding love for the country and purity of ideas in the public squares.

Using their publications as a rostrum, various Romanian intellectuals
sought to give an ideological basis to the fascist movements, break into
the people's consciousness, and determine their way of thinking. Poetry
shot through with rabid nationalism, hailing crime and glorifying death,
was read with interest, while the old scholar Gala Galaction,[30] in novels
woven through with deep humanism, showed life in its true light. *Take,
Ianke, and Kadar,* a play by Victor Ion Popa showing sensitive affection
and understanding for warm, clean, human feelings, was presented at
the theaters.

The democratic press struggled under difficult conditions for justice
and truth and against discrimination and hatred. Prominent Romanian
intellectuals, using for the struggle these platforms so besieged by fascist
propaganda, published articles showing concern and made heated appeals to reason and dignity. Meanwhile posters showing grotesque car-

icatures of Jews could be found everywhere, inciting anti-Semitic excesses.

In March 1936 another congress of the Legionaries took place at Tirgu Mures. Again the government supported this demonstration by making trains available and granting the help of the local authorities.

One measure taken by this congress inaugurated the notorious "Death Squads," intended to "avenge the nation" and "protect the Captain." The members of this organization were recruited with meticulous care, and their directives were clear. A number of political figures were directly warned that if the Captain came under attack, drastic steps would be taken without hesitation.

It is significant that although this organization had a clear-cut mission, Mihai Stelescu, who had been a close collaborator of Corneliu Zelea Codreanu, quit Codreanu's movement and founded a group with the same objectives, known as the Cruciada Romanismului (Crusade for Romanianism).

Stelescu wrote an open letter to Codreanu and published it in his movement's newspaper. For the first time the Captain was publicly accused:

The educational system that you and your father instituted has spoiled too many pure spirits. All have been dragged through the mud of immorality. Some of us have saved ourselves in time.... At Agapia, at the holy convent of Agapia, I received the first blow to my soul, and my confidence in your virtue and what you preached was jolted. I saw your debauchery. It is a crime for you to be so degenerate, you who hypocritically cross yourself so piously. The nuns were for the "musketeers," so the sermon was that even I should delight them.... When they started to build the dam at Visani, it was well known that it would be not permitted, but you sent young people there to be beaten black and blue, to advertise yourself. You were waiting at the Buzau railroad station, and you left for Bucharest when you heard that the clash had begun. Some fine Captain you are!... In Teius, the boys were defeated; at Mihalt, I was running between the bullets, and you were hiding behind a curtain in a house in the town. You did the same in Resita and everywhere else. Where is your courage as "Captain"? ...And just as it was in the real world, that's the way it is in Parliament. If you are such a great "Captain," why haven't you defeated the Chamber with your speeches? Who has listened to you?...You have sent some young men to the grave and others to the brink.[31]

This letter throws new light on a myth under the power of which people were killed and others were taught to kill, and for which people would give their lives with unparalleled bravery, fighting for an idea that was never clearly stated.

The punishment for this letter was prompt, taking a form that astonished everybody through its cruelty and having great repercussions among the masses.

On July 16, 1936, a team of ten Legionary commandos went into the hospital where Mihai Stelescu was recuperating after surgery. There, on his hospital bed, they riddled his body with 120 revolver bullets, and to complete their work, they butchered the corpse while hugging and cheering each other. After they surrendered to the authorities, the criminals were sentenced to hard labor for life, but no charges were filed against the party to which they belonged.

A volume entitled *For Legionaries*, written by Corneliu Zelea Codreanu, appeared during that period. With regard to this, Sir Reginald Hoare, Great Britain's Minister in Bucharest, wrote the following to Anthony Eden in a report dated March 26, 1937:

It is important to note that Mr. Codreanu bases his anti-Semitism not on ethnic prejudices, but on the theory that the Jews have stolen the land, which is the inalienable property of the inhabitants of this country. . . . It is hard to judge by the contents of this book what Mr. Codreanu's own opinion of his movement is. Its strength probably consists in the astonishing superficiality of its doctrine which does nothing but extol a nationalism of an extremely nebulous nature. In this connection, he makes a great thing of the fact that he never accepted any financial aid from a foreign source, stating that a movement which is not capable of supporting itself cannot survive.[32]

The events in Spain threw a new light on the Legionary movement. A group of seven Legionaries left for Spain (during the Civil War, 1936–1938) to fight alongside Franco's troops. General Granicerul-Cantacuzino, who was president of the Iron Guard party and later of the Totul Pentru Tara (All for the Country) party, left with them to deliver a sword to General Moscado, the defender of the Alcazar fortress.

During the fighting that took place at Majadahonda in January 1937, Ion Mota and Vasile Marin were killed. Bringing the earthly remains of these two Legionaries who had fallen on the front in Spain back to Romania resulted in a formidable show of strength by the Legionaries. Tens of thousands of Legionaries and their sympathizers arrived in Bucharest from all parts of the country to attend the funerals. On their way to the capital, when the train stopped at stations, groups of priests blessed the pilgrims, and mothers lifted up their children so that they could see those who were going to Bucharest.

The capital was animated by an unprecedented frenzy. Intellectuals, workers, students, people from all walks of life, and thousands of peasants in beautiful folk costumes gathered to give their last salute to the fallen. The group of priests gathered at the Ilie Gorgani church to perform the religious service was immense. There was a rumor that the Patriarch himself, Dr. Miron Costin, would take part in the service.

When the cortege was formed, it was really the movement of an immense mass in the same direction, all carried along by the same force. The crowd moved along the boulevards in perfect order, under the watchful eye of the Legionary police and the benevolent guard of the state police.

Somewhere in the Royal Palace a man was listening to the dull murmur of the crowd, which reached him now as a rumble, now as a groan. The songs of the Legionaries, the cheers, the noise and shouts resounded even in the depths of his soul and filled him with bitter jealousy. The king had been forgotten! He wanted this adulation by the people for himself! He thought that he was the one that deserved it, and he would do anything to get it.

Steps had to be taken at once. Ion Inculet, the old Bessarabian long in sympathy with Legionary ideas, was dismissed from his job as Minister of the Interior, and the courts received special orders to punish the Legionaries as examples.

New elections had to take place at the end of 1937. The Liberal government, led by Guta Tatarescu, had finished its term. Tatarescu received the order from the king to set up the elections.

In order to prevent the abuses that had taken place in previous elections, the National Peasant party, led by Iuliu Maniu, and the All for the Country party concluded an electoral pact intended to ensure fair and proper conduct of the elections.

Although Maniu was criticized, not without some justice, because this electoral pact really contributed to orienting his party towards fascism, what is obvious is that this "alliance" gave the All for the Country party immense credit among the masses.

It must be emphasized that the Communist party, which was then completely illegal, directed its members to vote for the National Peasant party. And so the members of the National Peasant party went to the polls supported by the Communists, although the alliance of this party with the Legionaries gave rise to strange analogies. Legionary representatives and members of the National Peasant Party could be seen at the polling places, watching the elections to see that everything was proceeding properly.

In these elections the Goga-Cuza party won 9 percent of the votes. Carol II had to make a decision! Since the Liberals had not received the mandate of the people, they had to leave. As a matter of course, Iuliu Maniu and his party were to come into the government. That was something Carol II could not accept. Ignoring the principles of democracy, for which he had never had any particular esteem, he solved the problem in a way that made the entire country hold its breath. A party with a ridiculous minority vote was given the task of forming the new government.

8

Considering that between two evils, the Iron Guard and the Goga-Cuza party, the king had to choose the one that best served his interest, he made an abrupt, direct decision and brought the National Christian party into power.

This step produced repercussions at home and especially abroad. A declaration by Sir Orme Sargent of the British Foreign Ministry sheds significant light on the whole situation: "[King Carol] has named Mr. Goga in order to reduce the importance of the Iron Guard, just as Hindenburg did when he named Franz von Papen Chancellor in hopes of getting rid of Hitler."[33]

The same diplomat remarked further that the violent anti-Semitic policy of the new government constituted one of its primary elements, but he considered the Iron Guard to be an even greater potential danger than the Goga-Cuza government. "What is more important than the ephemeral appearance on the political scene of the Goga-Cuza party is the increasingly powerful growth of the Iron Guard, a Nazi type of party in Romania."[34]

Indifferent to the situation and strictly following the king's directives, the Goga-Cuza government brutally put into effect its anti-Semitic program, not only because this was in fact the goal of its policy, but because it was the single most effective means of demonstrating to the people that their party was in no way inferior to its competitor, the Iron Guard. To this end, bands of "lancers" subscribed to true vandalism in the Jewish districts, and to the destruction and looting of property. Paradoxically, now that a party with a direct anti-Semitic program had come to power, the Iron Guard saw it as its own most dangerous adversary. Recriminations hurled at one another saying that each side had sold out to the Kikes became routine!

The coming to power of this party had taken by surprise not only the people, but the party itself! When it became perched overnight on the ministerial armchairs, it realized that there were not many leaders to occupy them!

The powerful disorders caused by the Blue Shirts, and the dilettantism of the new leaders, who were unable to face the complicated problems of administering the country, forced them to appeal to various political personalities belonging to the other parties. Many supported the new government, either from momentary opportunism or following hints from the leaders of their parties.

Before the decision was made to entrust Goga and Cuza with the mandate to form a government, discussions were held with Corneliu

Zelea Codreanu in order to form a coalition of the parties of the right. In this connection, the king had entrusted General Ion Antonescu with arranging for a joint conversation with Maniu and Codreanu. Antonescu began with Corneliu Zelea Codreanu, with whom he met at his villa in Predeal. The discussions did not lead to any result. "I did not ask for this audience [Codreanu declared] since I do not want it to be said that my attitude towards the Goga government has been influenced by His Majesty."[35]

When the king sought another formula, Armand Calinescu, a well-known figure in the National Peasant party, appeared in the new government; he took over the portfolio of the Interior Ministry. Antonescu occupied the post of Minister of Defense, and Istrate Micescu, an old anti-Semite, took over as Minister of Foreign Affairs.

As its first step, the new government dissolved Parliament and scheduled new elections for early 1938. This caused new problems, because prospective elections could bring the Iron Guard to power.

As a result, a series of draconian measures were taken, and laws were adopted against the Jews in every field of activity. Measures for the so-called Romanization of all economic, financial, and social activities were approved, and the famous Nüremberg laws were copied and applied strictly.

The law of citizenship review for Jews was brutally imposed, in total violation of the most elementary standards of legality. A series of formalities had to be accomplished in an extremely short time, and abuses of every kind spread through the hierarchical chain of all of Romanian society. Every document, every deed, every move had to be bought, with hard money; specific valuable items were demanded openly and without reservation, even in the offices of those who made the most elementary decisions.

In the Bar Association in Bucharest, where Istrate Micescu had been for years the leader and instigator of the most savage actions against his colleagues, lawyers could no longer practice their profession. In the field of education, Jewish professors were removed from the schools; some business enterprises were "Romanized" directly: they were seized without any compensation. In the governmental sector, the railroads, and other enterprises, where there were few Jews in any case, Jews were purely and simply thrown out into the street. Private firms were obligated to hire Romanian employees, who had to be paid during their period of training. When it was felt that these trainees could replace the Jews who had taught them their new jobs, the Jews were fired. With this state of affairs, the economy of the nation became totally paralyzed. Commercial activity virtually ceased, industrial plants no longer received raw materials, and foreign firms began to withdraw their capital from Romania.

A report entitled "The Political Situation in Romania",[36] which was sent to the British Foreign Office on January 24, 1938, by Sir Reginald Hoare, stated:

The present government in Romania is in a delicate position. . . . We have learned from Mr. Micescu that the coming elections, which are to take place in the first week of March, will be based on an anti-Semitic campaign. If the present government takes a moderate position with regard to this problem, it will play into the hands of the extremists in the Iron Guard. If however it takes a hard attitude toward the Jews, then it will stir up powerful resentment abroad. . . . The coming to power of the Iron Guard . . . would mean an alliance with the Rome-Berlin Axis.[37]

This fear expressed by the British Minister in Bucharest seems perfectly justified, given the declarations already made by Corneliu Zelea Codreanu in 1937.[38]

In view of the many irreconcilable points of view within the two rightist parties, preparations for the new elections in the spring of 1938 led the country to the brink of civil war. During that time, more than 200,000 Jews lost Romanian citizenship, and each one of them had to ask himself where he was going, and exactly what had to be done.

General Zizi Cantacuzino-Grancicerul, leader of the Iron Guard party, under the new name of All for the Country, candidly declared that the only possibility of solving the Jewish problem was to kill the Jews!

The tension between the Cuzists and the Legionaries increased, and in clashes between them, two Legionaries were killed and fifty-two wounded. As a result, 450 Legionaries were arrested. The situation became truly explosive, but it was tempered by General Ion Antonescu, who organized a meeting on February 8, 1938, between Octavian Goga and Corneliu Zelea Codreanu, where they both agreed on a model of action for the coming elections. After a short time, however, without giving any explanation, Codreanu announced that his party would not participate in the elections.

On February 12, 1938, the Goga-Cuza government resigned, and the king himself, with his solemn voice, proclaimed the principles of the new era which he heralded.

9

The new government installed by King Carol II, made up of so-called technicians, was in fact a conglomerate of switchovers from various political parties. Fed up by a prolonged stay in the opposition, craving power and riches, they did not see any other possibility of occupying the seats of power. The offer and the appeal of the king produced a healthy response and brought the adherence not only of their respective parties but also of sectors of the population frightened by the specter of civil war threatening Romania. In order to demonstrate its "impartial" nature, by placing the newly installed government above partisan interests, Carol II named the Patriarch, Dr. Miron Cristea, President of the Council of Ministers; incidentally, Cristea was known for his anti-Semitic feelings. Among the other ministers was Armand Calinescu, who in fact held complete power in his hands.

An exceptionally interesting personality, corrupt and demagogic, intelligent yet opportunistic, lacking scruples in his execution of the king's orders, a confirmed ally of the Allied Powers, Armand Calinescu took charge of the new cabinet from the start, which became known as "Carolist."

The steps taken led to at least a momentary relaxation of tension. Trade grew stronger, and forced industrialization reached an unprecedented stage of development. Around the king, a coterie headed by Elena (Magda) Lupescu and Ernest Urdareanu, the Marshal of the Palace, operated in the shadows.

A system of police surveillance, directly under the king's orders, was instituted. Its chief, Eugen Cristescu, had unlimited powers and was directly responsible to the monarch. Since Parliament had been dissolved as the first measure taken by the king, the state was governed by decree. The Constitution had been abrogated, and under the new Constitution every minister answered directly to the king. No one could be Minister in Romania without proven Romanian nationality for at least three generations. This measure was undoubtedly directed against Corneliu Zelinski, who later called himself Corneliu Zelea Codreanu in his capacity as leader of Romanian fascism.

What was surprising was Codreanu's docile attitude towards the measures taken by the king. On February 21, 1938, he issued an order to dissolve the All for the Country party. Codreanu understood the direction of international policy; it corresponded to his own interests, and he thought it unnecessary to clash with the royal dictatorship.

Although the Legionary movement was apparently dissolved, it continued to carry out its activities with vigor. Conscious of all this, Carol II decided even before the resignation of the Goga-Cuza government to assassinate Corneliu Zelea Codreanu. Istrate Micescu took charge of selecting the person who would carry out the plan, but he made a mistake. He chose the prefect of Neamt County, V. Emilian, who years before had set up a fascist-style political organization, and who later had gone over to the Goga-Cuza party; now Emilian betrayed the offer made to him by the Minister of Foreign Affairs.[39]

The scandal that exploded was quickly forgotten because of subsequent events: the dissolution of the Goga-Cuza government and the installation of the royal dictatorship. N. Iorga himself began to reprint his old daily, *Neamul Romanesc* (The Romanian People); in it he initiated a violent campaign against the Legionaries and, in particular, Corneliu Zelea Codreanu. Simultaneously, a series of draconian measures took effect against the Legionaries. A royal decree resulted in the arrest of all Legionary leaders and their internment in various camps for political prisoners. Codreanu was among this group.

Because of his arrest, the Captain designated other Legionary commanders to take his place. As soon as these were arrested, others took over the leadership, until finally Horia Sima became the head of the Legionary movement.

All these repressive measures did not satisfy Carol II, who wished to demonstrate publicly the secret ties between Corneliu Zelea Codreanu and Nazi Germany, as well as the material help he had received from them.[40] In the new court action brought against Codreanu, he was accused, among other things, of being the leader of a vast spy network in the service of a "foreign power." While the accusation of organizing terrorist activities was doubtless accurate, this further charge seemed to be unfounded.[41]

General Ion Antonescu's deposition at the trial in favor of Codreanu led King Carol II to order Antonescu's arrest; he was placed under house arrest in an elegant villa located in the romantic Lotru Valley in Oltenia, near the Bistrita monastery. "There for the first time the Germans had contact with Antonescu, with the support of Veturia Goga, the widow of the poet, who was well-known in Hitlerite circles."[42]

At this time Armand Calinescu tried to strike a mortal blow at the Legion. Through a vast police action, more than thirty thousand homes of Legionaries were searched and tens of thousands of Legionaries arrested. In view of this royal "offensive," many of the Legionaries sought refuge in the mountains, with the help of peasants, while others fled to Germany and Poland.

After a trip to England and France, King Carol II stopped in Germany to meet with Hitler, for the purpose of stabilizing the political balance in matters affecting the position of Romania. The discussions between Carol II and Hitler are not sufficiently well known, and there are different versions of them. What is essential is that the king received some assurances from Hitler regarding Hungarian revisionism. In any case, Carol II felt that Hitler had given him a free hand to take what he thought were proper measures against the Legion and its commander.[43]

The attempt by a group of students to shoot the Rector of the University of Cluj and the attempt in Cernauti to shoot Colonel Cristescu, an officer on special assignment, were the straws that broke the camel's back.

The reaction was quick and spared no one! On the night of November

29–30, 1938, Corneliu Zelea Codreanu, together with the three assassins of I. G. Duca and the ten assassins of Mihai Stelescu, were pulled out of the jail where they were being held and loaded into trucks, each with a gendarme at his back. The trucks stopped on an empty country road. The prisoners were strangled with ropes and then shot in the back. That night the corpses were buried in the vicinity of the Jilava jail, but no marker was put on their graves.

The next day the newspapers announced that Codreanu, together with the others, had been shot while trying to "escape under escort." Hitler's reaction was extraordinarily violent, and the press devoted entire columns to criticism of the assassinations:

During his conversation with Hitler, Carol II was called to the telephone [from Bucharest] several times to be told what had been done [to] the Legionaries. It appears that he did not mention to Hitler the subject of those conversations.[44]

The truth about the events in Hitler's office will probably remain hidden forever. It is very hard to assume that these conversations were not intercepted and Hitler not informed. The tense situation, however, was quickly defused, because of economic concessions granted later on by Carol II to Nazi Germany in order to obtain sympathy and good will.[45]

These events gave the royal dictatorial regime a certain degree of stability, especially in foreign affairs. The king's direct involvement in ordering these assassinations created a state of tension among the masses, and the terror campaign of the Legionaries still at large reached a climax. The situation suited Germany; that nation was subtly infiltrating all sectors of the Romanian economy, without making any extraordinary efforts. In their triumphant march through Europe, the Germans did not find anywhere "a more devoted Fifth Column or one more enthusiastic about bringing Germany's interests to reality."[46]

Some time later, in February 1939, Armand Calinescu, named President of the Council of Ministers following the death of Patriarch Miron Cristea, firmly asserted in an interview with the French daily *Paris Soir* that "the Iron Guard is now a story of the past. The Iron Guard no longer exists!"[47]

But the facts proved the contrary! Shortly before this interview, a clandestine Legionary workshop manufacturing grenades and bombs blew up, and a number of flame throwers were found in clandestine Legionary buildings. Later there was a plot to assassinate the king in his box at the Hippodrome during the horse races.

A network of couriers sprang up; they came and went on various missions between Legionaries who had fled abroad and those remaining

in the country. One of the most important of these missions was to avenge
the assassination of the Captain.

As a result of police infiltration into the membership of the movement,
some attempts were discovered in time. Nevertheless, on September 21,
1939, a group led by Miti Constantinescu, who had come from Germany
especially for the purpose, succeeded in assassinating Calinescu. Occupying the radio station, one of the terrorists announced to the people
in a choked voice, "The Captain has been avenged!" Then they surrendered to the authorities.

After a few hours they lay, shot dead, where they had assassinated
Armand Calinescu. The actions taken did not stop there; in every county
capital some three to fifteen Legionaries were executed by being shot
or hung from electrical poles. They were left there for days, with placards
reading: "This is how traitors are punished."

Once rid of his opponents, Carol II set up the National Renaissance
Front, Frontul Renasterii Nationale (NRF), offering new trappings to
the masses that were more resplendent than what the Legion had offered. He dressed the members of the party in elegant navy blue uniforms, differentiating them by rank and so forth. In order to drink
deeply from the cup of power, he organized a gigantic parade in front
of the Royal Palace. The populace observed, with surprise and ironic
smiles, Nicolae Iorga, Alexandru Vaida-Voievod, Mihai Ralea, and Mihai
Ghelmegeanu parading in NRF uniforms. While the country watched
this carnival of grotesque masks, war broke out. Romania felt itself increasingly isolated after the fall of Poland, although it continued to have
undiminished confidence in the support of France and England.

Agitation increased in the spring of 1940. The Russo-German pact
radically changed the balance of forces. The king felt obliged to make
a move that would change the direction of foreign policy. Renouncing
the guarantees made by England, especially after the collapse of France,
he set up a fascist party, the Party of the Nation, (Partidu Natiunei) and
Ion Gigurtu, an unknown engineer, appeared to lead it.

At this time a series of links were reestablished between the Iron Guard
and Carol II. Emissaries shuttled from one side to the other, seeking to
find solutions to the problems at issue. An amnesty gave the Legionaries
the opportunity to leave the camps where they had been concentrated,
and a declaration of obedience to the king signed by Horia Sima was
published on June 25, 1940. Horia Sima participated in the government
of Ion Gigurtu, along with two other Legionaries. Although he resigned
after a short time, the other Legionaries remained to continue their
activity, and a series of racial laws with an anti-Semitic character began
to be introduced. The day after the declaration just mentioned, June
26, 1940, the Soviet Union sent an ultimatum to Romania. It categorically

demanded the retrocession of Bessarabia, whose annexation in 1918 it had never recognized, and of Northern Bucovina.

The ultimatum had attached to it a map on which Molotov himself had drawn the new frontiers with red ink. Either because of a slip of the pen or because of calculated intention, the town of Herta and some twenty villages in its vicinity were also included in the Soviet ultimatum.[48]

10

The army and the entire Romanian administration had to leave Bessarabia and Northern Bucovina. Although the deadline for evacuation was four days, the Russians at once entered the territories, literally treading in the footsteps of the Romanian army, which was in full retreat.

During that time, subtle, perverse, well-cultivated propaganda spread tales that set minds afire—"The Jews are to blame!" "The Jews have insulted the Romanian army!" Never was any proof of these assertions produced. Since humiliation and deep pain must find a place to express themselves, and the civilian and military authorities could not be brought to respond, scapegoats were easily found: a large Jewish community had been living in Northern Moldavia for centuries. The Romanian armies, in retreating from the Ceremus to the Danube, showed differing attitudes and behavior. Those that retreated from Bessarabia, crossing the bridges over the Prut, generally behaved in a dignified and peaceable manner. But those that evacuated Northern Bucovina and Northern Bessarabia, coming into the country over the Prut and the Siret, perpetrated horrible crimes and massacres whose victims were the Jews, inhabitants of the cities, towns, and villages in Romanian territory. The signal for beginning these massacres was given on June 29, 1940, by a military unit under the command of Major Goilov, which began its sinister activity in the little town of Mihoreni in Dorohoi County. Without any reason, and not thinking it necessary to present a pretext that was at all plausible, they arrested several Jews, Sloime Wainer, his son User Wainer, and his daughters Roza Wainer and Fani Zekler. The latter was killed while holding a child in her arms. When they had been taken into the forest of Tureatca, the soldiers who had tortured, beaten, and raped those who had been arrested found a shoemaker named Moscovici, his wife, and two children, as well as his daughter-in-law, also with two children. All were lined up in front of a ditch and shot. The shoemaker's son, who was found later, was beaten until he died. The next day, June 30, 1940, troops of the 16th Infantry Regiment, commanded by Major Valeriu Carp (who later became famous for the massacres of Jews he accomplished), while on their way to their garrison at Falticeni, stopped in the village of Ciudei in Storojinet County. By the orders of this valiant military commander, a number of Jews were gathered in the center of the village. They included Moise Sechter, Dr. Conrad Kreis, the Hessmann brothers, Herman Gross, his wife, daughter, and a grandchild. All of them were shot. In order to satisfy his sadistic instincts, Major Carp tortured Dr. Kreis in a bestial manner; his body was literally torn to shreds.

On the same day, eighteen soldiers under the command of a lieutenant broke into the house of Suhar Lax in the village of Costina in Suceava County. After they tortured him, they tied him to the tail of a horse. With shouts of laughter, the entire group of murderers had him dragged through the streets of the village. After that, although he was dead, they riddled his body with dozens of bullets.

But the banner event of that sad period in the lives of the Jews of Romania took place on July 1, 1940, in the city of Dorohoi. On the morning of that day, the city learned of unusual activity that stirred up panic and uncertainty in the ranks of the Jewish population. A letter "C," written in chalk, had appeared on some houses, meaning that they were inhabited by Christians. Religious icons also appeared in some windows, attesting to the religion of the inhabitants.

On that day, the burial of a Jewish soldier was to take place in the Dorohoi cemetery. This soldier had died under heroic circumstances, and the military authorities asked that he be buried with military honors. In the little town of Herta an incident had taken place, between a Soviet tank soldier and a Romanian officer. The Russian, without hesitating, drew his revolver and prepared to fire it at Captain Boros, a native of Bacau. Beside him there was a soldier, Iancu Solomon. Realizing what was about to take place, the soldier abruptly put himself in front of his officer, shielding the officer's life with his own body. The Russian, undisturbed, fired, killing the soldier and the officer. When the military authorities inquired about the identity of the soldier, they learned that he was a Jew. Burial services were organized for the victims, the officer's in the Christian cemetery, the Jew's in the Jewish cemetery. The 8th Artillery Regiment sent a company made up of Jewish soldiers, under the command of Warrant Officer Emil Bercovici, in order to provide military honors.

The Jewish community of Dorohoi, wishing to honor the memory of the heroic soldier, encouraged an increasing number of Jews to participate in the ceremony, which was to take place at the cemetery at 2:00 P.M. In spite of the heavy, threatening atmosphere that prevailed in the city, especially since the news of pogroms and crimes committed in places where the troops had passed in their retreat had begun to spread, a large number of Jews, headed by the rabbi, took part in the burial service.

Taking advantage of the occasion, officers and soldiers of the 3rd

Grenadier Regiment, who were just moving out of the city along the highway leading to Suceava, which passed quite close to the cemetery, went into action. The honor company was just leaving the cemetery, having completed its mission. The soldiers of the 3rd Regiment ordered the Jewish soldiers to take off their military uniforms, and there, at the cemetery fence, they shot them all. After they shot Warrant Officer Emil Bercovici, they placed a machine gun in his hands and called on witnesses to show how the Jew had fired on the Romanian army. A group of soldiers entered the cemetery, opened the doors of a mausoleum, and under the pretext of looking for arms, pulled out the frightened Jews who had hidden themselves there.

Led along the Valea Cimpului highway, the entire group, which included a two-year-old child and seven-year-old, was killed by bursts of machine-gun fire. An old man of eighty-eight who escaped alive from the hail of bullets was killed with blows on the head from the butt of a gun. Fifty-three Jews were shot. The others succeeded in escaping. At the same time, the pogrom was continuing in the city of Dorohoi. Civilians joined the soldiers, and together they entered houses to plunder them. There were cases of bestiality never encountered until that time in Romania.

Avram Calmanovici, after being tortured, was killed by cutting off his genital organ. An old couple, Eli and Feiga Riezel, were shot after the old woman's ears had been cut off so that her earrings could be stolen. Herscu Ioina Ionas, an old man of ninety-four, was shot after the hairs of his beard had been pulled out.

Soldiers on trucks fired with machine guns on houses inhabited by Jews while the vehicles were moving. All this was brought to an end by a torrential rain that cleared the streets of the city.

It is worth mentioning that Captain Stino of the 24th Infantry Regiment made gigantic efforts to make sure that the Jewish soldiers in his unit were not killed. General Sanatescu and Colonel Ilasievici did the same thing. On July 1, 1940, Major Valeriu Carp's military unit arrived in the commune of Zaharesti in Suceava County. In the village there was one single Jew. So Jews that lived in neighboring communes, such as Vorniceni, Ilisesti, Vicov, Banila, and others, were pulled in, thirty-six persons in all. All were tortured mercilessly; many had their fingers cut off or their tongues cut out; they were beaten, and the women raped. Finally they were gathered around a ditch, where they were shot dead. In order to appease his perverse instincts, Major Carp ordered two Jews who belonged to his military unit to participate in the execution. One of them was a native of Burdujeni, and the other was a native of Suceava, and they knew many of the Jews who were to be murdered. In order to offer his daughter an opportunity for "amusement," the major set up a machine gun and she participated directly in the massacre.

Encouraged by the savagery committed by the military units, bands of peasants joined together and began, in their turn, to carry on pillaging and massacre. In the commune of Serbauti in Suceava County, Warrant Officer Bujica, the chief of the gendarmerie post, together with Hapinciuc, a peasant, broke into the house of Smil Getler, a Jew, where his wife and Leib Ellenbogen were present. All were shot, and the house was plundered. In the commune of Comanesti in Suceava County, Rabbi Leib Schechter was killed, together with his two sons and his wife, who was killed while she was saying a prayer.

In August 1940 the Jews were thrown out of the armed forces. Stripped of their military uniforms and dressed in the rags which were still to be found in the storehouses of the regiments that were in the midst of their retreat, they were sent home. On the trains they were easily recognized on account of their clothing, and in accordance with old practices, they were beaten and thrown from the windows of moving trains. The native population of Bessarabia and Northern Bucovina that was living in the country was obliged to return to the ceded regions. The crossing points were Galati-Reni and Dornesti in Bucovina. For the latter region, there was a Romano-Russian Commission functioning in Burdujeni, which completed its business in January 1941, when the frontier was closed. The Christians in this category who were at Burdujeni were returned to the cities from whence they had come. The 110 Jews who were there after the commission finished its business were kept there and housed in two rooms in the Burdujeni railroad station. They led a miserable existence, living off the small amount of help the Jewish community in Burdujeni could make available to them. Every evening groups of twenty to thirty Jews were pulled out and surrounded by soldiers, and were forced to cross the frontier into the ceded territories clandestinely. Because the frontier area had been mined, many Jews fell victim to explosions and to gunfire from the Soviets. By February 1941, only fifty-eight of the Jews remained alive. After intercession by Dr. W. Filderman, they were transferred from the hellish Burdujeni concentration camp to another one, the camp at Tg. Jiu!

11

The summer of 1940 was unusually feverish for Romania. The Hungarian claims on Transylvania came to be pressed more hotly, and following a visit by Ion Gigurtu and the Minister of Foreign Affairs to Hitler and Ribbentrop on July 26, 1940, the Germans advised them to begin direct discussions with Hungary to resolve their differences. The Hungarians demanded the cession of more than half of Transylvania, but the Romanians insisted on an exchange of populations. On August

24, 1940, the discussions being carried on at Turnu Severin were suspended without any results.

The Soviet Union encouraged the Hungarians to be intransigent in their demands, since they were interested in a weak Romania that would not represent a military force. Germany was in a difficult situation; on one side, it had promised support to Hungary, and on the other, it had material interests in Romania. An armed collision between these two countries could endanger the oil-producing region where it had vital interests. In view of this situation, Germany asked Italy to arbitrate and find a solution jointly with the disputing parties. The Romanian delegation, headed by Mihail Manoilescu, left for the discussions at Vienna. There they found Von Ribbentrop and Ciano in front of a spread-out map, where they had indicated exactly how much of Transylvania had to be ceded to the Hungarians. Representatives of all the political parties participated in the meeting of the Crown Council called by the king in connection with the cession of Transylvania. The vote was twenty-one for cession, one against or abstaining. The Crown Council had accepted cession! After the cession of Bessarabia and Northern Bucovina, the events in Transylvania amounted to a shocking cry of pain for the whole nation. Bitterness, sorrow, and deep humiliation filled the spirits of all. On August 30, 1940, it was a common thing for men to be seen weeping in the streets of Bucharest. As in Bessarabia and Northern Bucovina, a whole mass of people followed the army into the interior areas when it withdrew without firing a shot.

The public mood was unusually agitated. The army had been humiliated and was in a state of continuous movement towards its new garrisons. In various localities, great multitudes gathered to protest against the government, demanding the abdication of the king. Around the statue of Mihai Viteazu in Bucharest, the crowd demanded that Iuliu Maniu be brought to power. Green shirts began to reappear, and the country was splintered. Shortly afterwards, Bulgaria got Southern Dobrogia.

In view of this explosive state of affairs, Carol II called to the Palace General Ion Antonescu, the only military figure capable of being offered to the nation.

The Green Shirts had become more aggressive in the crowds that gathered in the public squares, and they expressed themselves more noisily in public. Shouts of "We want Lupescu!" and "We want the King!" were heard everywhere. In the regiments, manifestos began to appear demanding that the king leave, and on August 31, 1940, Horia Sima had a meeting with Colonel Dietrich of the SS, Himmler's authorized personal representative, who had been sent to Romania to prepare for the abdication of Carol II. On September 1 and 2, 1940, Ion Antonescu sought the support of Constantin Bratianu and Iuliu Maniu to form a national coalition government under his chairmanship. On September 3, Horia Sima demanded from Berlin the authorization for direct and effective action against those who had spoken in favor of a policy of national resistance. On September 4, 1940, the king again invited General Ion Antonescu to the palace, and after presenting the domestic and foreign political situation to him, and particularly the position of Romania under those circumstances, he asked Antonescu to form a new government. Following discussions held with representatives of the political parties, no result was reached.

Not seeing any other solution, the king agreed on September 5, 1940, after long hesitation, to grant full powers to General Antonescu. The mood of the country became even more agitated, and the population of the capital was in a fever. On the evening of September 5, gunfire could be heard, aimed at the Royal Palace and the office of the President of the Council of Ministers. The crowd moved en masse towards the Palace. General Antonescu visited the king again that evening, demanding that he abdicate. On the morning of September 6, 1940, at six o'clock, King Carol II abdicated after a reign of 10 years in favor of his son, Mihai.

On September 14, 1940, Ion Antonescu took for himself the titles of Leader (Conducator) of the State and Chief of the Legionary party. Horia Sima, the leader of the Legionary movement, became Vice-President of the Council of Ministers. All the political parties remained dissolved, including the Party of the Nation, Carol's last creation. The only political movements were the Legionary movement and the German ethnic group. The National Legionary State had been proclaimed!

3

"They Have Written a Page of Apocalyptic Shame in the Psalter of the Romanian People"*

1

The Legionary movement had come to power, having a serious and appreciable mass base.[1] The immense majority of the Romanian people looked with approving eyes on the "ascent to the throne" of the new regime. This was due partly to the fact that they were totally demoralized and disillusioned by the behavior and attitude of the former political parties that had succeeded each other in leading the country, and partly because they had faith in the enthusiasm of the young people who participated in the movement. To this was added the fact that members of the high Romanian aristocracy had participated in Legionary activity, and, later, had leadership positions in the government, which gave the Legionary movement some luster and a guarantee of stability.

The Legionary movement had succeeded in attracting some intellectuals, members of the middle classes coming from the ranks of the priests, schoolteachers, government officials, military men, and workers. This heterogeneous mixture, which rushed through the gates opened wide by the Legion was not an active, disciplined force educated in Codreanu's "school." On the contrary, they proved within a short time to be a disruptive element that contributed to the total destruction of the movement.

The government administrative apparatus, from the cabinet ministers down to the most minor functionaries in village mayors' offices, had a

*Traian Popovici, Mayor of the city of Cernauti, 1941–1942

long training in oppression and violence directed against the Jews. From the beginning of the Legionary administration they exhibited a servile attitude and extraordinary devotion in applying the orders that came from the "center." In their zeal, they many times went beyond them in their actions and tangled up the orders with regard to oppression of the Jewish population. This administrative "apparatus" formed the skeleton supporting the new administration.

In all these actions the prefects, Legionaries and later military men, and the mayors of the cities, villages, and towns had an important role, as did the police forces, the security forces, and the gendarmerie, which, instead of assuring the peace and safety of the citizens, placed themselves most of the time at the head of bands of looters and criminals.

The courts, under an appearance of neutrality and impartiality, were characterized by total obedience to the Legionary regime, to which they granted their support, as they had for so many years. The Romanian press had an important place in these complex circumstances. After the few publications in Romania with a democratic slant were suspended, and the members of a true journalistic elite were removed and denied the right to write and publish, the Romanian press in its entirety supported the fascist movement with all its resources and with newspapermen who were not lacking in talent.

Well aware of the role of the press and its power in a dictatorial regime, General Ion Antonescu declared in his first few days after taking power at a session of the Council of Ministers that he was giving extraordinary attention to the activities of the press; he asserted, "We have a controlled press in a controlled state."[2]

Having an old tradition in matters of anti-Semitic propaganda, the Romanian press identified itself with this ideology from the very beginning of the fascist regime, striving to shape a current of sympathy and approval for the actions against the Jewish population that followed.

What formed a backbone for General Ion Antonescu's regime and supported him in all his actions was the army. Its leadership in particular was made up of elements belonging to the aristocracy and upper middle class, and with rare exceptions, of members of the lower middle class in the cities and villages. It was conservative by tradition, held democracy in contempt, and was an old cradle of anti-Semitism. The Legionary movement favored the development of these feelings, and the officers, especially those of lower rank, and the NCOs and all ranks in the military units showed themselves openly opposed to the Jews.[3] To these were added a great number of priests, professors, and schoolteachers who had been preaching anti-Semitism from their high pulpits and teaching positions.

One of the first measures taken by Horia Sima was to reorganize the Corpul Muncitoresc Legionar (Legionary Workers' Corps). Instead of

Gheorghe Clime, a worker named Dumitru Groza, a former member of the Communist party, became the leader of this organization.[4]

In connection with the presence of the Communists in the Legionary movement or the collaboration between these extremist political movements, there had been hints of this long before the Legionaries came to power. For example, following some discussions held with Armand Calinescu,[5] Sir Reginald Hoare, the British Ambassador in Bucharest, wrote to Anthony Eden on February 7, 1938, as follows: "Calinescu asserted that Codreanu's party contains many strange elements, and there is not a shadow of doubt that when the Communist Party was declared illegal in Romania, the great majority of its members professed sympathy with the Legion."[6]

The same ambassador, in a report sent to his superiors in London on February 24, 1938, wrote with reference to a discussion held with General Ion Antonescu on that date that "the General then told me that he had held very serious talks with Mr. Codreanu about the presence of Communists in his movement."[7]

It is significant that among the points in the "Oath" that the Legionaries swore before the grave of Codreanu the following statement was made: "to struggle for the elimination of the exploitation of man by man."[8] This slogan, as became known only too well afterwards, had been a component part of the ideology professed by all the Communist parties.

Likewise, it is not at all surprising that on December 10, 1940, a meeting took place in the Caracal concentration camp for political prisoners between representatives of the Legion and Communist leaders who were in the camp, at which some proposals for collaboration were tried out by the Legionaries.

In this exceptionally favorable political and social climate, the Legion began its march.

2

From the first few days after the Legionary movement came to lead the state, a restless terror was released throughout the length and breadth of Romania. From within the walls of the torture chambers of the state police, the security force, the gendarmerie, the Legionary police, and the buildings of the sinister Case Verzi (Green Houses), stifled groans could be heard, and many of those who succeeded in escaping from these houses of torture were men who never recovered physically or mentally.

Tortures, beatings, torment, wrecking of private homes, searches in the dark of night, followed by total pillage of the houses that were searched, raping of women before the eyes of their helpless husbands, savage mistreatment of husbands in the presence of their wives and children, all these became routine happenings.

"We will make the country seem like the holy sun in heaven!" the Legionaries had proclaimed in the years before they took power. The slogan could be heard again when they were enthroned in the great ministerial armchairs and were organizing, guiding, and executing the measures which, in their minds, would lead to a "polishing" of Romanian realities until they would seem to "shine," even though the sun had hidden itself behind the clouds of Legionary terror.

An indescribable fear began to dominate the people, humbling their personalities and destroying their will. The proclamations of Ion Antonescu, written in a military style, with a soberness which asked for attention and sought confidence, proved ineffectual; the Legionaries purely and simply disregarded them!

Declarations of obedience, collaboration, and brotherhood between the movement and the General, during the first few days after they took power, sought to proclaim that a new era had opened up before Romania. After a short time, the reality proved to be totally different. The Legionary police and especially the Workers' Guards, along with their variant form, known as the Motorized Workers' Guards, made their presence felt even in the most remote places in the country.

Old quarrels were "liquidated" recklessly. The disciples of A. C. Cuza, the patriarch of the anti-Semitic movement in Romania, found themselves under direct attack by the Legionaries, and the homes of some of their political leaders were searched.

That was the least of it! The Legionaries asked General Ion Antonescu for three days in which they might liquidate all those whom they judged guilty of measures directed against the Legion in the past.

It was paradoxical that in spite of the outrages committed against the Jews, the regime took great care to legitimize crime and robbery. Thus those who were perpetrating them could work in the open; not only were they under the protection of the law, but they could claim that when they were acting in this manner, they were seeing to its application.

The Legionary legislation was characterized by the absence of any principle of right, of ethics, and particularly of juridical logic. Based on the principles of hate and violence, not knowing even the most elementary meaning of justice or real, true facts, it considered fiction as reality and denunciations as objective statements. On the one hand, the Legionary legislation was the instrument that gave a character of so-called legitimacy to the criminal acts of oppression, and on the other it was intended to hold under psychological tension the masses of Jewish people, who watched the daily appearance of this avalanche of laws intended to strangle them physically, morally, and materially. The Jews saw their existence crushed by a pressure they could not resist, and that being so, they gave way to every terrorist act and arbitrary demand for property.

In the provincial towns the terror was unleashed in all its brutality. Groups of Legionaries in front of Jewish stores blocked Christian customers from entering; posters reading "Jewish store" were seen everywhere. In the city of Buzau a group of some twenty young Jews were arrested on the charge of being Communists. However, when they were led before the judicial authorities, they were found not guilty and then freed. The presence of their names in the files of the Security Police later caused them to be sent to Transnistria, where they died. At Iasi, the Jews were subjected repeatedly to savage treatment, and the Jewish community was obliged to pay the sum of 6 million lei to stop the terror. The sum was deposited within a few days, and after a while everything went back to "normal".

The Mosaic religion was expelled from the group of religions recognized by the state, and its rabbis were subjected to harassment, beatings, and even assassinations. The property of the Jewish congregations was confiscated.

The Juridical Statute for the Jews, originated by Carol and approved and applied by the Legionaries, drove them out from under the protection of the laws. Anyone could attack their lives, liberty, or property without fear of being punished. In order to understand the mentality of some of the preeminent figures of those times, one significant example may be cited: Ion V. Gruia, the Minister of Justice, who framed these sinister racial laws, later appeared as a lawyer representing some Jewish firms before courts of justice to defend them against the laws he had originated.

Everywhere Jews were driven out of their jobs. The first step was taken by the First Bar Association, the one in Bucharest, an old citadel of anti-Semitic agitation. And so, of 1,479 Jewish lawyers, only 177 were left with the right to practice their profession, and even those were obliged to represent only Jews in the courts.[9]

These "promising" actions did not escape the attention of the press abroad. On September 30, 1940, the Romanian dailies reprinted an interview General Ion Antonescu had given to La Stampa, an Italian daily. The reporter wrote a series of laudatory comments on the Leader's speech and made hate-filled references to the Jews. On that occasion General Antonescu himself precisely defined his attitude towards the Jews publicly for the first time: "In Romania, it is first of all Romanians who must live and be advanced; the others [the Jews] come after them, if any free spaces remain."[10]

In the period that followed the Legionary "honeymoon," Legionaries infiltrated all Jewish enterprises, in the so-called battle to take over the

Kike stores organized by General Petrovicescu, the Minister of the Interior.[11]

It became a typical occurrence that when the proprietor of a Jewish enterprise was "invited" to the Legionary police headquarters and freed after a night of "convincing discussions," physically and morally destroyed, he would be met by a "well-wisher," usually a former friend, a neighbor, or the proprietor of a similar enterprise, who would offer to rescue him by "buying" his property for a ridiculous sum. Even these "compensations" were not paid.

In a country where a huge part of the population was undernourished and ravaged by social ills, where tuberculosis, pellagra, and syphilis were destroying thousands of lives, the Legionary government forbade Jewish doctors to give assistance to Christian people and drove them out of the small towns where they had practiced their profession.

What followed those months of preparation of a so-called legal basis was the systematic undertaking of acts of despoliation. The entire month of November 1940 was characterized by unprecedented acts of violence. Despite all this, it can be considered only a "training" period. In all the towns in the country a veritable competition began in the application of laws to "take over" Jewish property. After all the agricultural properties, vineyards, residences, and industrial and commercial enterprises were taken over in October, there remained one final objective for the Legionaries to achieve.[12] It was a typical occurrence in the regions of Transylvania and the Banat, where there was a large German population, for the Germans to come into possession of Jewish property before the Legionaries could. In view of this "disloyal competition," the Legionaries took action with utmost cruelty. The Jewish owners of properties that the Germans had taken possession of were arrested, and in the jails belonging to the Legionary police they were beaten until they agreed to issue a statement cancelling the "sales" they had made to the Germans. The Germans, seeing themselves done wrong by, in turn organized guards to watch over the real estate and enterprises they claimed as their own.

On November 10, 1940, an earthquake laid waste a good part of the country, and Bucharest in particular. In the center of the city, a high building, the Carlton, crumbled, burying the tenants under the ruins. Wishing to take part in the operation to rescue the injured victims, G. Cucos, a Jewish doctor, appeared at the site of the disaster. His "colleague," Dr. Ruptureanu, beat him savagely for daring to come to do his duty as a physician.

At Ploiesti, a city heavily hit by the earthquake, the Jews were hauled out on November 11 to clean up the wreckage of damaged buildings. In the morning of that day some sixty Jews, headed by Rabbi David Friedman, were arrested in the synagogue during the time of prayers.

After a few days, Horia Sima, who was visiting the city with Alexandru Ghica, the Director of the Police and the state security force, ordered that those who had been arrested should be freed. The Ploiesti police chief, disregarding the order, continued to beat and torture those who had been arrested and locked up in a barn for greater "security."

A few days after this visit, eleven of the Jews arrested were shot, together with Rabbi David Friedman. It should be pointed out that Professor Nicolae Iorga and Virgil Madgearu, the economist, were assassinated at the same time by a detachment of Legionaries. The irony of fate had it that on the floor of the Prahova gendarmerie headquarters, among the corpses of Rabbi David Friedman, a humble pretzel maker named Smil Smilovici, the barber Max Mendel, the dentist Mendel Mayer, the students Iosif Avram, Joffre Margolius, and others, lay the mutilated and violated corpse of the man known as the "Apostle to the Nation."[13]

He had been killed by the people whom he had raised and educated in a spirit of hatred and chauvinism. Nicolae Iorga's opposition to the Legion must not be seen as a change in his feelings towards the Jews. He was not in agreement with the pro-German orientation of the Legion and the methods it used to resolve political differences.

As one action organized by the Legionaries to exhume the bodies of those that had been killed by King Carol II, there took place the exhumation of the earthly remains of Corneliu Zelea Codreanu and his comrades. At the same time some sixty-five former dignitaries, political men, high-ranking officers, and gendarmes were held under arrest in the cells of the Jilava jail. On orders, they had performed assassinations of Legionaries. Deep discontentment was evident within the Legionary movement with the attitude of General Ion Antonescu with regard to these detainees. He had not agreed to give the Legionaries the right to set up special tribunals where the prisoners could be "tried." The fact that a Commission of Inquiry had been instituted and had begun its slow procedures, but with indecisive results, irritated them unspeakably.

On the night when the operations to exhume those who had been killed were taking place at the Jilava jail, a group of Legionary Workers' Guards under the command of Dumitru Groza broke into the jail. Pressing into the cells where those who had been arrested were held, they shot them, one after another. The group of murderers then lined up before the graves where the corpses were, and with voices transfigured with joy they cried, "We have avenged you, O Captain!" The news hit like a bomb. The Romanian bourgeoisie learned with surprise that the Legion had its eyes turned upon them, too. Their feelings were of total surprise, and aligning themselves with the actions of the Legion was considered a perfect remedy for proving their total acceptance of the Legion's practices.

All these things did not hinder the preparations for the burial of the remains of the Captain and the other Legionaries, which took place on a scale never seen before. A huge multitude gathered in the square in front of Cathedral Hill (Dealul Mitropoliei). Peasants from all corners of the country in handsome folk costumes, men and women of all ages, Legionaries in their green uniforms with pistols on their belts, and priests in solemn attire mingled somberly in the streets of the capital. Ion Zelea Codreanu and Horia Sima walked beside General Ion Antonescu. In the midst of the multitude, a group of women in mourning, the families of those who had been killed, addressed the people as a sign of deep, silent threat.

The arrival of the German army in Romania, under the pretext of training the Romanian army, gave new dimensions to the activity of the Legion and especially that of its leaders. The events that had taken place up to that time had led to greater dissension between Ion Antonescu and Horia Sima. They had tried to present a semblance of unity, at least before the nation, through direct discussions and a series of letters they exchanged with each other. From this date the problem was, exactly which one would have the German army's support? After the Jilava assassinations, Himmler wrote a personal letter to Horia Sima in which he congratulated him on the "performance" during that macabre night, remarking that "the measure was necessary, because it could not have been accomplished by an ordinary court of justice."[14]

After the funeral for Corneliu Zelea Codreanu was over, the representatives of Hitlerite Germany who had officially participated in the solemnities, Baldur von Schirach and Bohle, had a long conversation with Horia Sima, encouraging him to move at once to carry out other even more spectacular actions; they took the occasion to invite him to come to Germany to have an interview with Rudolph Hess. These discussions gave a new source of support to the Legion for carrying out its future actions. It appears that prominent persons in the leadership of Nazi Germany did not know of the support that Hitler had personally given directly to General Ion Antonescu. It is an indisputable fact that Antonescu enjoyed unusual esteem on Hitler's part. It can be asserted that after Mussolini, Ion Antonescu was the chief of state who enjoyed the greatest attention from the Führer. After the first visit the Leader had made to Hitler, the relations between the two became very cordial. From time to time Ion Antonescu had doubts with regard to Hitler's attitude towards him and the Legion, but he realized that in fact Hitler was deeply interested in a calm, peaceful Romania. Particularly at that time he needed an immense reservoir of raw materials and oil. He had still not told Antonescu of his intention to attack Russia. All these things made Hitler look with unusual sympathy on the general, for whom he had reserved an important role in future events and of whom he had such great need.

The approach of the new year, 1941, was awaited by the Legionaries as an unusual event. They wanted to organize a real "St. Bartholomew's Night" on New Year's Eve, to enter the new year "clean and purged." This idea of purging was connected with the assassination of all the former political leaders in the country. On December 29, 1940, General Ion Antonescu sent a secret order to all the county authorities in which he said, in part:

Having information that they have decided to execute the politicians of the old regime in your county on New Year's Eve and in the morning of New Year's Day, I invite you urgently to take the most severe measures to guarantee the lives of all those politicians who are in your county.[15]

Significantly, on finding the order, Horia Sima sent a new order in which he said in part, "The order in this form [that is, the one sent by Antonescu] must be considered as null and void."[16]

During that period and thereafter, the Jews continued to be maltreated and robbed, but no order was sent to the civilian military authorities in the counties such as might protect a peaceable population against the abuses and arbitrary actions to which it had been subjected.

At this time economic chaos had engulfed all sectors of public life, and prices were rising dizzily. The German army was emptying the warehouses, especially those containing foodstuffs, and trains loaded with parcels were heading to Germany.

Cultural life had begun to disintegrate. The schools were not functioning, and the professors and students were not coming to classes.[17]

In order to add new variations to the violence, the perverse imagination of those New Men took on insane forms. In the town of Hirsova a Jew, Alexandru Spiegel, had been brought from Constanta. After being savagely beaten all night long, stripped of his trousers and shoes, he could not get his feet into his shoes because of the beating. He was tied to a so-called post of infamy the next day and kept in the frightful cold until it got dark. The guards were changed every two hours because of the cold, but the helpless Jew who could no longer hold his head up had a splinter put under his chin to help him do so. Throughout the day children were brought from the school and encouraged to throw snowballs or pieces of frozen earth. At 9:00 o'clock in the evening Alexandru Spiegel died, but the chief of the Hirsova sector of the Legion declared proudly that he had "killed a Kike!"

At Braila the Jews were thrown into the Danube so as to "baptize" them for Christmas. An industrialist in Bucharest, after agreeing to turn over everything he had to the Legionaries, following horrible torture, was killed. His slashed body was dumped at the edge of the city.

The disestablishment of the Romanization Commission, the organizer of the looting of Jewish enterprises, led to a violent reaction by the members of the Legion. This step taken by the Leader, dispossessed them of the "legal" instrument which had given them the possibility of stealing to get rich. The disbanding of the Legionary police, which had been organized according to Gestapo principles, had no practical result, because General Petrovicescu, the Minister of the Interior, incorporated them into the ranks of the state police.

The relations between General Antonescu and the Legionaries became more and more discordant, and a special detachment was organized to assassinate him. New slogans began to be circulated, such as " 'Bourgeoisie' cannot find a place in Legion terminology,"[18] and "The Legion will radically solve the bourgeois problem." And one daily, the *Legionary Worker*, wrote, "For the first time in history the Romanian worker has triumphed over the exploiter." Foreseeing the future, the newspaper for the Legionary workers added, "The children of the workers will be those who will become the leaders of the Romanian nation."[19]

General Ion Antonescu made an urgent trip to Berlin. The meeting with Hitler at that time went beyond the limits of customary courtesy and had important consequences. The discussion turned on the excesses of the Legion and on the relations between Ion Antonescu and Horia Sima in particular. The Leader asked exactly what was to be done with such fanatics, and Hitler replied quite clearly, "One needs to get rid of them," and then talked about the way a machine gun must be used.[20]

The lesson was perfectly well comprehended! Hitler informed Antonescu about Plan Barbarossa, and Antonescu promised that Romania would be totally aligned with the Nazi plans. When he returned to Bucharest, Antonescu understood the situation perfectly, but the Legionary commanders did not. They simply enjoyed the sympathies of some members of the German Embassy who prodded them and encouraged them. As a result, the activities of the Legionaries became more and more directly aimed against the Leader.

During this period, a German major was shot in front of the Athenee Palace Hotel in Bucharest, "without the General Security Force nor the Police Prefecture having even one surveillance agent or any information to warn of the attack."[21]

As a result of this act General Petrovicescu, the Minister of the Interior, Al. Ghica, the director of the Police Prefecture, and Maimuca, the director of the General Security Force, were dismissed. All these men, however, refused to leave their posts and barricaded themselves in the buildings where they performed their duties. The assassination of the German major gave a perfect pretext. The Legionary leadership called the masses out into the streets to demonstrate against Ion Antonescu. In a manifesto addressed to the students, Viorel Trifa, the future bishop of the Romanian Church in America, wrote in part, "The understanding between the Romanians and the Germans is being imperiled by the Jews and Masons who have killed the German major."[22]

Considering the fact that events were hurrying along, Horia Sima ordered a "Legionary alarm" on January 19, 1941. All the organizations were in a state of alert, and the actions that took place were intended to win German sympathies at any price; and in any case it was a good occasion for the Legionaries to be kept in groups, ready to act on orders.

In order to ensure quiet in the provincial cities, and particularly to cut off the possibility of the Legionaries' receiving support and aid from their organizations in the counties, General Ion Antonescu ordered that the prefects and mayors, who were all Legionaries, be changed. Rebellion was imminent! In organizing it, absolute measures were taken in time, and special emissaries were sent to various places in the country, carrying verbal orders. The police arsenals in the country were seized, arms found in special warehouses were bought, and every means was used to get the most comprehensive and varied sorts of armaments possible. At a meeting of the "den" chiefs in the capital, Nicolae Patrascu, the Secretary General of the Legion movement, declared:

A divorce between the Legion and the General is inevitable. . . . The Legionaries are many and General Antonescu is a single individual. We know that we will be dominated by the military. We know that the senior officers are with him, but the junior officers are with us. . . . There will be firing from every window.[23]

On January 21, 1941, Horia Sima ordered the call-up of the armed Legionary Workers' Corps. As a result, columns of armed workers moved towards Roma Street, where Alexandru Ghica was barricaded, and he took command. His aides were Viorel Trifa, Gaina, and Cutzamina. The last weapons were pulled out of the Police Prefecture and the General Security Force where Inspector Baciu was located with fifty Legionaries. At the same time Legionary workers occupied the telephone building, the radio station, and other buildings at various points in the capital.

The Legionary rebellion had begun!

3

In Bucharest the situation deteriorated rapidly. The first exchange of shots took place between the Legionaries who had barricaded themselves in various buildings and public institutions and the army, which was trying to break into those places. Since the radio station was occupied by the Legionaries, it broadcast continuous appeals to rebel and incitements to pillage and commit crime, together with bulletins announcing that several entire corps of the army had left for Bucharest to join with the Legion. Names of generals and commanders of major military units began to circulate. At the same time, an atmosphere of agitation was stirred up by groups of Legionaries in the Motorized Workers' Guards who rode through the streets on motorcycles transmitting orders, and trucks loaded with Legionaries and banners fluttering in the wind moved through the districts of the city, singing songs extolling death.

All these things did not affect the residential districts, the streets with quiet villas in the vicinity of Herastrau Park, the comfortable houses in Dorobanti Park and Bonaparte, the Cotroceni district, and others. That was where the aristocracy and the high Romanian bourgeoisie lived, whom General Ion Antonescu stood wholly in need of for his future actions.

The same calm did not reign in the districts inhabited by the Jewish population: Dudesti, Vacaresti, and the neighboring streets. Throughout the period of the serious massacres, pillaging, and arson that took place there, not one military or police unit was sent to assure one small semblance of security for a desperate populace totally lacking any support.

The Legion finally had those "three days," to which they added three nights of sorrow, tears, and fury. However, they did not use this fury against those who had oppressed them, those who had tortured them, those who had interned them in concentration camps, those who had broken their backs, but against the Jews! They were the ones who were killed. The assertion made through perverse, subtle propaganda that in fact General Ion Antonescu had suppressed the Legionary rebellion in order to save the Jews is a sinister twisting of the truth.

The facts have confirmed that General Ion Antonescu needed this rebellion. He repressed it, executing the orders of Hitler. The Führer became uneasy with the situation in Romania and did not want it to get out of control. The Jewish districts in Bucharest were left for a period of three days and three nights at the mercy of the vilest and most harmful fascist elements, which had been educated, incited, and trained for years for that "great" hour!

Legionaries, students, young people and old, priests, intellectuals of every kind, women, and children started out from all the districts of Bucharest in a rush to get things without working. They descended like a curse on the Jewish districts, devoting themselves there to a veritable competition of death and destruction. They knew perfectly well that nothing and no one would stop them or hold them responsible. In order not to create "confusion," the houses of Christians had illuminated icons and other such religious decorations placed in the window. When these were lacking, an inscription, "Christians live here," was sufficient. Other inscriptions began to appear: "Kikes live here!" In their own way the local people helped those who came from other districts and were unfamiliar with the area.

People who had been neighbors of the unfortunate Jews, people who for years had lived in the same district and on the same streets, were transformed into informers and now worked with the gangs who were pushing into the houses, from which groans and screams of fright issued.

Gasoline was poured along the streetcar tracks and set afire. The district took on the image of an apocalypse. The street was burning! The houses caught on fire too, and the mobs crowded in through the broken shutters of stores to plunder them. A soldier was seized on the street by the Legionaries. They soaked him with gasoline and set him afire.

General Ion Antonescu was waiting! He did not make one gesture to stop this incredible outrage, of which he was perfectly well informed.

Fighting between the Legionaries and the army continued around some of the government buildings. The General needed this. The German Embassy was following the course of the fighting closely. German patrols began to circulate through the streets, without intervening.

In the quiet of his office, General Ion Antonescu was waiting. After a while, the telephone rang. The general lifted the receiver and a smile appeared on his ruddy face. Hitler was on the other end of the line. He asked him to restore order. "I don't need any fanatics. I need a sound Romanian Army."[24]

Hitler asked *him* for this, not Horia Sima!

For a period of more than seventy hours the Jewish districts were at the mercy of the masses. During this interval, several thousand Jews were hauled out of their houses, arrested in the street and in houses of prayer, and transferred to Legionary headquarters, police precinct houses, or even to some synagogues, for example, the Malbim synagogue, which had been occupied and converted into a torture center.

While the wrecking and destruction was continuing in the districts mentioned, groups of Legionaries who had the exact addresses, another proof that the actions had long been planned and prepared for, pulled out of their houses leaders of the Jewish community, rabbis, religious workers, synagogue personnel, personnel of the Jewish Congregation, and along with them journalists, writers, doctors, and engineers. These people were carried to different destinations and subjected to savage treatment. Some of those held under arrest at the Prefecture of the Police of the Capital, like D. Aschenazy (Ashkenazi) and Dr. A. Aftalion, were not able to stand the torture and threw themselves from the third floor of the building.

The workers at the Parcomet factory behaved in a bestial manner. Among those arrested by these people was a group of young men who had been hauled out of the Zionist organization on Anton Pann Street. For the space of three days they were beaten until they lost consciousness, and then they were made to drink a mixture of bitter salt mixed with gasoline, kerosene, and vinegar. Later they were shut up in the basement of the jail and left to lie in their own filth.

At the headquarters of the Legionary Workers' Corps at 37 Calarasi Avenue, more than two hundred Jews were held under arrest, men and women, including H. Gutman, the venerable rabbi, and his two sons, Joseph and Jacob. After they had been robbed of everything they possessed, the whole group was subjected to a new system of beating. They were forced to run up the stairs to the upper floor. Legionaries armed with sticks were posted along the stairs, and the people being beaten had to run up and down under a rain of blows. The women were led to the basement of the building and beaten on the face and head with ox sinews, and then they were freed!

The others who were arrested after this were beaten and tortured from 7:00 o'clock in the evening until dawn, and were then forced to do calisthenics. In that hard, chaotic dawn of January 22, 1941, they were divided into groups, made to climb into trucks, and sent out in an unknown direction. The first group of Jews was transported to the Jilava forest, where they were shot. The second group was taken to the so-called Captain's Farm in the Straulesti district of Bucharest, where they too were shot. In that cursed place seventy-nine more Jews were rounded up, and in time they got the same treatment. The drama that befell Rabbi H. Gutman had truly Dantesque aspects, because of the magnitude of the tragedy and suffering to which a man, a rabbi, and a father was subjected.

Rabbi Gutman and his two sons were in the last transport vehicle sent from the Engineer Gh. Clime Local Headquarters of the Legionary Workers. When the truck stopped at the edge of the woods, shots could be heard which came from the massacre of the Jews brought in the other transports. The Rabbi got out, together with his sons. As he held both of them by the hand, they were made to lie face down on the ground. Many bullets were fired at all three of them. The father felt nothing in his body, but in his hands which were squeezing the hands of his children, their pulses beat slower and slower until they stopped. . . .

The murderers left, and silence settled over this empire of the dead. The Rabbi, the only [one] left alive among dozens of corpses, got up from beside the inert bodies of his children, and walking to the highway, he encountered two gendarmes who uged him to leave. As he walked in a daze along the highway, he was spotted by German sentries who took him to the Jilava town hall. Seven other Jews were there, four of them wounded. All were kept at the town hall all day Wednesday, and in the evening were taken to the forest again, stretched out with their faces to the ground and shot. For the second time, the Rabbi was not hit. He stayed in the darkness among the corpses until two Legionaries came;

they were stealing the clothes of the dead. They wanted to shoot him again, but in the end they let him off, urging him to leave the woods for the village of Darasti. Towards daybreak he arrived once more at the Jilava town hall. Enraged by the fact that he had not died, the Legionaries there tortured him all day Thursday. He was mocked, beaten, and the hair on his head and in his beard was plucked out. They told him that at night he would be shot again, and that this time he could not work another miracle so he could get away. Before then, he was freed by four gendarmes! (The Legionary rebellion had been ended!)

Accompanied by a lieutenant, he returned to the forest once more, where he again found his sons among dozens of corpses completely stripped of their clothing. After moistening the cold skin of the corpses with his own saliva, he wrote their names on their bodies so they could be identified with a pencil borrowed from the officer.[25]

At dawn on January 23, 1941, a truck from the Podsudeck sausage factory happened to load on fifteen Jews from among those held under arrest at the Prefecture of the Police of the Capital, and transported them to the city abattoir.

The statements by Reserve Lieutenant I. N. Vladescu, the military prosecutor, in the report he made at the inquiry after the Legionary rebellion, stir the emotions:

TO THE ABATTOIR. Under the pretext of a movement of a political nature, the Legionaries did mass murder [at the city abattoir, at Baneasa]. More than a hundred men were assassinated. All were found with their bellies deeply slashed by the despicable assassins, who used a butcher's knife for this purpose. As masters in the art of torture, they took the intestines they had plucked out of their victims' bodies and tied them like neckties around the necks of those murdered.[26]

All this took place inside the abattoir, while outside it a great number of Legionaries were singing, making a mockery of Jewish psalms of prayer. A fifteen-year-old girl was killed and hung on a meat hook. The others were killed in the same way, following the procedure used when cattle are slaughtered. The bodies of the victims were later chopped up, and hunks of flesh were hung on butcher's hooks, carrying the inscription "Kosher meat."

At the same time, entire families were murdered when houses pointed out to Legionaries were broken into. One event among so many stood out for its cynicism and cruelty. A family of Jews were living in a building at 4 Petre Locusteanu Street. On the first night of the rebellion, a number of Legionaries attacked the house. The tenants were Oscar Andrei, an engineer, and his wife, as well as his son and daughter-in-law with their eight-month-old son. Hearing the Legionaries smashing open the door with hatchets, they got out by the roof, using a skylight. From there they came down to an adjoining building, which they entered through the attic, and from there they knocked on the door of some neighbors, begging them to shelter them. The householder, who worked at the Conservatory of Music and was a great lover of sonatas, refused to open up for them and sent them away with insulting remarks, threatening to denounce them. Not having anywhere to go, they returned home. All were hauled away, and later they were found shot and stripped of their clothing beside the bridge beyond the Sabar River.

The building of the Federation of the Union of Jewish Communities was one of the targets of the Legionaries. It was invaded by a group of twenty-four Legionaries. They smashed in the doors to the offices and wrecked them. Later they went up to the apartment of the Chief Rabbi, Dr. Alexandru Safran, where they stole everything that had any value. Beginning the next day, while the Legionaries were still in the building, they arrested all the people who came into the building for one reason or another, and locked them up in the cellar.

Other groups busied themselves especially with destroying, pillaging, and burning the synagogues. Religious artifacts of great value were lost, Torahs were torn and trampled underfoot, and in the delirium that had overcome him, one Legionary thrust his knife into the sacred parchment of the Torah. In this manner, twenty-five synagogues were destroyed and burned. The property losses were immense, but the sorrow was even greater for the houses of prayer, some of them dating back to the beginning of the nineteenth century, which burned like torches.

Ion Antonescu waited calmly as the masses of Legionaries moved towards the North Station to occupy or to destroy that important node in the rail network. Although the German command begged the Leader to send out the army en masse and take firm action, he waited to be asked to do this by high German authorities. On January 23, 1941, Hitler again called him on the telephone, offering him the help of the German army. "The Romanian army is sound and will restore order!" General Antonescu replied. From the other end of the line was heard a highly satisfied exclamation of "Heil Antonescu!"[27]

It was then that the Leader decided that his moment had come! Several military units, escorted by light tanks, changed the situation immediately, and the "New Men" began to appear in front of the institutions occupied by the Legionaries, with their hands up.

From the comfortable place where he had been hiding throughout the rebellion, which was kept secret from everyone, Horia Sima issued his communiqué of capitulation. The news went through the city, and for a moment people held their breath. Could it be true?

A light snow began to fall over Bucharest, and then the sun rose, turning everything into mud. Those who recall it, those who lived through those hours, cannot forget! Their steps took them to the districts

that had been worst hit, Dudesti and Vacaresti. It was the image of an
apocalypse. There were men with their heads bandaged; everywhere
things were thrown about and destroyed; pillaged stores looked through
smashed panes at streets where people had lived and worked, and once
had smiled. The walls of the houses, riddled by bullets, looked exactly
like faces ravaged by measles.

Cars belonging to news correspondents and foreign ambassadors began to appear on the streets; they were filming the disaster, but the
people were silently moving towards the morgue, seeking out their dear
ones. Several tanks surrounded the building in order to protect them
from new violence, but the people could do nothing more than cry.
Robert St. John wrote:

Accounts of the atrocities committed by the Legionaries during the pogrom
might never have been believed by anyone, except that we saw some of it happen,
we counted the corpses, we noted the mutilations, we inspected what little was
left of the seven once-beautiful synagogues, we saw the whole quarter in ruins,
and we took careful notes on exactly how the Jews of Bucharest were killed that
afternoon, that night, and the next day.... The actual number of Jewish cas-
ualties is not important. Thousands survived to taste of Nazi cruelty later. Nor
is it important at this late date to try to describe what a ruined ghetto looks like.
After the desecration of the Jewish quarter of Bucharest I saw many other ruins
during the war.... But I do remember the sick feeling I had in the pit of my
stomach when I saw fire engines arrive in front of a synagogue which had just
[been] set afire and legionaries with guns in their hands forced the firemen to
drive away [the great Sephardic synagogue known as the Spanish Temple, a
structure dating from the nineteenth century].... For sixteen years I have [been]
trying to forget some of the little snapshots my mind took that day.[28]

In front of the North Station there was a holiday stir: from elegant
cars descended dignitaries in formal clothing, many senior officers in
full dress, and the personnel of the German Embassy in particular. On
the platform, a red carpet contrasted with the puddles of water and mud
all around, but appearances had been saved. The train came into the
station carrying silvery snow that had fallen on it when it was crossing
the Carpathians.

Those present waited tensely. The doors of the official car opened,
allowing a wave of perfumed vapor to escape from the well-heated interior. Baron Manfred von Killinger, the new ambassador of Nazi Germany to Bucharest, stepped down, a massive man in the resplendent
uniform of a high dignitary of the Reich.

It was January 24, 1941.

In the cemetery on the Giurgiu highway, 128 Jews killed in the pogrom
were buried, and in front of their tombs were buried the Torahs that
had been desecrated by the Legionaries.

It is significant that although some of the Legionaries succeeded in escaping and others were imprisoned, the Legionary spirit, its anti-Semitism, and all the aberrant forms under which it manifested itself, continued to exist among the people. When they had the opportunity, this anti-Semitism was practiced in ways even more destructive than ever before.

Afterwards there was a period of calm, during which the German mission installed itself firmly, exploiting Romanian resources of raw materials, foodstuffs, and oil; its entire attention was directed towards training and instructing the army.

The majority of the Legionaries, who held various ranks in the military hierarchy, were mobilized and found their regiments situated in the border areas. Under of the anonymity of the military uniform they wanted to slip by unobserved, and if they could be forgotten, that would be a good thing for the time being! Ion Antonescu was perfectly well aware of the situation and knew that these people would be shock troops on which he could count when the moment came!

On June 11 and 12, 1941, the accords between Romania and Germany were signed at Munich and later at Berchtesgaden. By these agreements the Romanian government undertook to participate with all its forces at the side of the German army in the struggle against the Soviet Union.

On the evening before the operations on the front began, the Jews between the ages of sixteen and sixty in the towns located in the vicinity of the Prut and the Siret were forcibly evacuated and interned in the concentration camps for political prisoners at Tg. Jiu.

At dawn on June 21, 1941, one could hear the voice of General Ion Antonescu on the radio, addressing the army: "I order you to cross the Prut!"

4

Romania moved into the whirl of events leading up to World War II and later participated in it unconditionally on the side of Hitlerite Germany as one of the countries with a powerful and well-organized anti-Semitic movement.

The events that took place after the outbreak of the war against the Soviet Union were not, as such, spontaneous actions, manifestations of anarchy, or frustrated desires for revenge. On the contrary! Everything had been prepared beforehand, even in the finest details, by men who were perfectly educated and trained for this purpose. These people had broad, substantial technical means available for organizing and carrying through the "missions" entrusted to them. That they were accomplished with such punctuality and such "remarkable" results is due partly to this organization and partly to the broad support of those parts of the Romanian population that were mobilized and sent to the front during that period. In the army there were Legionaries, Cuzists, fascists, and fascist sympathizers from the other political parties, and to these was added a large number of individuals who considered the moment to be opportune for getting rich.

World War II was marked by the horrors done by the Nazis. This is a well-known fact, and commentaries are useless! But here we are not speaking of a comparison between the crimes of the Nazis and those perpetrated by the Romanians, both civilian and military, in Bucovina, Bessarabia, and later in Transnistria. Of course, their magnitude has to be taken into consideration. But what must be borne in mind is that in the years 1940–1944 more than four hundred thousand Jews were killed in Romania, the liberated provinces, and the territory occupied under the name of Transnistria.

Romania never had an "organized," scientific system of "liquidating" the Jewish population. What was clearly known and approved of, from the highest authorities of the state down to the humble civil servant in the village offices, was that these people had to be killed! This business was carried out in Romania before the extermination camps began to function in Europe, before the death trains began to cross countries to take victims to the concentration camps in Poland, and before the ovens began to smoke in Auschwitz, Maidanek, Treblinka, and elsewhere.

Not having any "scientific" means of extermination—the lack of which, by the way, was never felt—they used the classic means, the ones they had available: beating, torture, the noose, the pistol, the machine gun, in turn or all at once. They were applied to individual Jews, to groups of Jews, or to entire communities.

On the completion of these "operations," everyone had his reward. People were robbed before they were killed, their corpses were plundered, their homes and their shops were emptied. Whatever could not be carried off was destroyed. General Ion Antonescu's order to cross the Prut was not carried out immediately, like a glorious military parade on a holiday. The Soviet army put up stubborn resistance, and the losses of the Romanian army were severe. Merely mentioning the fighting at Tiganca (on the Prut) to the right of the small town of Falciu would be sufficient!

The bridgehead at Tg. Sculeni (Skulyany) was occupied by Romanian and German troops with heavy sacrifices. In this sector the 6th Ranger Regiment was operating, which had been garrisoned at the city of Balti (Bel'tsy) in Bessarabia. Its commander, Colonel Maties Ermil, requested permission to participate directly in the fighting to take revenge on the Jews who had humiliated it during the retreat in 1940.

Immediately after the seizure of the bridgehead by two battalions of the German 305th Regiment commanded by Colonel Buck and one battalion from the Ranger Regiment commanded by Major Garaiac, a counterattack by the Soviet infantry pushed the German troops back across the Prut. The Romanian battalion and the Command Company of the 6th Ranger Regiment, headed by Captain Ion Stihi and Second Lieutenant Eugen Mihailescu, remained on the spot. They spread the rumor that the defection of the Germans was due to an attack by the Jews in Sculeni.

Buck, the German commander, threw other battalions into the fight, regained the position, and ordered that the civilian population be evacuated. Those who were to execute the order were Captain Stihi and Second Lieutenant Mihailescu. They evacuated the Christian inhabitants of Sculeni to neighboring villages, but took the Jews to a place known as Stinca Roznovanu. There all the goods they were carrying were seized from them; a tent was filled with jewelry, money, gold, and everything that the people considered of value and had taken with them.

It is worth emphasizing that both the Romanian officers were from the local area, and Eugen Mihailescu, a theology student, in other words, a future priest, was the son of the notary at Tg. Sculeni. He had been a child with many of the Jews who were killed, he had gone to school with them, and afterwards, he liquidated them.

Some forty Jews were forced to dig several graves. These two officers, with the help of a sergeant who was a butcher by trade, killed every living Jewish soul in Tg. Sculeni!

In connection with this mass murder, Colonel Mihai Isacescu of the 6th Ranger Regiment was heard as a witness at the trial of these criminals after the war, on June 18, 1947. He declared, among other things:

It is not true that the population came out with white flags, after which they attacked Capt. Otel's company together with the Russians. The truth is that a Russian unit, about the size of a company, attacked Capt. Otel's company on the flank and put it to flight, but the Russians withdrew, taking with them Capt. Otel, who was wounded in the foot. The position which was made up afterwards by the regiment was invented to justify the lack of reasoning in the regiment, which had sent out the company, without trustworthy intelligence, toward the heights to the Northeast . . . where [they were] required to hold the position until the regiment arrived.[29]

The liberation of Northern Bucovina and Bessarabia was accompanied over the whole route of the Romanian army in its advance by deeds exceeding the most perverse imagination.

In order to organize, coordinate, and execute these actions, a special unit trained for this purpose had existed as early as the time of Carol II; from the beginning, it had precise directives. This unit was taken over by General Ion Antonescu with all of its personnel.

The Special Intelligence Service, known by its abbreviated name, the SSI, which strongly resembled its German counterparts in Himmler's SS, had a political mission of internal espionage directed against political figures and particularly against Jews. In order to strengthen these "institutions" in their sphere of activity, senior officers were detailed to them, who had among other missions that of drawing up exact lists with the names of Jews who lived in various regions, and in Moldavia in particular.

Eugen Cristescu was at the head of this organization. He was known for his total obedience to King Carol II, and he served Ion Antonescu with the same subservience and loyalty. He gave the order, before the operations began on the front, to deploy a special unit which was later known by the name of Operational Echelon I. More than 160 men were deployed in a column made up of automobiles, trucks, and other means of transportation. Cristescu was surrounded by senior officers, a staff perfectly qualified for the coming operations; even his brother, Gheorghe Cristescu, was not missing from it. The Echelon left for Moldavia on June 18, 1941, armed with all the necessary documentation with regard to the situation, location, and living conditions of the Jews in Moldavia. Likewise they had available immense quantities of posters representing Jews of hideous appearance or which plainly called them spies or saboteurs. This sinister Echelon left a giant trail of blood along its path as far as Rostov on the Don.

The second part of the Echelon which left for Moldavia was stationed in Piatra Neamt as a command post, since it was in the vicinity of the place where Ion Antonescu was but for its resident headquarters. At Iasi, Major Emil Tulbure and Major Gheorghe Balotescu received the order to begin the "action."

These officers reported that they had recruited, instructed, and trained a first group made up of about thirty to forty Legionaries from Iasi, whom they introduced into an apartment specially rented from a lawyer on Florilor Street in the Pacurari district.

They can further report that Mircea Manoliu, a Legionary who was mobilized as sergeant of the 13 Dorobanti Regiment, had the mission of testing by noisy acts of violence the possible reaction of those authorities who could not be warned of all the preparations that had been made. . . . On that very night Manoliu shot three Jews, but he succeeded in killing only one. On the following night he was to kill 6 others, and Saturday morning to stir up the entire Abattoir district, inciting the suburbanites to pillaging and excesses against the Jews. . . . Legionary mercenaries were sent to occupy every point that had been fixed in all districts of the city. They were well equipped. They had sidearms, Flaubert guns, and blank cartridges which only make the noise they need, but they also had deadly weapons.[30]

On the evening of Saturday, June 28, 1941, the air raid sirens were heard. It was a false alarm that had been ordered beforehand by those who were organizing the "actions." Later the sky was lit up by a rocket.

It was the signal to begin the pogrom!

By the number of its victims, by the bestiality of the means used to torture and kill, by the vast scope of the pillaging and destruction, by the participation of the agents of the public authorities to whom the life and property of the citizens w[ere] entrusted, the pogrom at Iasi marked at the local level the crowning of an accursed, injurious effort which has violated the Romanian conscience for a period of three quarters of a century, and it opens at the world-wide level the most tragic chapter in history.

It became the signal, not only to the Romania of the Legion or of Antonescu, but also to all fascist or quasi-fascist Europe, for massacres which during the following years were to kill six million Jewish people.[31]

5

Why did the curse fall on the old and sorely tried Jewish community in Iasi?

Long and detailed historical research is not needed on the life and existence of the Jews in the old capital of Moldavia. The eyes need not be turned back to past times covered with the mists of history, but only to more recent years. It can be clearly shown that in this city, precisely because of prolonged anti-Semitic activity, there had accumulated such a quantity of hatred that it had become a force which had to be exploited in the interests of the leaders of Antonescu's state.

Iasi was where A. C. Cuza, the patriarch of the anti-Semitic movement in Romania, lived, and where Corneliu Zelea Codreanu began his political career. Iasi was where Xenopol, Vasile Conta, Mihai Eminescu, and others like them lived, taught, and incited others to hatred and anti-Semitism. Iasi was where the League of National Christian Defenders was organized, which wore the swastika as a symbol, and where the Legionaries declared the city to be a "Legionary City."

Since they were in an area right at the front, the population went through moments of panic and unease because the military operations at the front did not go off, at the beginning, according to expectations, and the raids by the Soviet air force had brought into the open the lack of anti-aircraft defense for the city.

In order to divert attention from the realities of the course of the war and in order to explain failures that could not be hidden, a full-scale campaign of anti-Semitic agitation was set in motion. The famous SSI, under the leadership of Eugen Cristescu, excelled in matters like this;

it was aided by the similar German organizations who had their own resident headquarters in Iasi.

Placards and posters were exhibited everywhere, urging: "Citizens, this is who is guilty of this war!" The lithographs pictured Jews with the most outlandish appearance. In order to achieve the best degree of professionalism, "specialists" were sent for this purpose from the Ministry of Propaganda in Bucharest, and vehicles with powerful loudspeakers moved through the streets of the city informing the populace that the Jews were signalling to the Soviet air forces places that ought to be bombed. In time, the Christian population was urged to mark their houses with a cross and to write on them "Christians live here."

Reports appeared in the newspapers in which it was announced that electric lamps had been "discovered" in the chimneys of houses where Jews lived with which the Jews could signal at night to the Soviet air force, that gigantic quantities of weapons and munitions had been "discovered," and so on. At the same time, every representative of the government and military authorities was a direct participant in this campaign to disseminate rumors to enrage the populace and incite it to be ready for any deeds that could frustrate the so-called criminal activities of the Jewish population.

This campaign, senseless in its magnitude and criminal in its consequences, was sown in favorable soil. The light of a rocket that launched the call to death and destruction had not gone out when shots were heard in every district in the city, and particularly in the Jewish districts. The time was perfectly chosen; protected by darkness, Romanian and German troops moved towards the front. The rumor spread like lightning that "the Jews are firing on the Romanian army!" Panic was unleashed, and the troops that had been marshaled in silence began to fire at houses from which they supposed they were being attacked.

It must be mentioned that not one Romanian or German soldier was found killed or wounded as a result of the "attack" by the Jewish population, although a serious search was made for this purpose. Those who began the firing were clearly the organizers and mercenaries of the SSI.

Immediately, patrols of Romanian and German soldiers, public guards, and gendarmes, assisted by a great number of inhabitants of the city and all the renegades that could be found, rushed towards the residences of the Jews, pulling them out of hiding places, cellars, and the trenches that sheltered them from the air attacks. Then the massacre began!

Throughout the night the Jews were arrested wherever they were found and taken to various concentration centers, especially the Police Headquarters of the city of Iasi. At dawn more than two thousand people had been rounded up; by noon about five or six thousand Jews had been crowded in there.

The same barbarious deeds took place in the other concentration centers for the Jewish population, which were located in the courtyard of the National High School, the Wachtel School, and the office of the Inspector General of Security. All these people were later transferred to the immense courtyard of the Police Headquarters, where they were beaten and killed exactly like those who had been taken there during the night.

The next day, Sunday, June 29, 1941, became the bloodiest day in the history of the Jews in Romania! What happened on the premises of the Police Headquarters of the city of Iasi, an institution whose purpose was to defend and preserve the life of the citizens, goes beyond all imagination. The possibility of describing these horrors appears futile, not only because a tragedy of such proportions cannot be contained within a few words, but because every person killed, every person beaten, represents by himself alone an inexpressible tragedy, a sorrow which cannot be soothed. They fired, wholly without mercy, on an amorphous mass of people who died on their knees like cattle. They died as a result of beatings, they died after being shot, they died smothered by the corpses that covered them. Their shrieks, groans, and wails had no response in the souls of those who carried out the crime, those who had ordered it, and those who watched impassively, exactly as if they were at a spectacle. At the same time the pogrom was going on in the city, insane in its dimensions, and with a cruelty that made everything that had ever happened before pale.[32]

The Jews that lived in the districts near the Police Headquarters were arrested and taken to the Legion of Gendarmes, where they were thoroughly beaten by soldiers in the indifferent presence of their officers.

The entire drama of "that Sunday" took place under the eyes of the civilian and military authorities: General Gheorghe Stavrescu, the commander of the regional army; Colonel Constantin Lupu, the commander of the garrison; Colonel Dumitru Captaru, the Prefect of the County; Lieutenant Colonel Constantin Chirilovici, the delegate of the Chief of Police; Gheorghe Leahu, the titular Chief of Police, and others. No one took a single step, no one gave a single order to stop the pogrom! When the massacre was almost over and the perpetrators were tired out, General Stavrescu outlined some moves to stop the Romanian soldiers and went to General Schobert, the German commander, whom he brought to the Police Headquarters; Schobert gave the order to withdraw his few Germans.[33]

The Jews who were alive remained under arrest, under guard by the Romanian soldiers. After a little while a municipal truck began to transport the corpses in the courtyard of the Police Headquarters to the cemetery. Evening fell on the old city of Iasi. Convoys of Romanian and German soldiers continued to move towards the front. In the houses of the Jews, where there was still a flicker of life, there was silence, darkness, and fear, a fear of death that even strangled breathing. In the streets, loudspeakers ordered the scattered soldiers who were still continuing to shoot and rob to report to their units. The order addressed to the soldiers did not forget to ask the populace to be quiet and to indicate that all doors and windows were to be open!

Meanwhile the railroad cars necessary for transporting the Jews out of the city were obtained. The Supreme General Staff allocated fifty cars, of which twelve were refused for the reason that they were cattle cars, that is, with shutters for ventilation. They required freight cars for them, which could be sealed airtight!

The Jews in the courtyard of the Police Headquarters were lined up in a column and headed towards the railroad station under the escort of Romanian and German soldiers. The whole distance they were beaten without mercy, especially those who could not move along at the desired pace because of their torture. In the plaza in front of the station they received an order to lie down with their faces to the ground and not to move. One gesture, and the person who made it would be shot!

It got dark. Before they were loaded into the cars out of which the majority of them would never emerge alive, they were robbed of everything they had on them. Then they were counted, and one by one they were headed into the cars that awaited them, shoved along with the butts of weapons and pricked by bayonets. When a car was filled until it would hold no more, the doors were sealed airtight, and the next car was brought up. In this way 2,430 persons were crowded into thirty-three cars. The train, that is, the first section of it, was under a powerful guard placed under the command of Second Lieutenant Aurel Triandaf, a lawyer by profession, and counsellor of the Court of Appeals.

The attitude of this "delicate intellectual" made history because of the cruelties and crimes perpetrated along the route of that sinister train, which was known, quite rightly, as the Death Train.

6

To imagine that there are principles of humanity in a world that has fallen into a convulsion of insanity seems to be an effort that is truly ridiculous and tragically useless.

To try to transpose into words the tragedy of those 2,430 people loaded into the first train section on that night in June 1941 at the Iasi station is a rash endeavor. After they had been beaten for three days and three nights, and tortured, and had watched helplessly the murder of those around them, among them parents, brothers, and people with whom they had been brought up; after they had been held for entire hours with their faces pressed down to the pavement, knowing that any gesture or any movement could bring their death, to describe these facts seems to be an endeavor which goes beyond not just the usual means of expression, but even the most exalted imagination.

But all this grows dim in view of the unimaginable journey to death of a mass of people assembled by force and crowded beyond any possible limits into a few freight cars lacking any ventilation and with floors covered with carbide.

The inferno on the Death Train that left from Iasi, for an unknown destination, is grafted into the souls of the survivors, the wives and children of those who were killed—a train that moved at a snail's pace from one station to another through torrid days and nights filled with delirium; a train that was carrying human beings who were still alive, but who were obliged to reach their destination only as corpses; a train guarded by soldiers who spoke the same language as those who were locked in the cars but had no right to live because every means of human communication had disappeared from among them.

In the cars, men were dying! They were dying of thirst, because even the urine which they came to drink was not sufficient; they were dying because they could no longer bear the pain and suffering; they were dying because of their open wounds, which had become purulent. They were dying because they no longer had anything to live for!

The train would stop at the railroad stations to unload the corpses, and from within one could hear heartrending cries for "water, water!" No one would bring a drop of water. They would throw themselves down to the puddles of rainwater to drink the damp mud, but a bullet would nail them where desperation had driven them. Emptied of cadavers, the car would be refilled with those who were still living taken from the other cars, so that there would not be enough room to feel comfortable. The doors were shut, and the train continued its winding route over that beautiful plateau of Moldavia, past Tg. Frumos, Podul Iloaiei, Mircesti, Roman.

At the moment the train would stop at stations where no one was expecting it, a pestilential odor from the opened cars, now holding corpses, would envelop the surroundings. The Jews in the respective communities, who came in haste, with death in their souls, would pull out the lifeless bodies and prepare a resting place for them.

At the Tg. Frumos station, the military commandant of the station asked the local authorities that the Jews who were still alive be turned over to him so he could execute them. The intervention of the mayor saved them, that time. At Roman, a woman in the Red Cross, one of

those marvelous Romanian women with a soul of gold, showing dignity
and courage, and going against the orders and warnings of the sentries,
ordered the cars to be opened. What she first caught sight of made her
tremble! But only for a minute, until she could catch her breath.

Then she ordered that the people be made to get down out of the
cars and washed with a hose. There was no other way! Then the cars
were cleaned out, the people were fed, and their thirst was quenched.
They were given water to drink, lots of water!

Their souls had dried up; their bodies had been squeezed thin; their
eyes were glazed with madness.

The train went on, but the echoes of humanity had broken through
the layers of hatred. At the other stations the cars were opened; members
of the Jewish community were present and helped as they could, with
what they could.[34]

A second train followed the same itinerary, with slight variations—
with the same hellish life, with the same corpses, with the same desperation and slow death.

About eight thousand Jews died in the bloody pogrom at Iasi. The
exact figures will never be known. But the "victims" were the tens of
thousands of Jewish inhabitants of the city of Iasi. They were the ones
who remained alive, with their souls snuffed out and their eyes looking
into space, hoping that a miracle would occur and that those who had
left would return, after all! They were the ones who could not mourn
the dead, because their graves were scattered from one part of the
country to another along the railroad lines. At the common grave in the
Iasi cemetery, people would gaze with eyes that could not weep, and
their groans were stifled in handkerchiefs, because the authorities had
clearly ordered that everything must return to "normal"!

In the summer of 1941 one single color predominated in Iasi: black!
Yellow was the color of the stars that they wore sewn onto their clothing
to announce publicly their identity as Jews.

This action was not devoid of publicity. In all the capital and provincial
newspapers, a government communiqué announced emphatically that
"in Iasi 500 Judeo-Communists were executed. They had fired on German and Romanian soldiers from houses." On July 3, 1941, the newspapers announced similar measures and warned that "any attempt to
repeat these acts of cowardly aggression will be repressed unsparingly.
For every German or Romanian soldier, 50 Judeo-communists will be
executed."[35]

Eight hundred twenty-four Jews returned from the concentration
camp at Calarasi. That was how many escaped alive. How many had
died? Who ever made the count? Jewish communities, in the cities where
the train stopped, brought food, and in those conditions of misery, these

gestures were welcomed. Those who came with this kind of help themselves wore the yellow star on their clothing, and each one was asking himself, "When will my turn come?"

On August 31, 1941, the train with the Jews returning from hell reached the station at Iasi late at night. D. Pacu, the Chief of Police, was waiting for them on the platform, at a table lighted by two lanterns specially provided by the railroad workers. They were deloused under orders, and then the Chief told them, "Boys, you have been tried and found innocent. You are honorable men, so that each one of you can return to his own home. Be just as you were before."[36]

A young man dared to ask, "Mr. Chief, we left Iasi several thousand in number and only 824 of us have come back. Those others, were they too found innocent?"[37]

Curzio Malaparte, a journalist who witnessed everything the Iasi pogrom represented, has written pages charged with emotion and dramatic realism. Walking down the streets two days after the pogrom, he had the feeling that he was moving through a city of shadows, in which the silhouettes of people were moving about in silence, gathering up the corpses on the streets, carrying them to the cemetery, and burying them wherever there was a grave available.

The city breathed heavily under the torpor of the July sun. Packs of vagabond dogs were wandering through the streets, and they gave the journalist the picture of a nightmare.

At Iasi, life went on. It had to go on. Those who were still alive, and those who had returned from the concentration camp at Calarasi, wore the yellow star on their breasts in order to be recognized from afar. Later they were sent to other concentration camps, those for forced labor.

After he was present with Sartori, the Italian consul, at the arrival of the Death Train at Podul Iloaiei, where he tremblingly watched the cadavers being unloaded, Curzio Malaparte described the scene with a sharpened pen, dipped in gall and disgust. Later, he went to Warsaw.

In his book *Kaputt*, in the chapter entitled "Cricket in Poland," the journalist was present at a discussion between Frank, the governor general of Poland; Fischer, the governor of Warsaw; and Wächter, the governor of Krakow, one of the assassins of Chancellor Dollfuss of Austria.

Seated comfortably, sipping the drinks they had been served, Frank asked the journalist:

—"How many Jews were killed that night? In the official communiqué Mihai Antonescu, the Deputy Prime Minister, mentions 500 dead."

I replied: "But the unofficial figure sent up by Colonel Lupu is 7,000 Jews massacred."

—"That is a respectable figure," Frank answered, "but we must be sincere. That wasn't nice!"

—"No, it wasn't nice," said Fischer, the governor of Warsaw, shaking his head in disapproval.

—"It's an uncivilized method," said Wächter, the governor of Krakow, with a tone of disgust.

—"The Romanian people are not civilized people," said Frank, contemptuously.

—"That's right, they have no culture," said Fischer, scratching his head.

—"When is necessary, only when is necessary," Frank repeated, emphasizing each syllable, "we use the art of surgery, not that of butchery. Has anyone ever seen a massacre of Jews in the streets of a German town?"

—"It's a question of methods and organization," said Fischer.[38]

Situated on a level height at the edge of the town, the Tg. Jiu camp, the concentration camp for political prisoners, which had the fame of having been set up for a long time, stretched over an immense area. Built by the Polish army, which retreated into Romania after Poland was occupied by German troops, it could shelter several tens of thousands of people.

The order to evacuate Jews from localities in the vicinity of the front was carried out with excessive severity; the local authorities sought to exceed many of the limits set in the orders that were given. Thus, for example, in the town of Husi, the Jewish population sixteen to sixty years of age were arrested at one time at nightfall, and at dawn, when the offensive against the Soviet Union began, they were forced to leave the city. In other places, such as the town of Darabani, the Jews were granted two hours to get out.

In localities where the Jews within specified age limits were evacuated, those who remained, youths and old people over sixty years of age, were free to move about only between the hours of seven in the morning and eight in the evening. The columns of Jews, after they had slogged on foot for dozens of kilometers to reach the stations to board the trains, were surprised, on entering the Tg. Jiu camp, to find imprisoned within its perimeter, separated by barbed wire fences, Communists, Legionaries, those suspected of communism and—evacuated Jews.

Those last, the Jews, were transferred immediately to the now notorious Bumbesti-Livezeni railroad construction camp. Required to perform impossible work quotas, they labored, hungry and almost naked, under the surveillance of armed guards. Their commander, a schoolteacher in civilian life, was famed for his sadism and cruelty. It was sufficient for it to be heard that Lieutenant Trepadus had arrived at the camp for terror to be felt by all. For the most minor infraction, he had the habit of having the guilty person bound to the trunk of a tree at a height of several centimeters from the ground, so that the whole weight of the body would hang by the ropes, which would cut into the skin of a person exhausted from labor and hunger, producing indescribable pain. Similar camps existed in the cities of Caracal, Lugoj, and Turnu Severin.

In the summer of 1941 large forced labor detachments began to be organized. These camps, which were real concentration camps according to the form of their administrative organization, had begun to operate as early as the summer of 1940, when Jews were excluded from the army.[39]

The first labor camps contained more than one hundred fifty thousand Jews, men and women who were forced to perform hard labor in the stone quarries, repairing the highways and cleaning them of snow in the wintertime so that the motorized military units could move around. The women swept and washed the streets, cleaned floors in the hospitals, and washed the clothes of the sick and wounded. Everyone wore his own clothing and footwear. Medical care was nonexistent or was provided, to a certain extent, by Jewish doctors who had been sent to the labor camps.

Because of a total lack of organization for the work, there were serious accidents in which innumerable Jews perished. It is sufficient for us to recall the accidents in the stone quarries of Turcoaia, Iacob Deal, and Greci, among others, in Tulcea County.[40]

In order to prevent possible attacks or acts of sabotage, local camps were organized in which the best-known people of their respective towns were locked up; as hostages, they were responsible with their life for any act of sabotage, or what might be considered as such, that took place in their respective region. The majority of the Jews in the cities of Galati, Ploiesti, Husi, Focsani, and Falticeni were locked up in this way. It is worthwhile to mention that out of the entire population of the country, including members of various political parties and the other nationalities living in the territory of Romania, only the Jews were held as hostages. Their food was to be provided by their families, who were obliged to wear a yellow star to move about on the streets. There were situations, such as occurred in the city of Husi, where some of those who were locked up were sent to trial by the War Council under the accusation of having carried on "Communist agitation."

Pushed outside the law, Jews not only did not have any personal protection, but the inviolability of their dwellings became a "right" which was disregarded; anyone could walk in! At any hour, day or night, and under the most absurd pretexts, houses were searched, goods confiscated, and most of the time their owners were maltreated.

Their situation became so precarious that the local authorities, wishing to prove their total obedience to the central authorities, issued orders of an abusive nature, the cruelty of which exceeds imagination. For example: in the city of Arad, Jews were forbidden to buy milk and sugar. This state of affairs was due to a series of antireligious measures. Jews were forbidden to take part in religious services held in synagogues, under the pretext that subversive meetings had been held there. Although the Jewish religion was considered by law to be a "tolerated" religion, many synagogues were closed, their sites becoming state property. Jews were forbidden to own radio equipment and cameras and were obliged to turn them over to the police authorities, under the threat of severe penalty of law. Lawyers who still had the right to practice their profession could do so by giving legal assistance only to Jews. The same thing happened with doctors, who did not have the right to treat Romanian patients. Jewish cemeteries considered to be "farm lands" were confiscated, as in the town of Buzau, and the open space between the graves was cultivated.

All these arbitrary actions took on the power of law when the Supreme Court of Appeals rejected the suits of Jews who pled that the confiscation of their property was unconstitutional. This decision of the highest court in Romania put an end for this whole period to any plea connected with an abusive application of the laws. It was considered that any action taken against the Jews was legal and hence constitutional!

This decision was hailed by the entire Romanian press, which emphasized, in different articles, the fact that Romania was the first country in Southeastern Europe where a radical solution had been made to the Jewish problem, considering that it was not only a problem of a religious or economic nature, but a racial problem, with all the consequences thereof.

That pauperized population, down on its knees but not broken, bore its difficult existence, and with immense sacrifices kept up its basic morale. Despite the lack of material resources, special care was taken to provide for the education of young people, who were excluded from the Romanian educational system. Although all real property belonging to the former Jewish congregations had been confiscated, including the synagogues, and the culture halls had been destroyed, means were found to ensure regular education for young people of all ages, who did not come under legal provisions ordering them to be sent to forced labor camps. Out of this group of youths there later arose a brilliant constellation of intellectuals.

Having been ejected from the stages of the theaters of Romania, Jewish actors, directors, set designers, musicians, painters, and others gathered on the ancient boards of the stage at the Baraseum in Bucharest, which became the "Jewish Theater," and staged new shows. Burning like a flame, the Jewish spirit of culture was maintained, and in the darkness of a terrorized existence these miraculous people lighted in the souls of the spectators the lights of laughter and the smiles of belief in oneself.

In those years, the curtain went up on the stage of the National Theater for a delicate and romantic play, *The Nameless Star*. The author? An unknown. But some actors knew the truth. The real author was a sensitive and subtle writer, Mihail Sebastian!

Since he was a Jew, he did not have the right to present a play on the stage of the most prestigious theater in the country. A Romanian friend did it! On opening night, Mihail Sebastian, hidden somewhere up in the balcony among the spectators who were following the action on the stage with their hearts in their mouths, was living the drama of his own hero, Professor Miroiu, who in a dirty world of stupidity, wickedness, and mediocrity had aimed his sights at the dome of heaven, seeking a star! It was in fact liberty, decency, and humanity, for which the dramatic poet cared so much.

The last lines were said, and the spectators who had laughed and cried along with the actors gave frenzied applause. When, as usual, they cried "Author! Author!," no one came onto the stage!

The actors gathered in front of the curtain, bowed to the spectators in appreciation, and then, raising their faces to that obscure place in the gallery where there was a soul burning like a flame, living the drama of his existence as a Jew in Romania in those years, they bowed as if in supreme homage.

Mihail Sebastian could not even give his thanks. Seeing everything that had happened there, he was lost in his loneliness.

What had happened that evening on the stage of the National Theater was a gesture of the supreme dignity of the Romanian people. The news was spread by word of mouth and became a legend!

7

"I can promise the Jews of the whole world one single thing: they will lose the wish of ever laughing again." These words, pronounced by Hitler in a speech given on October 4, 1942, had a direct result on the Jewish population of Romania.[41]

Ion Antonescu, the Leader of Romania, had anticipated and gone far beyond Hitler in this respect. A few days after the war broke out, at a session of the cabinet on July 8, 1941, he clearly stated:

At the risk of not being understood clearly by some traditionalists who may still be among you, I am for the enforced emigration of the entire Jewish population of Bessarabia and Bucovina, which must be pushed beyond the frontier.... It makes no difference to me that we will go down in history as barbarians.

The Roman Empire performed a series of acts of barbarism according to our present standards, and nevertheless it was the most magnificent of political establishments. There has not existed a more favorable moment in our history. If it is needed, shoot all of them with machine guns![42]

On July 2, 1941, on the eve of the general offensive along the whole front, Romanian troops made a feint to sound out the resistance of the Soviet armies and went into the little town of Noua Sulita. Using the classical pretext that the Jewish population had fired on it, the Romanian army arbitrarily executed more than eight hundred Jews who made up the population of that village.

The general offensive took place on July 3, 1941, and encompassed the whole area from Southern Bucovina to the Danube. On the same day, Mihai Antonescu, the Deputy Prime Minister, gathered together at a secret conference at the Ministry of the Interior all the administrative inspectors and county prefects who were later to be sent into the territories that were to be liberated, Northern Bucovina and Bessarabia. They were given guidance based on decisions that had been taken with regard to "ethnic and political purification" and on the severe and unbending attitudes the Romanian authorities had to maintain towards the Jewish population in those provinces:

We are in the most favorable and broadly opportune moment in history for total ethnic purification, for a revision of national life, and for purging our race of all those elements which are foreign to its soul, which have grown like mistletoes and darken our future. In order for us not to let this unique moment slip by without any gain, we must be implacable.... The campaign for ethnic purification will be developed by driving out all Jews and isolating them in labor camps and in places where they can no longer exert their destructive influence.... If there comes a need in order to complete the work of ethnic purification, the provincial governments will also advise us on measures for enforced emigration of the Jewish population.... It must cross the frontiers, not being wanted in Bessarabia and Bucovina in these moments of restoring national rights forever in these territories.[43]

The entire campaign that followed the directives adopted in the period when the war was being planned, and all that took place afterwards in Bucovina and Bessarabia in connection with the deportation and extermination of Jews,

was wholly a Romanian Fascist operation. It is true that many of these unfortunate people were victims of German savagery. It is fair that note should be taken of some peculiarities in method and some time limits which the Romanian authorities, great or small, generally exceeded only very sporadically.... But the sufferings of approximately 450,000 people, of whom 350,000 died, were not caused at the request of Germany or under German pressure. The massacres in Bessarabia and Bucovina in July and August 1944, which caused the greatest number of deaths, were carried out by the Romanian armed forces. Among their ranks there was also the German XI Army under General Schobert, but its sector of attack was limited to the area of Balti County. On the rest of the front, from Ceremus to the Danube, only soldiers of the Romanian army were in action.[44]

The first locality reconquered by the Romanian troops was the village of Ciudei, located very near the frontier. One year before, in the summer of 1940, when the territory was occupied by Soviet troops, the 16th Infantry Regiment, commanded by Major Valeriu Carp, found time during its retreat to kill several Jews. The following year, the same regiment destroyed the entire Jewish population of Ciudei. Major Valeriu Carp was responsible for the death of 450 Jewish inhabitants in only a few hours after occupying the village of Ciudei.

From this obscure point on the map, the line of march of the Romanian army to liberate the Romanian territories occupied by the Russians was covered by the scattered corpses of those they killed.

It is a gigantic mountain of human pain and suffering! To desire and need to write about all this seems impossible. What must be understood is that every place liberated meant the beginning of terrible sufferings for the Jews, ending with their extermination or deportation.

The first town liberated in Northern Bucovina was Storojinet. Hardly was the occupation completed when the massacre began. Driven out of their houses, cellars, and attics, Jews were shot on the spot without regard to whether they were women, children, or old people. Common people, merchants, and intellectuals were killed. Rabbis, cantors, and other people belonging to the priesthood of the Mosaic faith were killed after being humiliated. Whole families were exterminated, and afterwards the looting began.

Although directives had still not come from the central authorities with regard to the measures to be taken against the Jews, Flondor, a landowner, assisted by the mayor, Dimitrie Rusu, and the assistant mayor, Stefan Tomovici, who had been a liberal senator, went on to organize the ghetto. Thereafter all the houses and property of Jews were pillaged by their neighbors.

There were mindless crimes along all the highways leading to Cernauti, the capital of Bucovina, which passed through places such as Rapocea, Iordanesti, and Patrauti, and along the side roads.

In order for the "business" to have even greater extent, the Romanian army, performing its role as liberator, was fully assisted by the local population in the crimes and looting that took place. There were cases where these actions began even before the Romanian troops arrived in the respective locality.

It must not be forgotten that Bucovina and Bessarabia were both provinces where for years and years the "archangels" of the Legion (Iron Guard) and the "lancers" of the Cuzist party had been appearing to incite the people to hatred, crime, and violence. Partisans of these people, now placed in impressive numbers at every level of the military hierarchy, found among the population of these places people who had been well trained and indoctrinated in a religion of hatred and ready for the most debased acts against humanity. It was a perfect symbiosis, which was sealed with incomparable crimes.

On Saturday, July 5, 1941, the inhabitants of the village of Banila, near Siret, headed by Moscaliuc, the mayor, and somebody named Barbaza, killed fifteen Jews, including M. Satran, a blind man more than eighty years old. Jacob Brescher was also one of the Jews killed; his body was cut into pieces, and the criminals anointed the wheels of vehicles with the blood that ran from his corpse.

The next day, July 6, 1941, Stefanovici, the priest of the commune of Banila, refused to go into the church to perform the mass. Looking up at the sky, the priest asked whether God still existed! He went on to ask what kind of flock he was the shepherd of, that was capable of doing such a thing! To such a God this honest priest of Banila refused to bow.

Before the Romanian army entered the village of Milia, the people there had rounded up 176 Jews and had killed them, some because they had been urged to, some using their "imagination." Among those killed was Dr. Jacob Gelier, a well-known Zionist leader from Cernauti who had taken refuge in that village with his family. They had killed him by picking him up with the tines of hayforks and pitching him up and down, watching the blood run out of his body. Afterwards his wife and child were killed. The kosher butcher (sochet) of the village was killed, pierced with bayonets. Others, as at Banila, were cut up with bucksaws meant for cutting wood. It seems that this "operation" was a local one, given special esteem. So it was that there was a write-up in *Viata* (Life) by a reporter who accompanied Ion Antonescu to Bucovina. He reported a conversation that the Leader had with a peasant: "These Kikes don't deserve to die by bullets; that way they would die as heroes. They have to be taken out on the main road and cut up with a saw by lazy people so they will suffer longer."[45]

Places continued to be liberated by the massive advance of the Romanian army, followed by a parade of acts of violence committed in the sight of everyone.

At Stanesti eighty Jews were shot, including Rabbi Friedlander and his two sons, and at Jadova Veche Rabbi Gutman was considered "lucky" because only his beard was cut off. At that place women and girls were raped in front of their aggrieved families. The peasants, overjoyed at being liberated, encouraged the army in its "operations" and pointed out to the police and the gendarmerie places where Jews had gone into hiding.

In the village of Herta, where in the summer of 1940 a Jewish soldier had tried to shield the life of his superior officer with his own body, more than one hundred Jews were shot at the orders of the county chief.

On July 5, 1941, between 4:00 and 5:00 p.m., the Romanian army entered Cernauti. The tragedy of the Jewish population in Romania began to take on new dimensions.

In Bessarabia, the Romanian troops occupied Tg. Edinet on July 6, 1941. After two days of a veritable massacre, 500 persons belonging to the Jewish population of that town were missing. Women and girls had been brutally raped, and many had committed suicide. Their dead bodies were buried on the next day. Mass graves were dug in the cemetery by the Jews who survived, and after the corpses had been buried, they too were killed. The Jews who were still living were forbidden to move about on the streets and in particular to enter the marketplace to buy the food they needed.

A small unit of troops of the 5th Infantry Division entered Tg. Pirlita. Their first concern was to identify the houses of Jews, and then the looting began, after which the victims were killed.

This criminal act was carried out with such brutality that, surprisingly, it was reported to the Romanian Supreme General Staff by the commander of the German XI Army, which was operating in the region. The investigation that was ordered was carried out in such a manner as to find that the guilty parties were the Jews who had been assassinated![46]

In the village of Vlad in Balti County, peasants armed with clubs and scythes broke into the houses of Jews and beat them so hard that many of them died. After this they stole everything and set fire to the houses.

One isolated unit of the 14th Infantry Division made up of about twenty soldiers commanded by a corporal, while marching along the Falesti-Chiscareni highway in Balti County, met a group of about fifty Jews, including forty-two adults and six to eight children, between the villages of Taura Veche and Taura Noua. After they were looted of everything they had on them, they were forced to go into the marsh and lie face down on the ground, and then were shot. Only two women escaped the massacre; they were found by a patrol of German soldiers. These soldiers showed them the way to the hospital at Chiscareni. Again the commander of the German XI Army became aware of this criminal act, and he stated the following in a report forwarded to the Supreme General Staff: "The attitude of some representatives of the Romanian forces serves not only to damage the prestige of the Romanian army, but at the same that of the German army in world public opinion."[47]

In the village of Cotmani Jews were thrown straight into the Dniester after they had been killed at the instigation of a local fellow named Dragan. Among the corpses was that of Rubin, the old rabbi.

In the city of Balti, at that time under German command, a clandestine brothel was opened for the homosexuals among the elite SS troops, where Jewish boys were forced to satisfy the perverse appetites of these representatives of the "New Order."

As soon as they were installed in the city, the German-Romanian authorities executed ten hostages in the public park. One of the survivors, Bernard Walter, the last president of the Jewish congregation of Balti, has given dramatic testimony about these events:

The city of Balti was occupied on July 9, 1941, by the troops of the German XI Army.... As soon as this action was completed, the Jews who had survived the massacres in neighboring villages began to come into town, and as they arrived, the Jews were gathered into two camps, one set in the courtyard of the Bank of Moldavia building, and the other in preventive arrest. On the evening of July 11, 1941, at the excuse that the Jews had fired weapons at a German truck, ten Jews were pulled out of the camp and shot.... Meanwhile Prat, the [German] captain, formed a committee in the ghetto made up of twelve Jewish leaders with Bernard Walter as chairman.... At 5 P.M. on July 15, 1941, all the members of the community were taken down to the headquarters of the German police, where Captain Prat demanded that a list of twenty Jewish Communists be drawn up so they could be executed. The committee did not waver in this moment of danger, and speaking through their chairman, they expressed to Captain Prat their refusal to lend themselves to such an infamy. All the members of the committee were immediately arrested.... The members of the committee were held for nearly half an hour by the guard of the camp, tortured, insulted, and photographed by the German soldiers who were guarding them. Later 44 more Jews pulled from a group of 150 prisoners were hauled in as hostages.... The convoy party was accompanied to the gate by other Jews who were tearing their hair from their heads and praying and throwing themselves at the feet of those whom they were seeing for the last time.... Only the chairman of the committee, Bernard Walter, escaped from this massacre. Since he enjoyed many friends in Romanian circles in the city, he was rescued by the spirited energy of Dumitru Agapie, the Romanian chief of police, who gained favor of Captain Prat and pulled the victim out of a group that had already been made up, that is, two to three minutes before he was to be shot.... Afterwards the German troops and the Gestapo left Balti.... The fate of the surviving Jews was taken over by other brutal hands, those of Major Ion Gradu of the Territorial military unit. Under his supervision the Jews were interned in a camp in the forest of Rauta, twelve kilometers from the city, surrounded by barbed wire and under military guard.[48]

In two columns, one coming from the direction of the towns of Iasi and Sculeni and the other coming from Husi, Albita, and Hincesti, the Romanian army liberated the city of Chisinau on July 17, 1941. And as it did to the Jews of Cernauti, the liberating army brought to the Jews of Chisinau blood, tears, and death! The number of victims of that first massacre will never be known. But it can be estimated from the number of Jews killed in the Chisinau ghetto, where more than ten thousand Jews were killed in the first few days!

8

Once the Romanian troops made their massive entry into Cernauti, they went into the Jewish quarter, where they began "cleaning the city of Jews." In less than twenty-four hours they had killed more than two thousand Jews on the spot where they were found, in courtyards, cellars, attics, anti-aircraft shelters, and dugouts. The corpses were hauled out of the city in garbage trucks and buried in four common graves. In the same time patrols of gendarmes rounded up more than three thousand Jews, who were hauled under escort to the dungeons of the gendarmerie. They were beaten throughout the day by the gendarmes in the presence of their commander, Major Cicandel. Late at night searches of the bodies of the Jews were made and the women given a genital inspection, after which the latter were freed. The men were kept and sent to hard labor. After a few days, "negotiations" began to free these wretched people. At the beginning, Teodorescu, the police commissioner, accepted between sixty and seventy dollars per person. Later, the price went down to between fifty and sixty dollars. Those who had no dollars could buy freedom for themselves by exchanging things of value such as gold or diamonds. These "transactions" took place openly, without any trouble.

From that date on it was no longer a question of deliberate individual acts of robbery by isolated persons or groups. It was a question of methodical seizure of the goods belonging to a whole population.

A veritable swarm of individuals fell upon Bucovina, and upon Cernauti in particular, in a short time winning the fine but significant name of Californians or gold-rushers.

For ridiculously small amounts, anyone who was a "certified" Romanian could obtain any store, factory, or dwelling he might wish. A request was made to Engineer C. Campeanu a Legionary, and the way to riches was open. This "Director" of Economy of the government of Bucovina became the absolute master of the property of the Jews, which he disposed of at his pleasure.

Industrial enterprises were transformed into the property of some government employees, many of whom had written recommendations from Ion Antonescu; private dwellings, with all their furniture, were "sold" for ridiculous prices.

Ion Antonescu declared on one occasion that he wanted to make Bucovina and Bessarabia "model provinces," and he succeeded.

A short time after the occupation of the city of Chisinau by the Romanian forces, a strange campaign took place, organized by the Romanian civilian authorities in close connection with the army.

On July 25, 1941, as a result of this "initiative," more than twenty-five thousand Bessarabian Jews were sent across the Dniester, into the Ukraine. Part of the convoy arrived in the village of Coslar, where the people were crowded into the marketplace; an order was given that no one should leave there. The least infraction was to be punished by shooting. This action, organized by the local authorities, had a double purpose. On one hand it was a means of getting rid of a considerable number of Jews, and on the other hand it gave the German troops on the other side of the Dniester the possibility of liquidating them. It was an attempt to get this business done without attributing any real responsibility in case the plan was carried out.

The military situation in the Ukraine at that time posed serious problems for the German army. Its commanders did not have any desire at all, particularly in these specific circumstances, to get involved in liquidating Jews, and especially to be responsible for a number of people near the front in a state of total physical decay who were potential carriers of epidemics and other infectious diseases.

Hence the German military authorities categorically opposed the presence of these Jews on the east side of the Dniester, and demanded that the Romanian troops return them to Bessarabian territory. In this way a sinister game began between these two armies, one throwing the Jews across the Dniester, and the other not wanting to accept them. Thus the mass of Jews wandered from place to place, trying to cross the Dniester back into Bessarabia; at every crossing Romanian gendarmes and soldiers immediately opened fire.

And so when they arrived at Moghilau, more than 4,000 Jews of an initial group of 25,000 had died. In face of the categorical refusal of the German army to permit the Jews to remain in the Ukraine, the Romanian authorities agreed to take them back. On August 17, 1941, those who were still living crossed the Dniester. At that time the convoy was comprised of 16,500 people. Before they crossed the Dniester, between Iampol and Scazinet, the Germans killed another 800 Jews who had not succeeded in crossing the river by the prescribed time.

A few days later, in the little town of Marculesti, which had a flourishing Jewish colony, there was another massacre. More than one thousand Jews were shot and buried in an antitank ditch at the edge of town. Similar massacres took place in the towns of Falesti, Gura Kamenca, and Gura Gainari.

At that time the Chisinau ghetto constituted an attractive point for any authorities who wanted free laborers or women. On August 1, 1941, 450 Jews were pulled out of the ghetto, especially intellectuals and beautiful women. They were taken outside the city, and 411 of them were shot. Some of the women and girls pulled out of the ghetto were sent to a military brothel of the Soroca. It was about this "institution" that Guido Malaparte, the Italian journalist, wrote pages full of deep compassion, in a chapter entitled "Girls of the Soroca." In a discussion he had with the supervisor of the brothel, the latter candidly told the Italian journalist:

"Making love to these girls does not cost anything," Schenk said. "It is a free service."
"Compulsory labor, you mean."
"No, it's a free service."[49]

Since the Italian journalist wanted to learn the conditions under which these girls and women who "offered" free services to the German troops were living, he visited them during the evening. He found there a group of cultivated girls, with whom he discussed art in French; Susana, Zoe, and Liuba told of their dreams, which were shattered when they were "liberated." "Then they began to tell me that they had learned French in school at Chisinau, and Liuba had studied music and played the piano like an angel."[50] The conversation went on through the whole night, and when the dawn timidly began to appear, the journalist departed. The girls had a day of "work" ahead of them.

Romanian journalists similarly moved about the front, sending their papers the most sensational stories, which were not lacking in "crimes committed by kikes." The reading public needed them, and awaited and read such pieces with interest:

Recently, the newspaperman Dumbraveanu reported, someone had the idea of arranging for a fast train to take the journalists from the capital dailies to the front.... Chisinau had been occupied. A group of journalists got out of the train and was taken in automobiles to the outskirts of the city, which was still smoking. The Germans had set it afire with airborne bombs and artillery shells.... The tent encampment where the soldiers stayed was of course quite quickly thrown up, frugal, and improvised. But when it had grown quite dark, the journalists came to realize they had been mistaken in their assessment.... There was a supper table that had been arranged for the journalists.... They ate as if [in] a restaurant in the capital in good times, with a real band. And after the supper was over, someone gave a terse order, like a hiss: "The dance of the dead"! From behind the tents in a corner which had been concealed until then, a fantastic parade entered of groups of women. Pale, altered figures, with torn clothing, hardly able to stand. And there were children along with some. Holding onto their skirts, both they and their mothers sensed the storm which was approaching.

"The dance of the dead" hissed again. And when the accordions began to play and the gypsies in [the] band began to shout, those fantastic shadows began to move in a kind of dance, to turn about, and to make pirouettes.

But the dance did not last very long. The song was as short as the life of the dancing shadows; the women were pulled from the grassy carpet and shot in the darkness behind the tents. . . . There was still a little boy, just one, who was still alive, near the table with the food and drinks.

He was picked up in someone's arms, tossed up like a ball, and was shot while his little body was still in the air.

It was certainly the strongest number in the show.[51]

The first columns of Jews from Bucovina arrived in Atachi on August 2, 1941, and tried to cross the Dniester. The same sort of incident occurred as with the Bessarabians. The German military authorities refused to let them cross into the Ukraine. In view of this situation the train prepared to return to Cernauti. At 9:30 p.m. the people, with their baggage, got down out of the cars at a railroad section cabin. The Jews were divided up into groups of about ten, and the first group was driven into the water of the Dniester under the fire of the gendarmes. After they were killed, the corporal who had the responsibility of guarding the train promised the remaining Jews that the shooting would stop if they would give money and jewelry. More than 100 rings, watches, and other pieces of jewelry were collected, amounting in value to 15,000 lei. All of it was given to the corporal in charge. Immediately thereafter, all the Jews were driven into the water of the Dniester and shot. A few who knew how to swim escaped with their lives.

Their testimony makes up pages of indescribable human suffering. It is worthwhile to mention that the Provost Marshal of the army, General Ion Topor, was informed about this base crime.[52]

Death extended its shadow over the length and width of Bucovina and Bessarabia. The pieces of testimony regarding these crimes are countless. Where they were killed, where they were buried, and especially by whom they were killed will never be learned.

9

The idea that the Jewish population ought to be defended or protected from those who were threatening their lives, their property, and their security was totally excluded!

Bucovina and Bessarabia were liberated. After the first wave of terror had washed over, work began in the places under civil administration the "organize" the lives of the Jews who had escaped momentarily from the ordeal through which they had passed.

In every locality camps were set up where Jews were concentrated after being forcibly evacuated from the surrounding villages and towns. These camps centralized the Jewish population in a given place, making it easier to "supervise" or rather exploit.

Hostages were drawn from the ranks of those shut up in the camps who were to guarantee with their life the quietness of life in their town and the region around it. Most of the time these hostages were executed with no justification.

Ghettoes in the strict sense of the word were set up in the capitals of the two liberated provinces, Cernauti and Chisinau.[53] The purposes were the same: in the long run, the camps and ghettoes became not places where the Jews had to live, in conditions of bleak misery, but points of departure for the extermination sites in Transnistria. Until the time of these deportations, the camps and ghettoes where the Jews were crowded to suffocation became places where theft, bribery, and influence-peddling were practiced openly and completely undisturbed.

The Chisinau ghetto was set up in an area that included several streets in a bombed-out district where not one piece of property was unscathed and the houses had no roofs or windows.

The survivors, crowded twenty-five to thirty to room, began a night-mare existence without water, without any means of providing them-selves with food, and especially without the most elementary health facilities required.

Not having the right to leave the ghetto, the internees were constantly subject to the whims of the authorities, the police, and the local gen-darmerie. Visits by the officers of the garrison or those who were in transit through Chisinau to the ghetto, where they were living the life of grubs, became a sort of ritual, and choosing Jewish girls and women for their orgies became a habit practiced on a large scale.

All the Jewish inhabitants were shaken down when they were interned, but this activity continued even after they were inside the ghetto, even though the Jews had not been able to bring with them any more than they could carry on their backs. When the house of Captain Ion Par-aschivescu, the commandant of the police force who had held that duty in the ghetto for only fifteen days, was searched a veritable bazaar of stolen objects were found, including furniture, carpets, table silver, and tableware.

These Jews were interned in the camps and particularly in the ghettoes by number, not by name. No one knew which individuals were present and which were missing. An attempt made in the Chisinau ghetto to reconstruct the identity of the Jews interned there proved to be in vain and was totally lacking in interest for those who were administering the ghetto. Various representatives of the German army and various Ro-manian authorities appeared before these ghetto authorities every day, seeking Jews for labor. These people were never asked by whose authority they were acting or about what had happened to the Jews who were not brought back to the ghetto. A simple statement to the ghetto authorities that it had been necessary to shoot the Jews on account of "insubordination" was sufficient.

At the same time entire trainloads of stolen property were being sent to towns in the Old Kingdom, to places where these officers had their homes. Their houses began to be furnished with stolen furniture and carpets, the wives of the "heroes" came to be adorned with Astrakhan fur coats, and pianos sounded in the houses. Not even the slightest qualms were felt that these things, which were shown as real war trophies, had belonged to human beings, men and women who been beaten to death, naked and hungry, along the endless roads of Bessarabia and Bucovina, and later of Transnistria.

An event of unusual importance for the life of the Jews in the liberated provinces took place on August 10, 1941, when it was established through a protocol signed by representatives of the Romanian and German armies that the territory between the Bug and the Dniester, known under the name of Transnistria, would be transferred to Romanian administration. A governor, Professor Gheorghe Alexianu, was named.

In Cernauti, in less than eight hours after the decision by the Governor of Bucovina, a population of about fifty thousand people was moved out of their homes, from which they could take only what they could carry on their backs. People of all ages, men, women, children, the sick and infirm, were herded in a mute exodus towards the district which was destined to be their hearth and home. Within a few hours this district was surrounded with nets of barbed wire, and compulsory entry gates were established to control any movements by the interned Jews. But the drama began at the moment when this sad, silent populace began to try to find space to shelter itself from the coming winter. Some fifty to sixty persons in an enclosure, and they were considered "fortunate"! Those who came later sought to find bedding places in attics, cellars, and stables. Many never found even this; they remained in the courtyards, sheltering themselves under the eaves of houses, or staying purely and simply in the streets!

It was possible to move about freely within the ghetto, but once you entered this hell, there was no way out but to the cemetery or a common grave. Wearing a yellow star was compulsory.[54]

With regard to these events in Cernauti, Traian Popovici, the former mayor of the city, has made an impressive analysis of the set of situations in which these measures were to be applied. A man of high moral probity, with deep human feelings and with a sense of his unusual responsibilities as a Romanian in the chapter of history in which he was obliged by the force of events to participate, he writes—after describing his vain struggle with Corneliu Calotescu, the Governor of Bucovina, and other military authorities to get them to withdraw this inhumane measure for interning the Jews in a ghetto—as follows:

On the morning of October 11 [1941] a cold, damp day as mournful as the groaning of such an unfortunate person, I looked out the windows of my bedroom at the flakes of early snow and I could not believe my eyes. In the streets in front of the windows there was a whole flood of people in flight. Old people being helped by children, women with babies in their arms, infirm people dragging along their crippled bodies, all with bundles in their hands, hauling suitcases in little carts, or clothing on their backs, trunks hastily tied up, bedding, rags and clothing, were pushing along in a mute pilgrimage towards the vale of sorrows in the city, towards the ghetto. I became aware that the wheel of their misfortune had been set in motion. I dressed and hastened to the Mayor's office. . . . I took steps to provide bread, food, and especially milk for the children.

Referring to the conditions in the ghetto, the mayor noted farther on:

I will not speak of the health conditions. . . . It is a miracle that epidemics have not broken out which would endanger the whole city. . . . I do not know what the purpose was, but the effect is evident: an official and unofficial squeeze on the outcasts. Windows were set up at the National Banks to exchange national currency into rubles, in order to take away their valuables, jewelry, and other articles of value.[55]

To all this one can add robbery by the Christian population that continued to live around the perimeter of the ghetto, where a flourishing new activity began: that of "disinterested helpers"! Having the ability to leave the ghetto from time to time, they brought food and articles of clothing to its inhabitants, which they sold at exorbitant prices.[56]

After the Russian retreat their warehouses were plundered and after that shops, dwellings, and all the property to be found in them had been pillaged, the ghetto was was still an unexpected source of wealth. When the Jews were deported to Transnistria, a series of tables was set up on the platform in the train station. The Jews were required to pass by each table and to pay. At the first table rent was to be paid up to the date of the expiration of the lease for the house they had been forced to leave. If they had no money, they had to give as an equivalent amount their most valuable possessions. At the second table the balance of taxes due had to be paid; at the third table the electric light bill had to be paid; and at the fourth table the men paid the military taxes. At the fifth table an employee of the National Bank changed Romanian currency into rubles at an exorbitant rate. At the sixth table they were searched, and everything they had on them that had not been declared was taken away from them. It is worth mentioning that neither a receipt nor any proof of acceptance was given for all these amounts that were collected in an abusive fashion.

10

A name that arose from the necessity of locating a perimeter geographically was determined arbitrarily: Transnistria! The territory beyond the Dniester extending to the Bug and making up part of the Ukraine had been called the Moldavian Socialist Republic under the Soviet regime. This name, which had no historic basis, was given for political purposes and had never existed in the Russian administrative system.

Transnistria, as a geographical term, had never existed, and no one could find it on a real map. It certainly was not necessary for the territorial expansion of Romania. Transnistria was necessary for Antonescu's fascist government so that it could become the graveyard where the Jews would be liquidated and thus bring a substantial "contribution" to the solution of the Jewish problem! Transnistria has remained a name that inspires terror and is branded in letters of blood and fire in the souls who escaped with a desperate need to save themselves from that hell.

After the journey of those 25,000 Jews who crossed the Dniester in the summer of 1941 and were thrown back by the German troops, as a result of which action 12,000 of them died, General Ion Topor, the Provost Marshal of the Army, gave an order on September 2, 1941, to the Inspectorate of the Gendarmerie of Transnistria to get things ready to deport the Jews in the camps in Bucovina and Bessarabia across the Dniester; this action was to start on September 6, 1941.

The regime in these three camps in Bessarabia, namely, Secureni, Edinet, and Vertujeni, was frightful. Many of those imprisoned were almost naked, at the end of their strength, and without any possibility of buying a morsel of bread. Everything they had ever possessed had been stolen by the soldiers who were escorting them or by the country people in the villages through which their columns had passed along the road to the camp. It came to such a pass that the peasants could buy one Jew for a sum of about one thousand lei, choosing those who were best dressed. The gendarmes would shoot him, and those who had paid the money stole from the body everything that was on it. In the Vertujeni camp the brutish Colonel Agapie was in charge, aided by captains Buradescu and Radulescu, who later became famous for the atrocities they committed. The inhabitants of the camp had no shelter, because the command had given orders to make barrels out of the tin roofs to hold the soap and oil which these valiant officers would later send to their families in the country.

On September 5, 1941, the Union of Jewish Congregations in Bucharest received an order to obtain 5,000 complete suits of clothing (overcoats, shoes, etc.) for the Jews shut up in the camps in Bessarabia. This figure was greatly surpassed, but in fact the goods never reached their destination. The Jews in Bessarabia, naked and barefoot on the threshold of winter, were getting ready to set out for the hell of Transnistria. The causes for the high mortality rate in the Bessarabian camps were many. A population exhausted from traveling endless roads, hungry, naked, and desperate, had no possibility under these conditions of finding enough food to enable their bodies to remain resistant to disease. Although there were doctors among them as well as others with medical training, the lack of the most elementary material resources for preserving and maintaining an elementary level of care and hygiene contributed to this state of affairs. Thus it was that exanthematic typhus, scabies, and dysentery would cut down hundreds of unfortunate people daily. Besides these calamities, a whole series of people who had passed their limit of moral resistance killed themselves, believing that the struggle for existence under those conditions was no longer worth the effort.

Those who were still "healthy" were put to forced labor, especially useless labor, by those who had the mission of guarding them, under the protective eyes of Captains Buradescu and Radulescu and the supervision of Colonel Agapie.

On September 12, 1941, columns of Jews from the camps in Bessarabia set out for the Dniester. In their state of total exhaustion, they were required to cover thirty kilometers a day, with the right to stop for three hours during the course of a day. Those who could not keep up with the pace fell exhausted along the margins of the road and were shot. Peasants watching from the corn fields along the sides of the highway fell upon the bodies and plundered them.

But this tragedy had its saddest moment when families were split up before they departed, in a savage and totally inhuman way, without any reason and, worse, without any justification. Wives were separated from husbands, children from parents; old people were left abandoned. Shrieks and cries rose to high heaven, but those who had organized this action considered it a "successful" operation. The road was strewn with corpses, and no one knows how many died, much less who they were. The price of a cup of water was figured in gold, and nothing was considered too much, in order to make the suffering all the greater. On September 28, 1941, the camps in Bessarabia began to close. Their "tenants" had been transferred to Transnistria.

After a few days, the evacuation of the ghetto at Chisinau began. The first convoy was made up of more than one thousand persons who left for the Dniester by the Orhei-Rezina highway. This evacuation continued throughout the month of October 1941, although an order was received from Bucharest to halt the forced deportations beyond the Dniester in order to carry out a screening. Intellectuals, merchants, industrial workers, handicraftsmen, and those who owned urban or rural property were to be exempted from deportation. This order was not observed.

In these impossible circumstances, an act of incredible courage took place in the Chisinau ghetto. The details of how this mission was carried out will never be known. But the vice-president of the Jewish community in Chisinau, a lawyer named Sapira (his given name is not known), put on the uniform of a military officer and left with a military plane, with Bucharest as his destination. He knocked on every door, trying as hard as humanly possible to bring about a change in the provisions affecting the evacuation, and particularly the abusive measures of the local authorities, who failed to respect the order they had received. It was all in vain! The only thing offered him was the right to remain in Bucharest. Sapira refused. Using the same means of transport, he returned to Chisinau and was transferred with the first convoy. No one ever heard of him later.[57]

During this period, the Jewish concentration camps in Bucovina were evacuated under the same conditions as those in Bessarabia.

The National Bank sent Ioan Mihaiescu, a high official, to the camp at Marculesti to put on a "squeeze," using every means possible, to get jewelry, currency, gold, and precious stones; in short, everything that had any value belonging to the Jews who had been arrested and held under the surveillance of Colonel Agapie. Within a short time Mihailescu's "operation" began to bear fruit. Although he had instructions that the goods must be paid for at a very low rate, Mihailescu considered it to be too much. He would continually walk through the camp and, although he did not have the official authority to do so, he would take identity papers away from the Jews, saying to them, "You are all going to your death!"

Columns of Jews from places around Cernauti, on reaching a forest in the vicinity of the commune of Cosauti, found there the corpses of hundreds of Jews from a convoy that had passed a short time before. The gendarmes, who had just arrived, were engaged in a veritable orgy, shamelessly plundering the corpses. The convoy, which had halted for a moment, continued on its way to Atachi, the point for crossing the Dniester over into Transnistria.

More than 30,000 Jews were evacuated from the Cernauti ghetto before the departures were stopped on October 14, 1941. There still remained in Cernauti 15,600 Jews who had been authorized to remain by a screening commission, and another 4,000 Jews stayed on the basis of provisional authorizations issued by Dr. Traian Popovici, the mayor of the city. This is what he has written in connection with the evacuation of the Jews from Cernauti:

The population selected for deportation was first gathered into groups of about two thousand and then pushed through the mud and mire towards the loading

ramps at the main railroad station. There they were packed into the cars, about
forty and fifty in a car (the cars were under military guard, and the train was
under the command of an officer), and the convoy began to move towards the
Dnester, towards the concentration points at Atachi and Marculesti, whence they
were ferried across the river of Charon, into the kingdom of Hell.

Heartbreaking scenes took place on the embarkation ramps and when the
trains left. The separation of members of the same family, the children leaving
and the parents remaining, or else the separation of brothers and sisters, not to
mention of course husbands and wives, filled the air with wails and moved even
the most hardened hearts. It was a separation forever. Some were leaving for
suffering and death, the others were remaining in slavery and sorrow. The
exodus of the Jews from Cernauti forms a tragic chapter in the history of
mankind and this, the most serious injury ever done to the ideals of civilization
and culture, will be recorded forever in memory.

The Jews lived through this deportation in two seasons, in cold and rain and
snow in the winter of 1941 and in torrid heat and thirst in the summer of 1942.
How similar in suffering is their tragic destiny in leading them into Babylonian
slavery thousands of years ago and into the hell of hunger, sickness, and death
in Transnistria or the Ukraine beyond the Bug!

Traian Popovici continued the description of this tragedy:

The dead were dropped off the trains, abandoned in the stations, and left to
the services of local charity. Dispossessing them of everything they had on them
at the concentration points along the Dnester, taking away their documents and
destroying them so that all trace of them would vanish, starting them across the
Dnester in barges, marching on foot through rain, wind, sleet, and mud, barefoot
and hungry, these are pages of Dantesque tragedy and apocalyptic savagery. Of
one car with sixty nursing babies, one alone survived. Tired and tortured, they
were abandoned on the point of death along the edges of the roads, and left to
their fate, the prey of vultures and dogs.

Those who arrived at the destination in miserable conditions of health lived
there without housing, without firewood, without food and clothing, exposed to
merciless storms and the vexations of the guards and administrators. It was not
even an organization for hasty deportation, in the sense of providing any shelters
for human beings.

To abandon them with nothing save hunger, cold, lack of hygiene, exanthematic typhus and other epidemics, characteristics of a herd of animals, rapes of
the women and girls, prostitution for bread, and the hatred of the Ukrainian
population, this was the purpose of the "evacuation."

Their death rate increased to 50–70 percent, and even reached 85 percent in
the commune of Bersad in Balta County, where the deportees were held like
cattle in an unsheltered place under the open sky until December 20. This had
no "human" purpose other than to destroy them.

Forbidding them under penalty of court martial to bring food, clothing, and
medicine from home, punishing by death those who tried to escape and return
home, what other purpose did all this have than to destroy them?

Delivering them across the Bug to German organizations on the pretext of lending a work force, to be martyred there, torn to pieces and buried alive in common graves, what other meaning did this have than to grind them to dust?

This is the parade of martyrdom for those who went out on the march into Transnistria. And this all took place in the twentieth century, this century of lunacy.

Several times I told the governor [G. Calotescu] and other bearers of the torch of hatred that it would have been more humane for us to put them up against the wall and shoot them than for us to torture them in a cold and calculated fashion, with no qualms of remorse in the soul nor any fear of God.

This is one of the phenomena of the "holy war" for "liberation" and the "crusade."

History is not to be besmirched in the name of humanity, civilization, and a religion having forgiveness as its essence, nor in the name of a pagan Christ, a "Creator of our nation" and an "artisan of a good destiny."[58]

Popovici concluded his testimony:

With the blood of those martyred, with the souls of those grown into superhuman figures, with the terror of those bathed in the waters of death, the new priests of this savage religion have written pages of apocalyptic shame in the psalter of the Romanian people.[59]

On November 17, 1941, the pillage operations sponsored by the National Bank stopped. It is interesting that this "impartial" organization now became crowded by other authorities which had as "representatives" in the camps in Bucovina and Bessarabia none other than capable people like Ioan Mihaiescu, the "senior official" of the National Bank.

The immense amount of Jewish property gathered into the treasury of the National Bank was divided as follows after prolonged discussion: the gold was given to the National Bank; gold and silver coins and numismatic collections of great value were given to the National Mint. In order to simplify matters, it was decided to sell the jewelry and other precious articles at public auction. In order not to waste anything, the clock mechanisms that were taken out of gold watches were "donated" to watchmakers' schools that had been set up by the Ministry of Labor.

As a matter of ironic fact, the government of Bucovina, which had organized the evacuation and deportation and had blessed all the massacring and plundering that been done in that province, was excluded from this "impartial" allotment.

11

Defying dangers and accepting risks, Dr. Alexandru Safran, the Chief Rabbi of the Jews of Romania, organized at his residence a center for

underground activities seeking to save the Jewish population from the
calamities that had befallen them. For this purpose he used every means
at his disposal, contacting leading personalities in Antonescu's governmental apparatus, high personalities in the hierarchy of the Romanian
Orthodox Church, members of the diplomatic corps, the International
Red Cross, and others. The principal shape taken by the activity by this
resistance movement was the Federation of Unions of Jewish Congregations, headed by Dr. W. Filderman.

By drawing up and forwarding memoranda to different forums, soliciting permission to organize help for those people who were in total
poverty, a possibility was created for trying to save a large number of
human beings from death.[60]

It is of interest that on September 7, 1941, Section 1 of the Supreme
General Staff issued Communiqué No. 37871, stating:

The Supreme General Staff has ordered that you [Jewish organizations] are to
collect aid of all kinds, preferably in cash, which is to be transferred to the camp
through the Supreme General Staff, Section 2, which is in charge of the prisoners.[61]

On August 27, 1941, a few days before this order, the Military Command
at the city of Iasi asked the Jewish communities to deposit a large sum
of money to help the Jews in the camp of Vertujeni. The Jewish community of that city succeeded in collecting the sum of 200,000 lei, to
which the Federation of Unions of Jewish Congregations of Romania
added the sum of 300,000 lei.

This sum, which could have alleviated the suffering of so many people
in bleak misery and on the verge of complete despair, never arrived to
fulfill the purpose for which it was collected.[62]

Given these abuses by people lacking elementary human feelings towards those who had been brought to the threshold of complete despair
and physical and moral destruction, a new appeal was forwarded by the
Jewish organizations on August 28, 1941, this time directly to the Prime
Minister, Mihai Antonescu:

We have the honor of asking your kindness in ordering that we be permitted
to send delegates with food, clothing, medicine, and money to the Jewish camps
which have been set up in . . . Bucovina and Bessarabia. The Union of Jewish
Communities in the Old Kingdom has sent an order by telephone to the Jewish
Communities in Iasi for the sum of 300,000 lei and the latter organizations have
added the sum of 200,000 lei, thus creating a fund of 500,000 lei for the purpose
of helping the evacuees.[63]

These appeals remained unanswered at that time. The Leader, Ion
Antonescu, and the entire administrative and military apparatus had no

intention of improving sanitary conditions for the Jews despite the risk
of spreading an epidemic. They wanted to destroy them physically, and
the measures which were taken and applied with a perseverance and
conviction which exceeds all imagination reflected this policy exactly. On
October 4, 1941, Section 2 of the Supreme General Staff stated in Order
No. 6651, addressed to the local military command at Cernauti: "In
conformity with the orders of Marshal Antonescu all the Jews in Bucovina are to be transferred to the east of the Dnester [Transnistria]
within ten days."[64]

After two days, on October 6, 1941, at a session of the cabinet, Ion
Antonescu announced emphatically:

As regards the Jews, I have ordered a measure to have all of them removed
from this region forever. This measure is being carried out. I still have approximately 10,000 Jews in Bessarabia who will be sent across the Dnester in a
few days, and if circumstances permit, they will be sent beyond the Urals.[65]

Dr. Meier Teich, the President of the Jewish Communities in Suceava,
declared in a most dramatic memoir:

I left on the third train. I was thrust into a cattle car which had not been cleaned
up, crowded beyond measure. When our train was ready to depart, Colonel
Zamfirescu came and ordered that the departure be held up. Apreotesei, the
Chief of Police, and Major Botoroaga told me that Colonel Zamfirescu had
ordered that all those who could not be transported should also be evacuated.
In fact the old and the sick, invalids in bedclothes, without any baggage, had
begun to get into the cars. But [there] was even more! The chief physician, Dr.
Bona, had released from the hospital all the sick Jews, even those in [the] most
critical condition, as for example Isaac Mayer, a coach driver, who had been
operated on a few days before for amputation of a foot and was in agony. He
died later, one hour after departure.... Dr. Bona released his colleague Dr.
Bernard Wagner, who was more than seventy years old. Not being able to endure
the torture, he killed himself when we reached Moghilev.[66]

At that time, it was the Succoth holidays. From the beginning of the
war until the middle of September 1941, more than one hundred fifty
thousand Jews had been killed in the camps in Bucovina and Bessarabia,
along the roads of those provinces, in the camps and ghettos, according
to the statistics from the census of the Jewish population made in 1941.

In view of this situation, Dr. Alexandru Safran, the Chief Rabbi of
the Jews of Romania, tried a desperate move and addressed Marshal
Ion Antonescu directly, but with no results at all! Under these circumstances, he sought the good will of Nicodim, the old Patriarch of the
Orthodox Church.

Rabbi Safran asked for and obtained an audience with the high prelate, to whom he described the desperate situation in which the Jewish population in the liberated provinces found themselves. While he showed very little interest at the beginning, the old Patriarch nevertheless listened attentively to the fervent pleas of the young rabbi and gradually began to change his attitude. Trying to explain to him the terrible responsibility he would have before the Supreme Judge if he did not help to remedy this tragic situation, Rabbi Safran, despairing of his case, fell on his knees before the Patriarch, begging for his support! The spiritual leader of a Jewish community, which numbered more than 750,000 at the beginning of the war, had fallen on his knees, begging and imploring that his people should be saved.

Touched, the Patriarch asked the young rabbi to rise and promised him his support. For this purpose, Patriarch Nicodim made contact with the Queen Mother of Romania. She understood the situation and arranged a dinner at the Palace to which King Mihai was invited and at which Patriarch Nicodim and Manfred von Killinger, the German Ambassador to Bucharest, were present. Making use of the occasion, the Queen Mother spoke warmly, pleading with Killinger to intervene to save the Jews of Bucovina and Bessarabia.

The Ambassador was insensitive to the plea and refused brutally. Discouraged and disgusted, Patriarch Nicodim ceased to concern himself with this problem any more. Understanding that the fight could not be given up, Rabbi Safran, making use of the fact that Tit Simedrea, the Metropolitan of Bucovina, was in Bucharest, requested an audience with him.

The rabbi had been acquainted with the Metropolitan from the time they had both participated in sessions of the Senate. The Metropolitan of Bucovina, a well-known anti-Semite and an open adherent of A. C. Cuza, accepted his request for a meeting.

To his great surprise, Rabbi Safran found an attentive and favorable listener. Metropolitan Tit Simedrea promised his support, and in Cernauti he intervened directly with the Governor of Bucovina, General G. Calotescu. As has already been pointed out, the mayor of the municipality of Cernauti, Dr. Traian Popovici, played an important role in this gigantic effort to change the course of events that were known to be bloody and could only end in death. Dr. Traian Popovici continued his testimony:

It is of no interest who among those present approved or disapproved the deportation decision. Considering the fact that there was no civic courage, no one had the grit to protest against such an act, with its historic consequences for a whole people.... I asked for grace for those presented to the church for baptism, pointing out that our reason for this was that missionary work is the keystone of Christianity. I asked that those dedicated to high culture and the fine arts be spared. I asked payment for those who deserved the gratitude of the nation, the pensioners and the disabled officers. I asked to keep the master craftsmen in every branch of industry. I asked to make an exception for the physicians, in the service of humanity. I asked for engineers and architects, for construction workers. I asked for judges and lawyers. . . . The result was that the Governor accepted my proposals in part and in view of all this he authorized me to draw up a list of those who deserved the gratitude of our nation.[67]

On October 15, 1941, the mayor of Cernauti, together with General Ionescu and the German Consul General Schellhorn, waited in the ante-room of Governor Calotescu's office. When they were invited into the office, he told them this:

Gentlemen, I have just now finished a conversation with the Marshal, who has allowed a quota of up to 20,000 Jews to remain in Cernauti. I authorize you, General, Mr. Consul General, and Mr. Mayor, to proceed with this screening. You have discretionary powers. I reserve for myself a percentage and my personal signature on whatever authorizations are made.[68]

It was a gigantic effort, and one of great responsibility. Before carrying it out, the mayor wanted to give a ray of light to the people who were enveloped in despair, those who were awaiting the verdict from minute to minute: the transfer to death! Dr. Popovici went into the ghetto to bring this good news:

It was a dramatic scene that I experienced when I brought them the news of hope, the most solemn and the most emotionally charged decision of my life, and I do not believe that the future has a greater one reserved for me. Old rabbis, intellectuals of all ages, leading people from every walk of life in the community, merchants, and workmen, in a word, the entire living crowd knelt down to bless their God, giving thanks to Heaven for its pity, to the Marshal for the favor, and to me, trying to kiss my hands, my feet, and the hems of my clothing. Tears do not always shame a man. At that moment, touched by that spontaneous outburst of gratitude, tears sprang into my eyes and I cried, even I, one of the "town fathers." In order to relive that moment precisely, I call as witnesses all those who have survived tortures and who have shared with me the cup of hope for a better world. This gesture has not been taken from my people; that little thing like an apology for the future remains to release it in their consciences, those who cursed me, and persecuted me.[69]

There remained fifteen or sixteen thousand Jews with authorizations from the Screening Commission and about four thousand Jews who had authorizations issued by the mayor of the city, who were known as "Traian's Jews." Although the orders to stop deportations across the Dniester were clear, they still continued in the ghetto of Chisinau, even though bad winter weather had fallen upon Romania. The survivors of that hellish summer now found themselves on the threshold of winter, drained of all their physical strength, naked, robbed of all their property, without material resources to buy the most basic things needed to live, decimated by illnesses, and subjected daily to the most bitter vexations.

In view of this situation, Dr. W. Filderman wrote to Marshal Ion Antonescu, this time directly, a memorandum in connection with the departure from Chisinau of one final convoy made up of more than fifteen hundred Jews.[70]

The news of the suspension of deportations to Transnistria for some Jews in Cernauti was received with joy by the leaders of the Jewish congregations, and with a justifiable feeling of hope. On this occasion Dr. W. Filderman asked for an audience with Mihai Antonescu, and forwarded him another memorandum, which read as follows:

I am going to implore you to do an act of mercy which is not contrary to law ... that is, to order that those who have been sent away be sent back to their homes, all the more because among these who have been deported there are Jews from the Old Kingdom who were caught there, who wanted to be repatriated in time but were not able. Among them there are war veterans, decorated or disabled, and war orphans.[71]

This memorandum, drawn up with a deep sense of responsibility for the fate of the Jewish people, represented for those making the plea an important means of making themselves heard by those guiding the destinies of Romania. It had only one effect: Marshal Ion Antonescu replied in writing to the pleas made by Dr. W. Filderman!

It is the only case known when a leader of a fascist state in direct alliance with Hitlerite Germany had such a "dialogue" with the leader of a Jewish community. The occasion was perfectly chosen and had serious and harsh consequences for the actions planned against the Jews for an appropriate time in the future. On October 16, 1941, the troops of the Romanian army entered the city of Odessa.

Romanian public opinion was divided between those who saw the need for continuing military campaigns beyond the Dniester and those who favored halting them at the old, traditional boundaries of Romania.

The reply of Ion Antonescu to the memorandum from W. Filderman marked an escalation into crime such as has never before been seen. The letter, which was published in all the newspapers in Romania, says, among other things:

In two successive petitions you have written me about the "enormous tragedy" and have "implored" me in emotional words mentioning "conscience" and "humaneness." ... In order to inject yourself as an intervening tragedian you emphasize that this measure "is death, death, death without guilt, without any guilt other than that of being a Jew." ... I understand your pain, but [you] especially must understand, once for all, that my [concern] was for a whole nation. Will you think, have you thought about what happened in our souls last year when Bessarabia was evacuated? . . . The hatred with which the people of your religion treated us during the retreat from Bessarabia, how they received us when we returned. In direct response to the generosity with which you have been accepted into our society and treated, you Jews, joining the Soviet commissars, by terror without equal, witnessed by the Russian prisoners, pushed the Soviet troops in the region of Odessa to a useless massacre, only in order to cause us new losses. . . . Do you ask yourself about such hatred on the part of some Russian Jews with whom I have never had anything to share? But this hatred of theirs belongs to all of you. It is your hatred.[72]

The letter had an obviously political nature. The deportation measure was presented as an act of justice, and all the crimes, as usual, were by the Jews. There had never existed any tangible and undeniable evidence proving hostile activities by the Jews against the Romanian armies during their retreat in 1940.

Everything that has been said, everything was based on rumors carried by the retreating armies, made up and launched by their commanders, who were frustrated by the humiliating situation in which they found themselves and in order to be able to present a "proof" having some credibility for the disaster which the authors of the rumors themselves had witnessed.

The letter in question, dated October 19, 1941, was received by Dr. W. Filderman on October 20, 1941. But it appeared in the press on October 27, 1941, and not by chance. It was one more pretext for "justifying" the massacres at Odessa! The press campaign that followed the publication of this letter constituted a climax in the propaganda activities of the anti-Semitic authorities, and, as has been pointed out, it represented a landmark pointing to events which were to follow.

After a short time, Ion Antonescu, being discontented with the activity of the Federation of Unions of Jewish Congregations, decided to disband it and to establish a new organization that would be perfectly submissive and ready to carry out the wishes of the Marshal, without grumbling and in complete obedience. In the place of this Jewish organization the Jewish Center (Centrala Evreilor) was set up, to be a faithful copy of other organizations set up by the Hitlerites in the occupied countries.

12

The conquest of Odessa was a climax point in the self-made Marshal's execution of his expansionist policy, and the occupation of the Russian port on the Black Sea represented the beginning of an unimaginable tragedy for the Jewish population.

On October 22, 1941, a few days after the entry of Romanian troops into Odessa, the building located on Engel Street, which housed the headquarters of the Romanian army, and which until the evacuation of the Soviet administration had housed the Russian secret policy was blown up. Some of the occupants of the building were killed, along with General Glogojeanu, the Commandant of the City of Odessa. In addition, sixteen other officers, thirty-five enlisted men, and nine noncommissioned officers and civilian employees were killed in the explosion.

Three hours after the explosion occurred, the new Commandant of the city of Odessa, General C. Trestioreanu, reported to the 4th Army: "I have taken severe measures to hang the Jews and Communists in the public squares of Odessa."[73]

Just how one could determine under those conditions exactly who was a Communist and who was not never caused a problem. Prolonged propaganda and training for fighting against Judeo-Communism and the association of every Jew with Communism solved the problem simply.

On October 23, 1941, the reprisals began to be carried out. They were organized and performed as a result of Order No. 562 sent by Marshal Ion Antonescu from the Military Office, in which it was clearly specified that "for every German or Romanian officer killed, 200 Communists are to be executed, and for every enlisted man, 100." The order adds, "All Communists in Odessa, as well as one member of each Jewish family, are to be taken as hostages, and in case of a similar event, they will be executed."[74]

That order had an application that far exceeded its own dimensions, unleashing *real* hatred and sadism exercised against an innocent populace held collectively responsible for deeds no one had ever done, deeds no one has ever proved actually were done.

On the same day the order was issued more than five thousand Jews were executed on gallows set up in all the squares and on street corners, on tree branches along the boulevards, or on electric and telephone poles. After lunch the police and gendarmes pulled another twenty thousand Jews out of their houses to herd them into the Odessa jail, which in a short time became unable to take any more. The next day, October 24, 1944, the great massacre began in the city of Odessa!

Execution by shooting and hanging proved to be extremely slow. Hence the civilian and military organizers of the massacre decided to have recourse to more "efficient" measures. Jews arrested and dumped in the Odessa jail were taken out at dawn on October 24, 1941. Lined up in long columns, they were led outside the city to a place known as the Dalnik Barrier.

As soon as the columns arrived, the Jews were halted at the edge of the antitank ditches dug by the Soviet army to defend the city. In that way groups of about fifty to sixty people were shot and fell into the ditch. Nobody stopped to see whether those who fell were dead or not.

Even in this case, the means of execution seemed slow. There was need for something faster! The commander of a battalion of the 10th Division found a solution that was quick and cheap. There were some empty warehouses at the port of Odessa. The Jews were routed to them and packed in to the point of suffocation. Some embrasures were cut into the walls of the warehouses, and machine-gun barrels were placed in them. Then, calmly and very precisely, they opened fire on the crowd shut up in those sinister warehouses.

Alexa Neacsu, an assistant in the Faculty of Letters and a reserve second lieutenant in the 23rd Infantry Regiment, witnessed the massacre. He declared at the trial of Ion Antonescu and his ministers as war criminals:

I believe that the order to open fire was given by Colonel Deleanu or Colonel Niculescu Coca. The warehouses were taken in turn, which made the operation continue until nightfall, and all the warehouses were finished the same night. Next day, one of the warehouses where machine gun operation had not been completed was blown up, and so as to stand as a symbol and example, this blast was accomplished at the same hour as the explosion that blew up the Headquarters. . . .

Observing that by machine gun fire alone they could not succeed in killing all those who were inside, those who were in charge of this operation and who were visibly worn out and worried went into another conference and resorted to spattering the warehouses with kerosene for lighting and gasoline and setting them afire. When the fire broke out, some of those who were still inside the warehouses and who were only slightly wounded or unscathed tried to escape by jumping out the windows or to get out over the roof. The soldiers had a general order to the effect that [if] anyone should come out [they] should be shot. Some who were inside, as if to escape from the fire, appeared at the windows and made signs to shoot them, pointing with their hands to their heads or hearts; but when they saw weapons leveled against them, they would disappear for a moment from the window, only to reappear after a few seconds, making the same signals to the soldiers and turning their backs so as not to see for a moment when they were fired at. The operation lasted into the night, when even more gruesome scenes were visible by the light of the flames. Those who appeared were naked, because they had torn off their clothes, which had caught fire. Some of the women threw children out of the windows. I remember one scene when a boy four or five years old who had been thrown out of a window wandered for five to ten minutes with his hands up among the corpses, because the Romanian soldiers did not want to fire on him.[75]

Winter settled in with storms in 1941. The heavy winter, with deep snows and bitter winds that came from deep in the Russian steppes, completed the work of destroying the Jews physically and morally. Those who survived the massacres at Odessa, together with those from the southern counties of Transnistria, were gathered into camps and ghettoes that were set up and put under the command of Colonel Modest Isopescu, one of the most sinister figures in that whole bloody period. In Golta County, where Isopescu was the prefect, 48,000 Jews were interned in the camp at Bogdanovka, 18,000 at Dumanovca, and 4,000 at Akmicetca. In these camps, after they had been robbed of all they had, the Jews were subjected to a savage regime of extermination by hunger and misery. At the time of this massive plundering operation, when a slice of bread would be sold only for an article of gold, Isopescu began his infamous operation of massacring the 48,000 Jews in the camp at Bogdanovka.

Colonel Modest Isopescu gave the execution order to the sub-prefect, Aristide Padure, his faithful collaborator, who together with Vasile Manescu, the Chief of Police, began to organize the massacre. This was on the morning of December 21, 1941. All the able-bodied internees in the camp, who were living in abandoned barns, were separated from the old, the sick, and the infirm, who could not be removed from the wooden buildings where the crime was to be committed. Then gasoline was poured on two stables housing helpless people, and they were set afire. In a few minutes these two buildings, where four or five thousand Jews were gathered, were burning like torches, under the surveillance of the police sent for that purpose by Isopescu.

In the other barns, where the remaining 43,000 Jews were shut up, the scenes of desperation reached a paroxysm of panic. While the two stables were burning and the screams and groans could be heard growing weaker and weaker from within, the remaining Jews were pulled out of the barns and sent to a forest in the vicinity.

The place had been chosen with care. In this forest there was a depression, with a cliff, and at the edge of it the first columns of Jews to arrive were halted. They were shot in groups of three to four hundred people, with explosive bullets. The massacre lasted through the days of December 22 and 23, 1941. On December 25, it was Christmas. The crime was suspended until December 28, when those who were still alive were killed to the last man.

The corpses were gathered up by a group of about two hundred Jews who were kept alive especially for this purpose. All of the dead were piled up in heaps two meters high and four to five meters wide. Then Colonel Modest Isopescu, the prefect of Golta County, must have wished that he could enjoy the benefits of Hitler's high technology, gas chambers and crematoriums. But he did not have such sophisticated means. On the other hand, he did not lack imagination. He ordered that the dead should be piled up in a particular way: the fat ones at the edge of the pile and the thinner ones inside,

so that setting the corpses afire could be done that much more effi-
ciently. After the corpses had been set afire, the two hundred Jews
that were kept for this job were killed too. The black column of
smoke rose towards the unsettled winter sky over Transnistria, mark-
ing like a seal the place where crime became virtue, and the fruits of
so many years of inciting anti-Semitic hatred and contempt reached
their peak! Later, in the postwar years, when it was again possible to
write the truth in Romania, the author Aurel Baranga wrote a book
entitled *Snowfall over the Ukraine*. Snow fell over the Ukraine, and
from the swollen bodies of the Jews the blood oozed, drop by drop.

They worked hard during the winter of 1941–1942 to "purge" Transnistria of Jews completely! In spite of the terrible winter, so bad that
even the trains stayed frozen in the stations, the Jews were evacuated
from Odessa and from other cities and were interned in concentration
camps.

At places where cold, hunger, desperation, and sickness had not completely destroyed the Jewish internees physically, and places where the
executions ordered by Colonel Modest Isopescu and those like him had
not succeeded in destroying every trace of human existence in camps
where Death became a daily visitor, exanthematic typhus did so. Lacking
the most elementary means of hygiene, without clothing, without soap,
and especially without hot water, afflicted with dirt, invaded by lice, the
people, human beings who dragged themselves through the snow with
eyes burning with fever and seeing hallucinations, died, cut down by
typhus.

Those who were helplessly present at the end of their friends' lives
followed them silently along the road with no return. On January 8,
1942, Dr. Lazar Grief died, a victim of exanthematic typhus. His wife
killed herself, together with their only child! On January 13, 1942, Mrs.
Therese Robinson died of exanthematic typhus at Shargorod. Her
brother, Dr. Robinson, was a presiding judge, and her sister, Dr. Mar-
bach, killed herself beside the corpse of her sister. These are examples
among the thousands and thousands of dead and the nameless dramas
that were played out in silence in the ash-gray existence in the concentration camps of Transnistria. By January 21, 1942, the epidemic of
exanthematic typhus had spread to all the camps in Transnistria. The
corpses could not be buried because of the frozen ground, and they
waited for weeks in the cemeteries where even the earth refused to accept
so many martyrs.[76]

The spring of 1942 was a cold spring, with damaging rains and strong
winds. The apple blossoms were shaken off before they set fruit, and
over the bare fields there prevailed a silence interrupted by groans which
the hardened earth carried like a call! Dr. Traian Popovici, the mayor
of the city of Cernauti, was dismissed.

Humaneness cannot coexist with crime, and he had to be "sacrificed." A "New Man" was introduced, Major Stere Marinescu. He had been the secretary of Interior Minister Paraschivescu, a Legionary, who had organized the Jilava assassins in November 1940. This man, not by chance, had been named Office Chief of staff and right-hand man for the Governor of Bucovina, General Corneliu Calotescu. A profoundly corrupt man, a drunkard and a womanizer, sadistic and perverse, he accepted a monthly "salary" of 500,000 lei from the Jewish congregations in Cernauti. This did not prevent him from becoming one of the initiators and the savage executor of deportations.

Once the mayor of the city was replaced, the problem of deporting the 4,000 Jews that had been saved by Dr. Traian Popovici was reinstated in a special way. The operation was prepared in advance. Under the supervision of Stere Marinescu, patrols picked up in the middle of the night the Jews who possessed the authorizations mentioned in accordance with a list that had been specially drawn up. On the first night of the raid 1,000 people were arrested and forced to leave their houses with what they could carry on their back. Gathered into the Macabi sports arena, they were searched down to the bare skin, and the women were even given a gynecological examination in order to look for jewelry or other articles of value. After they had been deprived of everything they possessed, they were taken under escort to the railroad station and loaded into cattle cars. Along with this trainload Stere Marinescu sent sixty-six mentally ill people to Transnistria, together with the Jewish medical personnel who were taking care of them.

Similar operations to "purge" the city of Cernauti took place on June 7, 14, and 28, 1942. The perversity and cynicism with which these deportations were carried out are hard to describe. For example, the leader of the County Jewish Centrale in Cernauti was invited to the government house on June 26, 1942, where Stere Marinescu himself informed him of an order calling off the deportation of the last batch of Jews. But at the very moment that he was making this hypocritical assertion, the orders to arrest and send away the last batch of Jews had been carried out with unusual brutality.

Major Marinescu made one more final inspection the evening before the departure of the train. Observing that in some cars there was still vacant space, he ordered the Jews of the suburb of Rosa to be pulled out of their houses and taken to the railroad station. Since the cars were not sufficiently loaded even after this, he gave another order, and the Jews living on the streets of Pitei, many of whom had authorizations to remain in Cernauti signed by the governor, had to fill up the spaces in the cars, and they left!

13

The differences between the military authorities and the various administrative organizations that were interested in organizing the activities of the camps for the forced labor that was done—free—by Jews were resolved in a basic fashion.[77]

In order for affairs to be given a larger showcase, Reserve General Constantin Cepleanu was recalled to duty and named inspector general of the Jewish labor detachments. This man, who was well known for the wickedness and brutality of his actions, even during the time of his active duty in the military, had plenty of people on his conscience. For example, while he was commanding the 6th (Mihai Viteazu) Regiment, several of his subordinates, unable to stand the regime of terror run by this paranoid maniac any longer, committed suicide.

Now the general had discretionary power! He was able to order any measure of punishment, and no one would require him to account for it. As his first action, he inspected one such labor camp in which the internees were working on the repair of highways near Tg. Neamt. Dressed in civilian clothes, he observed how the work was being stretched out, and at lunch time he introduced himself to the commander, showed his credentials, and called the roll of the detachment. As a result of this "inspection," where in fact nothing proved to be in violation of the provisions of the law, twenty-five young people were sent to Transnistria. His last operation, which made him famous, was on October 2, 1942, when, accompanied by a military unit, he blocked the entrances and exits of the Galeries Lafayette department store in downtown Bucharest, checking every customer and salesman. Those who were written up on that occasion by General Cepleanu were never sent to Transnistria. But that happened for reasons other than his desire. In the confusion he could not pick from the crowd, the Jews who had deserted labor camps.

In the summer of 1942 whole columns of Jews from the Old Kingdom were sent to labor camps that had been organized in Bessarabia. The plan was clear; Jews from the Old Kingdom had been sent to work there, replacing the Jews of Bessarabia, who had been deported to die in Transnistria. A whole series of such camps appeared throughout the country, but especially in Bessarabia. One of these, located in the commune of Cubei near Bolgrad, became famous for the slave work into which the Jews were pressed. The camp contained Jews from Husi, Vaslui, Tecuci, and Galati. They were men of different professions, and many had intellectual occupations, but they were unable to pay for the so-called labor exemption licenses. The train stopped at the Bulgarica station, because the town of Bolgrad had no direct rail connection. It was hot, being almost the middle of June 1942. At the station repellent odor of putrefying corpses struck the newcomers. The air was simply impossible to breathe. To whoever asked about it at the station, the answer was simple: "From the common grave." There was such a grave in the vicinity of the station, and there was not any idea of asking who had been killed!

The road to Bolgrad, about thirteen to fourteen kilometers, was taken on foot. On entering the city itself one saw a picture that struck terror into the soul. It was a dead city! The streets, houses, and stores were all empty. Not a person could be seen. Only in the center of the city, where the military headquarters had been set up with the duty of organizing the workers, were there a few soldiers and civil service employees. A hot wind carried the dust from the highway, and the newcomers looked with fear to the dead city, whose inhabitants had been killed and were lying in the common grave at the Bulgarica station. The mystery was explained.

Somebody told his story:

"Before the war, an artillery regiment was stationed in the town. I was invited along with other soldiers to the house of a Jew on the evening of Purim. All the Jews were accustomed to invite soldiers to visit their families on holidays. You see? There was the house where I spent Purim...." We entered the house, now inhabited by ghosts. The man stayed on the threshold of the door and did not dare to go inside. His voice was choked with sobbing that he was vainly trying to stop. "Do you see? Over there, there was a piano. The hostess had two daughters. One of them was playing the piano that evening.... Do you understand? The house was full of people, the tables were set, it was warm and light and there was the smell of fresh bread, just taken out of the oven...."

His voice was a whisper that could barely be heard. The young fellow was that soldier. A friend from past years of childhood and adolescence mutely looked at a world that had disappeared and could not understand that even ghosts could become realities!

What was certain was that the city was dead, stripped of its people, who had been killed or deported and robbed, pillaged down to the bricks their houses were built of. The work in the camps was done according to established standards that were severe. Not to meet these quotas incurred punishments. The work was like convict labor. Some worked directly in the stone quarries at Cubei, bringing up blocks of stone from the deepest excavations. Others carried these stones in their arms to the highway to be transported, and they wielded sledgehammers much beyond their strength.

At Turcoaia, in Dobrogia, in the stone quarries at Manole Hill, Greci, Piatra Rosie, and Iacob Hill, the workers were pushed to exhaustion. Captain Munteanu, the commander of the forced labor camp at Turcoaia, who was a counsellor in the Appeals Court in civilian life, a completely vicious man, a drunkard, gambler, and womanizer, was eternally looking for money. One day he organized a theft on a grand scale. All the Jews under his command were gathered together at Turcoaia; everyone was searched and all their money was confiscated. The money was required for "high patriotic purposes," the captain declared; and, quite properly, he issued receipts to those who had been shaken down. He succeeded in collecting more than 500,000 lei. Later in the winter, a problem arose because the Jews were to be sent home in order to get warm clothing. Then the claim became clear. Orders for leave were given in exchange for the receipts.

The camps at Doaga, Vadeani, Ciocardia, and elsewhere remain branded with letters of fire in the memory of a generation who learned the humiliation of being slaves at the age when people dream.

14

Through the mediation of Andreas Cassullo, the Vatican representative in Bucharest, who was performing the function of Dean of the Diplomatic Corps, Chief Rabbi Alexandru Safran passed to Queen Mother Elena a file of information and documents regarding the grave situation of the Jews in the camps and ghettoes where they had been shut up. The Queen Mother met with Mihai Antonescu and asked for his help in approving shipments of aid to the deportees.

Following these coordinated efforts and activities, the Supreme General Staff approved sending money, but what happened to the sums that were sent to the Jews in the Vertujeni camp made the leaders of the Jewish community intercede directly with Marshal Ion Antonescu to approve sending aid directly to the camps by special delegates.

In spite of so many hostile attitudes and acts against which courageous men were struggling, defying the danger, Order No. 259, officially authorizing the Federation of Jewish Communities of Romania to send money and medicines to the Jews that had been deported to Transnistria, was issued on December 10, 1941.

Incapable and most of the time not even desirous of solving the problems raised by displacing, supervising, and reorganizing the lives of this multitude of people, the administrative and political authorities in Mogilev County decided to set up a Jewish Committee which would concern itself with all these problems, and which could be called upon as a last resort to be responsible for everything that took place in the various camps.

This committee, set up on November 18, 1941, was made up of men who understood that no help at all could come from the authorities, and the only possibility for survival lay in the organization, discipline, and

responsibility with which they could bring to accomplishment what they
proposed to do. Leading this committee, made up of Jews from different
professions, was Siegfried Jaegendorf, an engineer.

Thanks to its competent and responsible actions, the measures taken
by the Jewish Committee in Mogilev began to take on a definite shape.
The concrete results, although few in proportion to the gigantic needs
of this uprooted and totally plundered society, represented from the
beginning an effective means of helping to preserve the existence of the
Jews in that region.

The most acute problem to present itself was that the deportees had
to demonstrate their needs tangibly to the local authorities, and especially
the advantage of their remaining in the same place. This was a necessary
first step for saving them. To move them across the Bug signified death,
directly and without any possibility of delaying or evading it!

For this purpose the deportees moved to rebuild the central electric
power station, making use of a group of Jewish specialists and skilled
workers. In their general state of desperation, the possibility of doing
productive work, even if it was done by a small group of the Jews, had
remarkable effects on morale. The city of Mogilev, which had been
abandoned by the Russian troops, was in almost complete ruin. Hence
there was an acute problem for assuring the operation of engineering
plants that would permit the continuation of productive activity. Several
days after the electric power station was put into operation, they went
on to rebuild the foundry, the machine shop, and the metal fittings
plant. After assiduous work and enormous sacrifices, these installations,
which had been in ruins, became within a short time an industrial complex of capital importance. The life of the workers was organized around
these industrial nuclei, and later they created a service supplying provisions, a pharmacy, and a bakery. This supplied the bread necessary
for the population and put an end to exploitative speculation. What was
especially significant was that within a short time the machine shop began
to make tools to repair trucks; this gave work to a large number of
people.[78]

Under these conditions, a shelter provided with 250 beds was set up
for old people whose family members had died or been killed. The
hospital for contagious diseases also had an important place in the life
of this community. The run-down buildings of the former Ukrainian
hospital were used for this purpose. There was nothing in these ruins,
which were penetrated by the wind, rain, and snow. Nevertheless, the
necessary resources were found to set up rooms in which 100 beds were
installed. During the end of 1941 and the beginning of 1942, when the
great typhus epidemics broke out, these rooms were the scene of an
inexpressible drama, stirring the soul with pain and anger.

There was no delousing room in the hospital, no soap, not even hot

water or gasoline to eradicate the lice. The dreadful cold of that unfor-
gotten winter, when people wrapped themselves in rags thoroughly in-
fested with lice in order to stay warm, made the epidemic spread like
lightning. The worst thing was that the doctors and health workers
engaged in this indescribable struggle to stop the typhus themselves fell
sick, and the number of deaths grew and grew.

The Health Service set up by the Jewish community made giant efforts,
but as they completely lacked the elementary means of fighting this
terrible epidemic, their successes were extremely slight. They appealed
to the local authorities to authorize the Jews to use the only local bath-
house, for which they agreed to pay an immense sum for only a few
days' use. But the authorities refused to make available to these unfortunate people the only means of keeping a trace of bodily cleanliness.
In this epidemic, 7,000 people perished!

Under these desperate conditions, a public kitchen was set up, which
served hot food once a day to those wholly lacking resources. This small
amount of food gave many the capability to resist and to survive. The
lack of funds available to the Jewish Committee endangered the operation of this canteen, which was the single source of existence for these
desperate and hungry people.

Among these people were orphan children whose parents had died
or had been shot or left exhausted along the evacuation routes, dead of
hunger, cold, or exanthematic typhus. They represented a problem
which needed a speedy solution. The committee succeeded in organizing
an orphanage where 200 children who had been living in horrible misery
were housed and cared for.[79]

In spite of the efforts made, on June 14, 1942, the Mogilev Jewish
Committee, headed by Engineer S. Jaegendorf, was dissolved by the
Romanian authorities and placed under other leadership. This group
was obliged to sign a declaration that they would be responsible with
their lives for any escape from the camp that might occur.

It was bitter, it was hard, but from the pure depths of some unspotted
souls among them who had still not lost the warm, human feelings of
hope and faith, there arose poetry and song like a murmur, like an
appeal, or, more exactly, like the whisper of springs and the roar of the
free-rushing water of spring floods. Modest festivals were organized for
the people, plays were staged, and artists, singers, and impromptu or-
ators sought with their modest means to disperse the sadness from their
eyes and to bring a smile to their lips, bringing life to those wounded
by pain and bitter humiliation. Some courageous young people issued
several numbers of a modest publication. They distributed it at the risk
of their lives, but people waited shivering for those six numbers of their
publication![80]

The conditions for helping the Jewish population in the forced labor camps as well as in the deportation areas reached a critical point in those years. In these two years after the deportations began, goods valued at 481,807,045 lei were sent to the camps, not counting massive aid shipments in the form of raw materials: salt (150 tons), coal (300 tons), timber (11,000 square meters), caustic soda needed for making soap (5,000 kg), and so on.

In addition to these sums, more than 25 million lei were sent into the regions in question in the period between October 1942 and March 1943. These amounts were sent individually from funds which came from abroad, from the American Joint Distribution Committee, through the representatives in Romania of the Jewish World Congress, W. Fischer, Dr. Cornel Iancu, and M. Benvenisti.

It must be borne in mind that this gigantic effort to aid the population that had been deported into exile to die rather than to live was coordinated with another series of activities which were to contribute materially, to some minor extent, to resolving this situation.

The Zionist leadership in Palestine found a means of sending aid, which was distributed through the efforts of the Zionist organization in Romania headed by M. Benvenisti. In addition, a separate effort was developed through intense effort, with results worthy of mention. A group of magnanimous people, as early as 1941, began to collect money and goods, which they sent especially to the city of Cernauti. The function of cashier of this group was carried out by a Christian engineer, Traian Prokopovici.

To those already in desperate need of help were added daily increasing numbers of Jews in the country who had been pauperized. Romanization had begun to show its effects! Jews who had been deprived of their property or occupations permanently swelled the number of those who sought aid. Severe and massive obligations were brought to bear on the Jewish population in the form of payment of sums in the order of billions of lei, the obligation to "donate" clothing, underwear, footwear, and barracks articles, all calculated on the basis of the income earned by the Jews before the Romanization of their property, although these Jews had practically no income anymore. To these were added the obligation to pay military taxes calculated on the same basis; this exhausted the material capabilities of the Jewish population of Romania. The last sum imposed on the Jews, 4 billion lei, destroyed the entire Jewish community in the material sense. The protest by Dr. W. Filderman, although he no longer retained any official functions, resulted in his deportation to Transnistria on May 26, 1942.

At the same time, the Jews in the forced labor camps, undernourished and naked, found themselves at the end of their physical endurance. The coming of winter posed difficult problems. In spite of the unfavorable weather, they were required to work in the stone quarries, on the dams, and at cleaning snowdrifts from military highways and city streets. The bombardments by the American air force in the spring of 1944 resulted in an obligation on the Jews to clear the cities out from under the ruins. The support of these slaves fell on the Jewish communities from which these forced labor detachments came, although they too were completely impoverished and had few material resources.

In view of this desperate situation, means of making contact with international Jewish organizations and seeking their support were sought and found. A letter dated June 1, 1943, sent to Geneva to Sally Mayer, the President of the Jewish Congregations in Switzerland and representative of the American Joint Distribution Committee for Europe, represented a first step on the difficult, twisting road to get possession of the aid sent. In February 1944 the Vatican sent the sum of 1,353,000 lei to aid the deportees in Transnistria. Since this money was sent to the Jewish Centrale in Bucharest, the way in which it was used is unknown.

The liaison between the real leaders of the Jewish community in Romania, that is, W. Fischer, M. Benvenisti, and others, was performed by Hans Welti, a Swiss journalist. He made several trips to Switzerland, bringing correspondence and various materials, and organizing a way of getting the funds so greatly needed into Romania. Through the mediation of this journalist, discussions likewise took place about organizing a vast network to assist the emigration of Jews. All these activities did not prevent the Jewish leaders from continuing contact with the governmental authorities.

Thus, thanks to their intercession, approval was given, through the leadership of General Radulescu, a member of Marshal Ion Antonescu's secretariat, for a commission to leave for Transnistria to investigate the situation on the spot. As a matter of fact, after a month, on December 16, 1943, a commission of the International Red Cross headed by Charles Kolb, accompanied by representatives of the Romanian Red Cross and delegates from the Prime Minister's office and the government of Transnistria, visited a number of camps in that dreary enclave of death.

This visit was a Potemkin show indeed. Only those whom the authorities wanted were designated as members of the commission, and everything was arranged and prepared long in advance. In spite of all this, suitable means were found for getting reports showing the real situation in the camps directly into the possession of those who had a right to them.

These activities were abruptly interrupted by the arrest of the leading Jews who were clandestine leaders of the Jewish population. On January 30, 1944, William Fischer, M. Benvenisti, Dr. Entzer, and others were arrested and taken to the Prefecture of Police in Bucharest, where Inspector Sava Dumitrescu subjected them to bestial treatment.

As early as December 1943, Hans Welti had ceased his liaison work

with the Jewish leaders. Richter, Eichmann's man and the Chief of the
Gestapo in Romania, handed over a dossier to the Siguranta (Security
Police) and gave daily attention, along with Radu Lecca, to the course
of the investigations.

After a week of torture, the interrogations began. A file was put before
the eyes of those under arrest which filled them with fear and conster-
nation; it contained copies of the entire correspondence carried by Hans
Welti, the journalist. He was in fact a Gestapo agent!

15

The actions taken and the methods used to "resolve the Jewish problem" in Romania, beginning with the Goga-Cuza government, the National Legionary State, and especially under Ion Antonescu, the Leader,
were satisfactory to Hitler's Germany in every respect.

The German Embassy in Bucharest was perfectly organized, with personnel that were "highly qualified" in liquidating the Jewish population.
It followed most attentively the progress of the deportations, by which
this population was displaced, plundered, and killed in the geographic
enclave known by the name of Transnistria.

This state of affairs could take on considerable magnitude, because
at that time the Germans had not started to call the concentration camps
in Poland "installations." These had gone into operation in the spring
of 1942.

Because of this fact, the Jewish population of the Old Kingdom had
been able to survive, in spite of all the economic and especially the
spiritual oppression exerted against them. Then these installations began
to go into operation. When trains originating from all the countries of
Europe, loaded with Jews, were headed towards the camps in Poland,
the Germans began to raise before the Romanian government and public
opinion the problem of liquidating the entire Jewish population of Romania, at first discreetly, and later more insistently.

On August 8, 1942, the *Bukarester Tageblatt*, the official newspaper of
the German Embassy in Bucharest, published an article entitled "Ru-
mänien wird judenrein" (Romania Will Be Purged of Jews), in which it
praised the new Jewish organization known as the Jewish Centrale,
which, as the newspaper remarked, had among its various missions that
of "preparing all matters connected with definitively purging Romania
of Jews."[81]

An article with a similar theme appeared in issue Number 151 of the
Donauzeitung, the Gestapo organ for the Balkans published in Belgrade.
Two days later, the *Völkischer Beobachter*, the official Nazi newspaper,

reproduced the same news item published in the German newspaper in Bucharest:

There are only 272,409 Jews [in Romania] altogether. This surprising result of the census of Jews in Romania is also a proof of the efforts put by the Romanian government into solving the Jewish problem quietly and without much noise. ... Because the number of Jews before the summer of 1940 was perceptibly greater.... The reduction in this number ... in [the] short time since the summer of 1940 is considerable. A complete purge of Romania of its Jews, which is one of the new duties of the Jewish Centrale, is now moving forward, and the first steps in this direction have already been taken.... This removal is now being pursued in large numbers. It is foreseen that a first contigent of Jews, limited to some 25,000 because of transportation difficulties, will be sent to the East, that is, farther off, in Transnistria, during September and October [1942]. Another contingent will follow in the summer of 1943, and the rest of the Jews in Romania, including those in [Southern] Transylvania, must leave Romania in the autumn of 1943. In the course of the next year, Romania will be completely purged of Jews.... The prospect that Romania will become a place that is forbidden to the Jews, a country that within a definite time will be completely closed to Jews, the first one in the Southeast, offers the Romanian people even further assurance that it will achieve the position in the new Europe which befits it, on the basis of its contribution to the emancipation of Europe from all Jewish influence.[82]

It is worth mentioning that the Romanian press did not write a single line connected with this article, which cynically revealed publicly the manner in which the Jewish population would be sent to death! This significant silence did not exclude total acceptance by the Romanian leaders of the manner in which the Final Solution would be applied. Moreover, deporting the Jews from Cernauti and Dorohoi in the summer of that same year, applying draconian measures affecting work in the forced labor camps, and imposing the payment of exorbitant sums on the backs of a people clearly indicated that their attitude towards the Jews in fact remained the same as before! Doubtless this set of anti-Semitic measures encouraged the Nazi authorities to insist on the application of the plan just mentioned.

With this purpose in mind, the German Embassy in Bucharest forwarded a note to the Romanian Ministry of Foreign Affairs on August 13, 1942, in which it clearly specified the following points:

The German Legation has the honor of informing the Royal Romanian Ministry of Foreign Affairs that the Director of the Ministry, Radu Lecca, has been invited by the Chief of the Security Police and the Berlin S.D. to a conference lasting several days which will begin on the 19th of the current month. (If he intends to follow up this invitation, he will be accompanied by Hauptsturmführer Richter

of the SS [Eichmann's representative in Bucharest].) The Legation request that
the competent authorities be advised about this.[83]

The visit took place between August 20 and 27, 1942. The openly
contemptuous attitude of the German authorities towards Radu Lecca
is doubtless explained by the fact that Martin Luther of the Second
Department of the German Ministry of Foreign Affairs had informed
Wörmann, Weiszäcker, and Ribbentrop about the complete assent of
Ion Antonescu to the deportation of the Jews to Poland. The operation
had to be begun with the Jews in Timisoara, Turda, and Arad. As a
consequence it was thought that Radu Lecca was not needed, nor did
he have to be given any special attention, since the problem he had been
invited to Berlin to discuss had been solved with the Romanian leaders
directly.

The return of Radu Lecca caused a chain reaction. Those governing
Romania were humiliated and furious, and determined on categoric
measures. Those in the German Embassy in Bucharest realized that
something stupid had happened in Berlin during the visit. An attempt
by von Killinger, the German Ambassador, to explain things in writing
had no effect at all.

Without doubt, it is difficult to accept the idea that the approximately
three hundred thousand Jews in Romania were not sent to the extermination camps in Poland merely because Radu Lecca was not received
with complete courtesy in Berlin, thus wounding the sensitivities of the
Romanians.

A whole series of factors at home and abroad contributed to this. The
Germans could not easily accept the idea that the Romanian refusal was
definitive. In September 1942 a meeting took place at Berlin at which
the manner in which the Jews would be deported from Romania by rail
was established. On the day the conference opened the Romanians requested that the meeting be postponed. The Germans did not think a
postponement was necessary and stated: "The station of departure for
the special trains is Adjud on the Ploiesti-Cernauti line, the station on
the frontier of the Gouvernement General [Poland] is Szniatyn, and the
destination is Belzec"[84] Then technical details follow with regard to the
manner in which the cattle cars needed would be obtained, and the
relations between the Romanian and German railroad authorities for
this purpose. It was likewise established that about two thousand Jews
would be sent daily.

The moral pressure on the Jewish population reached a peak. News
about sending Jews to Poland had the effect of a bolt of lightning. Urgent
steps were demanded!

For this purpose, a group of Jewish leaders from Timisoara, Arad,
and Sibiu gathered in Bucharest to begin some lobbying. They found

no help at all in the Jewish Centrale! Hence they made contact with the clandestine leadership of the Jewish resistance movement. The first contact was made with Dr. Stroiescu, Ion Antonescu's personal physician. Without seeking any personal advantage, he had obtained the sum of 100 million lei for the Home for Disabled Veterans, which was under construction and of which he was the director. His intercession with the Marshal had some results, but they were far from substantial. Simultaneously with these activities, Dr. Alexandru Safran, the Chief Rabbi, set up liaison through a special messenger with Metropolitan Balan of Transylvania at Sibiu, who was known for the influence he had over Marshal Antonescu. Although he was a man known to have anti-Semitic feelings, the Metropolitan responded to the calls and came to Bucharest, where he met with Chief Rabbi Safran at General Vaiatoianu's house. In the discussion which took place, Rabbi Safran explained the grave situation and requested support. Metropolitan Nicolae Balan did not hesitate and called Marshal Antonescu on the telephone to request a meeting.

At the same time, Queen Mother Elena was informed. There was a lunch at the Palace at which King Mihai, Marshal Antonescu, the Queen Mother, and Metropolitan Balan were present. On this occasion they spoke seriously and earnestly with the Marshal, asking that he cancel the decision on deportation.

Later a telephone rang in Chief Rabbi Safran's house. Metropolitan Balan of Transylvania told him this great news: the deportation had been postponed. A moment of respite had been gained!

As regards their attitude towards the Jews, the Romanian authorities began to prepare measures authorizing emigration of the Jews from Romania to Palestine. The price for each separate authorization was 200,000 lei.

In the autumn of 1942, the German pressure became stronger and stronger, and Eichmann himself traveled to Bucharest. It is possible that on this account the Leader of the State, without giving any explanation, sent directly to the Ministry of the Interior the order to begin deportations from the regions that had already been established during the summer, and seven categories of Jews for initial deportation were defined. The order was issued on the evening of October 10, 1942, and had to be sent with urgent priority to the police organizations in the respective localities. The minister of Police, General Piki Vasiliu, made the order known to Dr. Stefan Antal, one of the leading figures of the Jewish community to whom the Minister had shown his good will on many occasions by solving some problems which this courageous Jew had asked him to settle.

Dr. Antal understood that every moment was precious and tried by every means to persuade General Vasiliu to delay the release of the order and to cause Marshal Antonescu to cancel it.

It was late at night when Dr. Antal, desperate over his unsuccessful

efforts, decided to go to the residence of Dr. W. Filderman, who had
recently been liberated from Transnistria because of the intercession of
the Papal Nuncio, Andreas Casullo. He explained the situation to him
and asked him to come to the Ministry of the Interior so that they could
try together to convince General Vasiliu to take action to save the Jews
who were destined for deportation. They appeared at the Ministry of
the Interior and tried, with their united strength, to get General Vasiliu
to act favorably on their requests.

Finally, at dawn, the general agreed. He called Marshal Antonescu's
office and dictated to the colonel on duty a report which pointed out
that due to the rainy season and the approaching winter, it was hard to
carry the operation through to a conclusion, and asked that the deportations be postponed until springtime.

These two Jewish leaders were called to the Ministry of the Interior
the next day (in fact, the same day at lunch time) to be informed of the
result. When they came at the appointed hour, the Minister was not
there. An agonizing wait began, lasting until after 3:00 p.m., when General Piki Vasiliu came and advised the two of them that he had obtained
a delay in the deportations from Marshal Ion Antonescu.

These two prominent Jews took good note of the importance of the decision
which had been wrested from the Romanian Fascist leadership and felt the thrill
of an earth-shaking which marked the end of one chapter in the history of
Jewish sorrows.[85]

The deportation order, however, remained in effect; its execution had
merely been postponed. On the plea of Chief Rabbi Alexandru Safran,
the Papal Nuncio, Andreas Cassullo, departed in haste for Rome to
induce high authorities in the Vatican to intercede to have the order in
question cancelled. He induced de Weck, the Swiss Ambassador in Bucharest, Sefbarty Istinyell, the Turkish Chargé d'Affaires, and especially
Charles Kolb and Setinger, the representatives of the International Red
Cross, to join him in this action.

The idea of "selling" the Jews in return for approval of their emigration remained valid. They were awaiting the appropriate moment!

16

Desperate attempts by the Jews to escape the tightening noose of the
fascist terror in Romania and other satellite countries of Hitler's Reich
were rewarded many times with tragic results. Romania and Bulgaria
were the only two countries with an outlet to the sea, providing a chance

of finding a way to Turkey, that is, to freedom; some of these attempts succeeded because of perfectly organized efforts.

The drama of the vessel *Struma* gave these operations added dimensions. The steamer had left the port of Constanta on December 12, 1941, with Palestine as its destination. The first port of call was Constantinople (Istanbul), where it arrived on December 16. There the captain declared that it could no longer continue the trip because of serious defects in its engines. This old steamer, which was not fit for sea journeys, was used as a unique, desperate solution for a group of 769 people, of whom 70 were children, 269 women, and 428 men. The odyssey of this steamer and its tragic cargo is well enough known! The Turkish authorities refused to pass this group of refugees through their territory to Palestine, and the British authorities, hiding behind the so-called regulations for Jewish emigration to Palestine, refused to give them entry visas. In view of this situation from which no way out could be seen, the Turkish authorities issued an order to a vessel to tow the *Struma*, and it sailed out along the Black Sea coast. A few minutes after it left in tow, the *Struma* sank. Only two persons escaped by swimming.

It is worth mentioning that two days before this tragedy occurred, the British authorities had approved the debarkation of the children, but for reasons unknown this order was not made known, and all these people were found dead in the waters of the Bosporus on February 24, 1942.

There has been much speculation over the years about the causes for the vessel's sinking so rapidly. The truth seems to have come to light through a remarkably interesting and significant revelation which appeared in an article published on October 7, 1982, in the Boston *Jewish Advocate*:

Although the truth about the sinking of the *Struma* by the Russians was revealed as early as 1978 in a book published by the Ministry of Defense of the Soviet Union, it has only recently come to light. The book which reveals the truth is entitled "The Black Sea Fleet in the Great Patriotic War." Written by G. I. Vaneiev, it was published by Voenizdat, the publishing house of the Soviet Ministry of Defense ... The Soviet authorities have always referred to "reliable" persons in Nazi-occupied Europe who were chosen by "Zionist collaborators with the Nazis to be trained as spies and saboteurs and were later sent to Palestine disguised as immigrants. . . . " This remarkably interesting report, which also casts new light on the *Struma* tragedy, appeared for the first time in a translation by Emanuel Litvinov.

At the same time, the drama of the Jews deported to Transnistria and the persecutions against them continued to be consummated with diabolical tenacity and perseverance, even though the situation on the po-

litical chessboard had changed in many of its aspects on account of the
course of the war.

The speech made by Cordell Hull, the United States Secretary of State,
on the occasion of the Jewish autumn high holy days of 1942 offered
not only hope for the peoples held under oppression, but also a warning
to all of those who had made violence and contempt the only purpose
of their existence. It is significant that Nicolae Mares, the former Legionary minister and a personal friend of Ion Antonescu, when he was
asked by the latter to take a position in the government, replied with a
characteristically opportunist attitude that, in view of the international
circumstances, he could not accept the proposal.

In spite of all this, Jews continued to be sent to Transnistria from
Bucharest and other places in the country on the most fanciful charges.
In that period 600 Jews were sent to Transnistria, beyond the Bug, from
whence no more than 16 of them returned. After the Embassy of the
Soviet Union had been opened by the Romanian authorities, their names
had been found on some lists of those that had asked in 1940 to be
repatriated in Bessarabia, the region to which they in fact belonged.
Communist Jews who were imprisoned in the camp at Tg. Jiu and
hundreds of other Jews that still had their freedom but had been accused
of Communist sympathies were sent to the camp at Vapniarka, where
Colonel Murgescu was in charge. He was afterwards replaced by Captain
Buradescu, who had "tours of service" operating under the protective
wing of Colonel Agapie in the camp at Vertujeni.

The food ration was fifty to one hundred grams of bread per day and
soup made of beans normally used for fodder. Because this plant was
used for feeding the animals and also for feeding the Jews in the camp,
the results began to show themselves within a short time. The prisoners
suffered severe complications, which led to paralysis. In spite of the
protests, the leaders of the camp at Vapniarka continued their program
of liquidating the Jews undisturbed. "You have been brought here to
die, not to live!" screamed Colonel Murgescu, and Gheorghe Alexianu,
the university professor and Governor of Transnistria, asked the entourage which surrounded him, smiling innocently, "Are there still Jews
around here?"

But one of the most bitter aspects of the tragedy taking place in Transnistria was the state of the orphaned children! Living a vagabond existence, naked, hungry, sick, and uncared for, these children presented
a living image accusing a criminal regime of unforgivable deeds.

The problem became especially serious when some of these unfortunate little beings who had never known warmth and love began to get
sick. This finished the work of killing them. With extremely limited
resources and with a spirit of abnegation far exceeding the bounds of
Samaritan compassion, the Jewish Committees began to organize so-

called orphanages. In a memorandum forwarded by Dr. W. Filderman
to Ion and Mihai Antonescu on January 2, 1943, he states:

In one orphanage alone, with 140 children, 26 have died within a single month.
They are naked, sleeping on beds without any bedclothes, in unheated rooms,
without any windowpanes, so that they cannot get up out of bed to take care of
their needs; they live in a pestilential atmosphere.

The memorandum offers a single solution:

Return the children under eighteen immediately to Cernauti, where living costs
less than one-fourth as much as in Transnistria, and where public charity can
provide some results and they can be cared for [until] their emigration.[86]

17

The postponed order to deport the Jews from the Old Kingdom to
Poland continued to hang like a Damocles sword over the bowed heads
of the Jewish population!
Marshal Ion Antonescu wanted to get rid of the Jews in the country
with one blow, and at the same time to collect handsome sums of money,
which had long been needed because of the dried-up finances of the
country.
As early as November 22, 1942, Radu Lecca convened a meeting of
the Jewish Centrale with these aims, surprisingly including Dr. W. Filderman, although the latter no longer retained any public office. The
principal topic of discussion was organizing the evacuation of Jews from
Transnistria and the emigration of seventy-five to eighty-five thousand
Jews of Palestine.
The price of this operation would reach several tens of billions of lei.
Obtaining such funds raised many obstacles, and there was little chance,
under the conditions then existing, that it would be possible to act ef-
fectively to solve these complicated problems. On the other hand, the
problem of the five thousand or so orphan children who were continuing
to lead a miserable existence in the camps and ghettoes of Transnistria
was brought up.
With this intention a report was forwarded to the government, in
which approval was requested for the evacuation of these children, and
in addition, as a first step, the evacuation of the Jews from Dorohoi who
had been deported in such an abusive fashion, because that city had
never been under Soviet occupation. Furthermore, approval was asked
for freeing the people who had been sent beyond the Dniester on the

grounds that they had been withdrawn from forced labor, as well as those Jews named, as has been pointed out, on lists found in the Soviet Embassy, who had asked to return to Bessarabia in the fall of 1940.

In order to bring this extraordinarily important project to reality, in addition to getting substantial amounts of money, the approval of the Gestapo in Bucharest was necessary. The problem was to ensure the passage of the evacuees through Constanta and after that to guarantee their journey to Istanbul by sea, or by land, crossing Bulgarian territory. Constantin Bursan, a Romanian lawyer, had an important role in realizing this project. He departed for Istanbul to set up liaison with the international Jewish organizations, or with their representatives, and particularly to set up liaison between the representatives of the clandestine Jewish leadership in Romania and the Gestapo units in Bucharest.

On January 11, 1943, Dr. W. Filderman sent a letter to Jacques Salamanovitz, a leader of Jewish activities in Switzerland. After explaining the grave situation in which the Jewish deportees found themselves, he referred to the emissary who was about to arrive in Istanbul:

I will send Mr. Constantin Bursan, a good friend of mine and a great friend of the Jews, for this purpose. He will leave on the twentieth of this month. I beg you, I implore you to intervene personally, with no delay, to bring this project to reality. . . . This alone is not enough. There is also a need for money. More than 280,000 Jews still in this country are weighed down with a burden beyond human strength. They have borne it with dignity and strength of sacrifice in the face of things we must not reveal. They themselves can not do it all.[87]

Before his departure for Istanbul, Constantin Bursan organized a meeting on January 6, 1943, in which Dr. A. Tester, an influential member of the Gestapo in Bucharest, Colonel Lupascu, representing the Romanian administration, and Uterman from the German Embassy participated. The discussion had to do with the amounts of money the Jews had to pay, especially for the 5,000 children who urgently required evacuation. Dr. Tester complained that he had not received the promised funds, but the Jewish representatives reproached him for not having done anything to start this operation. It was decided to make the necessary representations to Ambassador von Killinger.

Several days after this gathering, there was another meeting, this time at Dr. Tester's house, in which Radu Lecca, Constantin Bursan, and Dr. W. Filderman participated. Lecca informed those present that the report of Dr. Filderman relating to the orphan question, which he had forwarded to Marshal Ion Antonescu, had been found correct with regard to its contents, and it had been decided that these orphan children would be moved from the camps to a sanatorium where they would be sheltered under hygienic conditions.

In order to speed up these measures, it was necessary to send a special delegate to Switzerland who would make contact with persons empowered to help Jews, and this raised the problem that perhaps Constantin Bursan would have to delay his departure for Istanbul and leave for Switzerland. Since his presence in Turkey was more important, it was decided that another person would be sent to Switzerland.

In the power of attorney which Dr. W. Filderman forwarded to Attorney Bursan, he wrote, among other things, "I hope that after today you, or rather we, will have the good fortune to meet in Ankara with authorities that are competent to help and make decisions."[88]

In Turkey at that time, in addition to representatives of the Jewish Agency for Palestine—a clandestine organization in Palestine prepared to bring in Jews, by any means, who had escaped from the hell of Europe—a personal representative of the United States was at work. His duty was to take direct action to rescue those held in the fascist camps. Since, in conformity with American laws, the official representatives of the United States did not have the right to make direct contact with representatives of states with which their country was at war, Ira Hirschmann, the representative of this organization, could do this job.

With the support of Gilbert Simond, the representative of the International Red Cross in Ankara, a meeting between Ira Hirschmann and Alexandru Creteanu, the Romanian Minister in Ankara, was organized.

This meeting, which was rich in consequences, took place in Gilbert Simond's house, after a whole series of preventive measures had been taken in advance, since the German secret police, with all its subsidiaries, was very active in Turkey under the direction of von Papen.

The meeting proceeded under dramatic circumstances. With regard to the tragic situation in Transnistria, which was made evident by President Roosevelt's representative, the Romanian Minister tried to throw blame on the Germans.

Later, Alexandru Creteanu asked directly, "What exactly do you want, and what exactly are you offering to give?"[89] The question was put unequivocally, and the man to whom he was speaking realized that his Romanian counterpart was ready to collaborate and to help. His reply was clear:

We ask first that those death camps in Transnistria be abandoned immediately, and those 48,000 survivors be returned to Romania proper, to their homes.... We ask, secondly, that 5,000 children be freed in Romania, and that they be helped to get to Istanbul, by giving every one of them exit visas for that purpose. The children will be transported from Istanbul to Haifa on steamers we will furnish for them. We ask, thirdly, that arrangements be made with Antonescu to issue an order without delay to put an end to all forms of persecution.[90]

The Romanian Minister listened attentively and noted down everything that had been asked. Then he replied quietly, "It's not impossible.
I promise to give warm endorsement to what has been asked in a telegram which I am going to send this very night. But . . . what are you
offering in return?"

I do not consider that it is necessary to offer anything to a government to free
its own citizens. Nevertheless, if you will stop the massacres of your own people,
I will offer you the good will of the government and the people of the United
States of America. These arrangements will receive wide publicity in the United
States, and will demonstrate decisive evidence of a change in the policy of your
government and the departure of your Nazi collaborators.[91]

At the moment when the two parties were saying good-bye, Ira Hirschmann told Alexandru Creteanu, "Your father had a period of brilliant
activity in Washington [as Romanian Minister between 1926 and 1929].
Who knows whether this tradition may continue in better times when
peace is made again?"[92]
    After a few days, Alexandru Creteanu, using the same representative
of the International Red Cross as an intermediary, requested another
meeting with Ira Hirschmann. The Romanian Minister arrived in haste
to bring the results of the first interview, and quoted to the American
delegate directly from a telegram he had just received and which was
not yet completely deciphered:

Antonescu has approved the requests that were made. Instructions along these
lines have also been given to General Gheorghe Potopeanu, telling him to close
the camps in Transnistria, and their inhabitants have also begun to leave. The
approximately 10,000 children will receive approval for leaving for Constanta.
All persecutions will stop in time.[93]

    This note deserves to be remembered. The day after this interview,
Gilbert Simond advised Ira Hirschmann, "I have just received a report
from our representative in Bucharest who writes to me that 'for reasons
unknown to me, the camps in Transnistria have been abolished.' "[94]
    By this time, Constantin Bursan had set up liaison with representatives
of the Jewish Agency for Palestine, who confirmed to him on March 1,
1943, that there were possibilities for receiving 5,000 children and their
escorts as soon as the Romanian government approved their departure
from the country. Likewise, material aid would be sent to them while
they were still in Transnistria, but only through the representatives of
the Jewish Agency in Bucharest.
    In this climate, the intercessions made within the country and abroad
found a positive echo. To all of this should be added that toward the
end of 1943 the Soviet army recrossed the Dnieper, reconquering the

city of Kiev and directing its divisions at full speed towards the areas where the Romanians had sent the Jews to die.

Marshal Ion Antonescu convened a special session of the Council of Order on November 12, 1943, to analyze the situation. With regard to the developments at this important conference, General Piki Vasiliu, the Minister of Police, prepared a detailed report regarding the situation in Transnistria, in which it was clearly pointed out that from 1941 until that date, of the 110,000 Jews that had been evacuated from Bucovina, Bessarabia, and the city of Dorohoi, only about 50,471 people remained alive in Transnistria.[95]

Following the conference, the Council of Order transmitted to the General Inspectorate of the Gendarmerie an order including directives with reference to the situation of the Jews in Transnistria, establishing certain categories with which to begin the evacuation operation.

On December 20, 1943, the repatriation of the Jews who originated in Dorohoi began. The first batch of 1,500 Jews left Transnistria via Mogilev and Atachi. All were naked and malnourished, and many could not even be carried. Even in that situation, in the final hour of their suffering, people were not lacking the thought that everything that had been done to those people, and everything they had undergone and suffered, was not enough!

In the localities from which the Dorohoi Jews were removed to be sent to the railroad stations or collection points, the local authorities, chiefs of police, gendarmes, and a crowd of minor functionaries accustomed to asking for money or always seeking bribes from the Jews whom they had at their disposal, feeling that they had been deprived of one of their "rights," devoted themselves to acts of true robbery. For example, Colonel Gavat, the commander of the Legion of Gendarmes at Balta, allowed only twenty-five Dorohoi people to leave, until he received a gold watch. Then, when they had nothing more to give, they were beaten savagely before they departed.

18

The year 1943 slipped into history, bringing a ray of hope to souls tortured by pain and waiting.

Then Marshal Ion Antonescu, the Leader of the Romanian State, spoke! On New Year's Eve 1944 he said in an Order of the Day for the army:

With your heads high, you stand before your deeds, those who would threaten you, and your God who will judge you. You have not punished the right even one time. Your fight is righteous. Your activity in the occupied areas and in the places you marched through has been kind and humane. Wherever you have passed, no one has been robbed or beaten. For us a man is a man whether or not he is of this nation and no matter how wickedly he may behave.... All those who have been found along your way have been helped and protected like men. ... We have not deported anyone and you have not thrust a dagger into anyone's breast. No one has been thrown into our prisons and no innocent people are lying in them. The faiths of all and the political creeds of everyone have been respected. We have not uprooted any persons or any families from their places for our political and national interests.[96]

In Transnistria thousands of Jews continued to be held in camps, and the bureaucratic machinery of the state moved with extraordinary awkwardness. Their repatriation was delayed, and pale hopes were dissipated in a vast desperation which enveloped every soul. A new attempt had to be made!

Indolence had to be given a jolt, despite the risks. On February 2, 1944, H. Clejan, an architect and a personal friend of Ion Antonescu, wrote as follows:

According to the data of the Ministry of the Interior, 55,000 survivors remained. Of these 6,300 Dorohoi people and 700 political deportees have been repatriated ... so that there are 48,000 remaining. According to the data collected in Transnistria there might be 58,000 remaining, and these are threatened with destruction, and are awaiting rescue from day to day. For them even destiny is unfavorable, and the whole Jewish community is suffering and being broken. For this reason I am standing before Your Excellency imploring justice for these innocent people, and imploring humane treatment and forgiveness for those who have done wrong.[97]

As to the previous letter addressed to him by Dr. W. Filderman, Marshal Ion Antonescu replied to architect Clejan using the same range of "arguments": "Although I had decided to evacuate all the Jews from Bessarabia and Bucovina [in Transnistria], I have been hindered in doing so by various intercessions and appeals. Today I regret that I have not done it."[98]

On March 14, 1944, the great Soviet offensive began. Russian troops were at the Bug. The United Nations radio stations gave categoric warnings that crimes against humanity were to stop. At the last moment, Ion Antonescu agreed to a general repatriation from Transnistria.

The leaders of the Jewish community hastily sent delegates with special plenipotentiary powers to take care of organizing this great transfer of people under pressure from an army that was on a full offensive. The commission that left for Mogilev had hardly penetrated beyond Atachi when the Soviet troops reached the Dniester on March 20, 1944, reconquering the Transnistrian area. The commission sent to Tiraspol succeeded in rescuing 2,518 deportees.

Following the Soviet troops, a portion of the deportees succeeded in reaching Romania. After this, at the end of June 1944, the Soviets closed the frontier. It was later reopened for some seven thousand deportees who succeeded in rejoining their families in their own country.[99]

No one has ever learned anything about those who remained in the Soviet Union!

19

How was it possible?

Nevertheless, the facts contained here and many, many, others not included in the pages of this book really happened!

The Romanian people are known for their humaneness, for their deep understanding and tolerance for the neighbor with whom they have shared joys and miseries, and for the hospitality with which they have shared bed and board with those who have knocked on their doors. They themselves have experienced a long series of shortages, burdens, humiliation, and frustration.

This people has suffered, like no other, at the hands of those who over a long history have invaded the country from the north and the south, from the east and the west. The years have changed the appearance of things and produced great changes in the spirit. Out of a people stooped and on its knees, there arose a free people. Deep love for the ancestral earth, fatherland, and people, the warm sentiments which, crossing the generations, led to the achievement of the country's independence, became transformed over time, because of subtle education and persistent propaganda, into a bitter chauvinism that took on truly morbid manifestations.

In Romania, particularly during the years after World War I, about 25 percent of the population was made up of other nationalities. The Jews remained in a comparatively unchanged proportion, comprising 4 percent of the population of the entire country. The Romanians had anti-Magyar feelings, especially those in Transylvania, and the attitude towards the Jewish, German, Bulgarian, Serbian, and other populations was always one of contempt and superiority. The jokes and anecdotes circulated, the butts of which were members of the respective minorities, demonstrated this abundantly. And never did the curse of hatred, mockery, and physical and moral destruction fall upon these populations with such persistence as upon the Jewish population.

Without protection and moral support anywhere, without effective legal protection within the country, the Jews were an easy target, a lightning-rod held responsible for all the calamities that befell Romania.

The spread of fascism in all its variations in the years between the two world wars led, as I have pointed out, to the exacerbation of some unique manifestations of anti-Semitism, which were otherwise extremely foreign to the specific character and makeup of the soul of the Romanian people.

The great pogroms, deportations, executions, pillaging, trains of death, ghettoes, forced labor camps, and hostage camps, the whole train of affairs organized by a governmental administration profoundly fascist in its features and anti-Semitic in its thinking, structure, and action—this sinister activity could not have been developed without broad mass support. The political figure Ion Mihalache, the leader of the National Peasant party, who had long since passed the draft age, put on a military uniform and left for the front as a volunteer. His photograph appeared in the whole Romanian press, but he did not make a sound or speak a word of protest about the nightmare through which the Jewish population of Bucovina and Bessarabia were passing, about which, without the least doubt, he was perfectly well informed. Writers, newspapermen, artists, teachers at every level, intellectuals of different backgrounds and professions, and others collaborated with the Cuzist, Legionary, and Antonescu governments either out of conviction or out of opportunism. Somehow they knew, they heard of, or they were witnesses to and participants in all that was done. But they kept silent, they accepted and took advantage of everything they could get, following after those who had been pillaging before them.

Then, when the first wave of euphoria had passed, and indeed much before that, the people began to understand reality! They observed that it was not the Jews that were guilty of everything that was happening or that had happened. Gradually the anti-Jewish feelings of the people began to change, and were replaced by warm feelings of compassion.

What is sad and painful is the fact that except for many, many studies about the golden vein of Romanian humanity, never has a single line been written about those rare but significant and extremely important manifestations that were experienced during the time when humanity became a crime!

Let us look back with humility and respect to those people who, in facing up to the times, to the terror, and to accusations of "selling out to the kikes," acted calmly and with dignity, most of the time risking life and liberty.

As early as the nights of blood and fire during the Legionary rebellion, nameless people, but with hearts of gold, hid in their houses the Jews that were being hunted like so many wild beasts. At Iasi, at the height of the pogrom, the Jews found shelter in the houses of some Romanians, who steadily, with dignity and persistence, protected them, saving their lives! Iacob Nahumovici, a lawyer, was heard on March 21, 1945, by Veronica Zossin, the Public Prosecutor. He testified as follows:

On the Wednesday or Thursday before June 29, 1941 (the famous Black Sunday), I met Ioan Dimitriu, a lawyer, on Lapusneanu Street. Despite the fact that he was a Cuzist, for various reasons, he was a good friend. When he saw me he told me to leave for my parents' place at Bacau. When I asked him to explain, he replied: you have to go even hiding in a snake pit. I have a clean conscience, and I have warned you! On June 29, 1941, we went out of our house and we were saved by inspector Mircescu and Policeman Sava Dobrota, who advised us not to leave the house. I know that these same men saved about two hundred more people whom they kept under arrest in the cellars of the police station.[100]

An officer in the gendarmerie who was billeted in the house of the Schneider family on Pacurari Street told his landlords a few days before the pogrom broke out, "It would be good if old Jews, and even young ones, left home to hide somewhere. Something is in the making."[101]

A sergeant in the 13th (Dorobanti) Regiment himself warned his friend, Herscu Iancu, a Jew, "Stay at home, because there is an order that all the Jews are to be shot."[102]

A significant thing occurred at the 2nd Police Inspectorate at Nicolina. Chief Inspector Suvei, together with Inspectors Mircescu and Cosnita, protected hundreds of Jews and sheltered them in a cellar, in hay ricks, and in an abandoned house, and even brought them bread, food, and medicine. Captain Darie of the Investigative Militia, seeing an old man beaten so that he could hardly crawl, brought him home.[103]

A police sergeant at Bivolari distributed a jug of water and a quarter loaf of bread to every Jew (the bread had been brought from Roman by the Medical Commission). They offered him money, but it was refused.[104]

The attitude of Richard Filipescu, a captain in the reserves, is interesting and full of dignity. On the day of the pogrom he was duty officer at the headquarters of the Iasi Legion of Gendarmes. He stated:

I observed a column of Jews being brought into the courtyard of Legion headquarters.... I was present at the horrible scene. Romanian soldiers and NCO's were beating Jews with gun stocks and kicking them.... Then, with my revolver in my hand, I intervened, shouting to the soldiers and NCO's not to make another move. At the same time Petru Serban, a lawyer in Iasi, also intervened quite strongly. He was a reserve captain that had been mobilized into the Legion of Gendarmes, and he gave proof of unusual courage and strength when he stopped the soldiers from beating them using just his bare hands.... Due to the courage and energy of Captain Petru Serban and my energetic intervention, we stopped the massacre of those 500–600 Jews.[105]

These officers were not the only ones who intervened to rescue those unfortunate people. Their actions were paralleled by those of Vasile

Panu, who later became Procurator of the Supreme Court at Bucharest, Emil Costinescu, the Counsel of the Appeals Court at Iasi, and Lieutenant Colonel Manole Alexandru.

At the same time, a sergeant in the 2nd Communications Regiment at Iasi rescued Etelca, the daughter of Lupu Meilic, a poor Jew from the commune of Codaiesti-Vaslui who was killed in front of her. The sergeant sheltered her and later turned her over to Captain Richard Filipescu, who took care of her until she was taken home by some of her relatives.

When the infamous Train of Death with Jews from Iasi arrived at Tg. Frumos, the mayor of the town, Aurel Totoiescu, made heroic efforts to dissuade Danubiu Marinescu, the captain of a unit of railroad troops, who wanted to kill the Jews who were still alive. The town physician, Dr. Gheorghiu, stood by the mayor in this action.

Paul Teodorescu, the parish priest at the commune of Razboieni, gave dramatic testimony to D. Saracu, the Public Prosecutor, on June 20, 1945. After describing the circumstances that brought him at that time to Tg. Frumos, where he was present at the tragic evacuation of the corpses from the railroad station, he went to the Jewish cemetery. There he saw several Jews standing before a common grave, which they had dug.

Then I heard the words: "I am dying, I am dying" coming from the grave. I spoke to one of the young Jews, saying: "Don't you hear? It's as if someone is crying in the grave."

"Yes, it sounds to us like crying, too.... But what can we do? ... If we go down into the grave they will say that we are robbing the corpses and they will shoot us." At that moment a German officer approached the group, and addressed the priest in perfect Romanian, saying not to meddle, warning him: "You should be ashamed." The priest, amazed by what had happened, asked: "You speak Romanian. Where did you learn it?"[106]

The German replied that he had learned it in the Commercial High School at Timisoara. After a lengthy discussion, the priest succeeded in getting the guards to allow a search for the person speaking from the grave. A completely naked man was pulled out from among the corpses.

At Vijnita, a place in Bucovina, all of the Jews would have been killed if a captain who was the son-in-law of Petruc, the priest at Vatra Dornei, had not intervened, using all his authority, and stopped the massacre. After things had quieted down again, he called the rabbi in the village and gave him food for the Jews who were still alive, asking him to pray for him; he was leaving for the front line!

When the Jews were being evacuated from the Cernauti ghetto, a soldier helped an old woman to walk. This simple, humane gesture was seen by Metropolitan Tit Smedrea, who was strongly moved by its beauty.

The Metropolitan had gone out into the street to watch the tragedy, which he had not been able to stop, working to the very last.

Likewise at Cernauti, Teofil Saveanu, the former Minister for Bucovina, as well as Gherman, the Counsel of the Court, protested with all their strength to Governor Calotescu over what was being done, but in vain!

Musat, a lawyer sent by the leaders of the Jewish Federation at Bucharest, left for Chisinau. He attempted the impossible, trying to save the Jews who had to leave for Transnistria in the depths of winter. With contempt for the risks, in spite of persecution, Attorney Musat, when he came to understand that he could not fight against the forces of evil that had been unleashed, sent a telegram to Bucharest in which he announced the failure of his activities!

Colonel Alexandru Constantinescu, the commander of the notorious Vertujeni camp, appealed to the Supreme General Staff to be relieved of his duties; he refused to be engaged in the crimes that were demanded of him! The Perfect, Colonel Stroiescu from Suceava, observing the evacuation measures and the cruelty exhibited by Colonel Zamfirescu, the commander of the Recruiting Center, testified, full of disgust, that "he ought to be arrested and locked up in a madhouse."[107]

In the ample testimony regarding the situation in Cernauti given by Dr. Traian Popovici, that rare figure of a man and a Romanian, he recalls, among other things, a discussion with Colonel Petrescu, who testified to him that "I recognize that in justice, evacuation is not required; so many [Jews] need to be kept, that it's a sin [about] those who have left." When Colonel Petrescu left the city of Cernauti, he told the mayor, on saying good-bye, "I am leaving but I do not want to lose your esteem."[108]

People could do nothing more. They were military people; they were under orders; the whole set of circumstances was against them. These evidences of humanity, even if they did not always have direct practical results in rescuing Jews or ameliorating their misery, were enough to demonstrate that in the darkness and gloom that covered a nation, there were still enough hearts and minds that were sensitive to pain.

In an audience Dr. W. Filderman had with General Dumitru Popescu, the Minister of the Interior, on September 13, 1943, Popescu told him:

Although you are not in charge of the leadership of the Jews, I believe that it is proper for me to address a plea to you. Surely you recall my repeated statements that I am not in agreement with what is being done against the Jews. But my authority stops at the Prut. Hence I can not to do anything . . . I beg you tell this to the Jews . . . I cannot help them at all.[109]

When General Gheorghe Deliceanu, as commander of the 5th Army Corps, received an order that the Jews in the area of his command should wear a yellow star, he sent, without any hesitation, a report to the Ministry of the Interior pointing out that he did not agree that the measure should be applied, giving as his reason that this would give rise to anti-Semitic agitation and disturbances. D. Popescu, the Minister of the Interior, replied, "Deliceanu, proceed as you believe is proper!" This same General Deliceanu, a man of great moral probity, disgusted by the anti-Semitic abuses, refused an offer made to him to become the Governor of Bessarabia since he was not in agreement with the massacres that had been recommended. Again in his role as commander of the 5th Army Corps, he sought aid for the Jews, releasing many of them from forced labor and making it possible for the Jewish doctors to practice their profession.

Later, when he was named prefect of Timis County, he sought to make the supply of provisions to the Jews easier; but the measure was harshly criticized by Jung, the Gauleiter in the Banat. It is worth mentioning that when the problem of applying the Final Solution was raised by the Germans in collaboration with the Romanian government and the evacuation operations were planned to begin, starting with the Jews of the Banat and Transylvania, General Deliceanu informed Dr. Ligety, a leader of the city congregation, who thus had the opportunity to leave for Bucharest to undertake his well-known activities to stop this order, which would have led to the extermination of the Jews in Romania.

Gheorghe Prisacaru, a warrant officer in the gendarmerie, who was chief of the gendarmerie section at Bogdana-Tutova, on receiving the Jews from the city of Husi on their way to the camp for political prisoners at Tg. Jiu, told them that he could not sit down to dinner knowing that they were hungry and thirsty. It was the day after the war broke out and the same day that the massacres began in Bucovina and Bessarabia!

A police sergeant was arrested at Mogilev on January 15, 1942, on the charge that he had brought money from the Old Kingdom that was sent to some Jews interned in that camp by their relatives. He was sentenced as a traitor. The same thing happened with another sergeant at the camp at Bersad. Petru Eftimiu, a chaplain serving at Mogilev with Contagious Diseases Team No. 47, had the same fate. He sought to help some Jews and was tried and condemned by court martial.

The illustrious personality of Dr. Chirila can never be forgotten. With devotion and a spirit of sacrifice that cannot be equaled, he fought with all his might, together with the Jewish leaders in their respective camps, to stabilize the serious epidemic of exanthematic typhus in Transnistria. Traian Procopovici, an engineer, became the cashier of a clandestine Jewish organization that collected money to help the Jews in the camps, and especially those from Bucovina.

The list could be lengthened greatly. It is not a question here of citing all the names of people whose direct, spontaneous actions as individuals characterized not the individuals themselves but an attitude towards neighbors in distress. Similar feelings also inspired Mrs. Viorica Agarici of the Red Cross in the city of Roman. With extraordinary civic courage and characteristic humanity, she gave an order on her personal responsibility to open the cars of the Train of Death to clean them up, and especially to feed those who had almost ceased to be human beings. The glorious personality of this Romanian woman and that of Major Gherman, who helped her carry out this act of humanity, hover like a blessing over this train in which Death had become king.

The fantastic trip from the Chisinau ghetto made by Sapira, the lawyer who went to Bucharest to ask for help for people of his own religion who were imprisoned and threatened with death, cannot be looked on as a thing done in isolation. This Jewish lawyer could not have undertaken this courageous action without direct material aid from some military men, who must have obtained for him the uniform of a Romanian officer. He needed authorization to gain entry to a military airfield, to use a plane to take him to Bucharest, and to wait there for his return to Chisinau. Who helped him remains a mystery! No one has ever tried to lift the veil on this exceptional deed. It is not just a question of a Jew who was determined to risk his life to rescue people of his own religion, but of deeds by Romanians in a period of exacerbated anti-Semitic hatred. They took a fantastic risk in helping him put into effect a plan that appeared to be insane!

Acting in different spheres and making use of the positions they held, important figures like Queen Mother Elena, King Mihai himself, and high prelates of the Orthodox Church, indifferent to the favorable or unfavorable feelings towards Jews they had grown up with, sought to help to curb crime, doing their duty as human beings and Christians!

On other levels, Attorney Bursan and Alexandru Creteanu, the Minister Plenipotentiary, and many others joined efforts to rescue Jews, or to somewhat curb the excesses of others and to aid in improving the living conditions of those who had been imprisoned.

Perhaps some of these people acted on the basis of self-interest or through temptations of a material nature, and others acted out of opportunism, realizing the political and military situation, and seeking certificates of good conduct for the years after the war. When their actions are seen through the perspective of time, their motives have no significance. The important thing was that in those situations, there were people who wanted to take action, and those people, defying laws and risking their life and liberty, gave effective help.

But besides those who held various positions in the military and administrative apparatus, there were plain, anonymous people, unknown then and completely forgotten now, who helped Jews quietly and patiently, defying the harsh and inhumane atmosphere that then existed!

With what can one compare the gesture of a Romanian who would take advantage of the darkness of night to slip into the house of a Jewish neighbor to bring him a loaf of bread, a little meat, and some vegetables, hidden under his mantle? What could be the price for these gestures of honest, sincere humanity, which not only helped some people to survive, but also demonstrated, without trumpets and fanfare, that Romanian humanity had not disappeared?

Where could there be such a gesture as that of those Dobrogean peasants who, on returning in the evening from their work in the fields, would make a long circle around the stone quarries at Turcoaia, Manole Hill, Greci, Iglita, and Piatra Rosie to offer the Jewish slaves the food they had saved up for them? Everything was done simply, naturally, without ostentation, and timid smiles would bloom on their sunburnt and wind-beaten faces. Before Christmas, everywhere in the village of Turcoaia could be heard the squeals of stuck pigs, and the smell of fried bacon rinds floated through the air. The peasants, and particularly their wives, would go out to the gates of their houses and insist that the Jews come inside to enjoy the pig's charity too. Certainly the meat was not kosher, but the hearts of those people were sincere and honest.

A modest tribute: On one such Christmas Eve (1942), on a night of cold and snow, in the wind-beaten port of Macin, a group of Jews from the stone quarries at Turcoaia were waiting for the ferry to take them across the Danube to Braila.

A man came up in the dark to the writer of these lines, saying that the ferry was not going to run any more that night. Then, as if hesitantly, he invited him to come home with him to eat something. His words seemed to be blown away by the wind and seemed improbable, but they reached the heart. The man addressed another youth who happened to be there. He insisted, and the two young men went with him, slipping through the night over the snow-covered streets. The front windowpanes of the house where they stopped were lit up and exciting to see; they had guests! Inside it was warm; an aroma of plum cake was coming from the oven, and when they came in there was an aromatic and pungent smell of stuffed cabbage.

The hosts watched the young men eat in silence, without pronouncing a single word. The wine was clear and lighted the spirits and urged them to talk. It got late, and the young men judged that it was time to leave. The hosts insisted that they stay and sleep there. It was too much! The young men refused categorically. They had to swear that they could not accept the invitation; they were full of lice! To sleep in a house that was as clean as a goblet they considered to be a sacrilege. But the hosts insisted. Things that aren't clean can be washed; anything else can't be cleaned.

The bedclothes were as white as hope and smelled of lavender. From a cupboard some quinces that retained all the gold of the autumn sun smiled at them in friendship. The youths stretched out their bones, worn out from labor and cold and twisted by hunger, in that house that was lit with humanity, and felt at home.

If Heaven has any material form, then those youths felt as if in Heaven!

With such people, and others like them, Hell sometimes could be supported more easily!

20

POSTSCRIPT

Somewhere in Transylvania, near the arbitrary boundary that separated Romania from Hungary, there is a village, Sarmas. Not far from it is another smaller one, Sarmasel. For centuries a modest community of Jews had led their lives in those places, where the majority of the population was Hungarian. The Romanians were present in smaller numbers.

The Soviet army, at that time allied with the Romanian army, was fighting hard to reconquer Transylvania. On September 5, 1944, the village of Sarmas was occupied by Hungarian troops. Two days later, a company of gendarmes, at first commanded by Lieutenant Balasz, and later by Captain Lancz Laszlo, aided by six subordinates, Lieutenant Vekardy, Deputy Lieutenant Fekete, Deputy Lieutenant Holosz, Sergeant Major Horvath, and Sergeants Polgar and Szabo, arrived from the Gendarmes' School at Zalau.[110]

As soon as this unit entered Sarmas, the population began to pillage the houses of the Romanians and especially those of the Jews. At this time the Hungarian counts and magnates from the neighboring communities, dressed in their folk costumes, crowded into the residence of Iuliu Varga, the druggist in the village. In a solemn scene, they decided to kill the Jews in the commune.

These were "heroic" times, and they, the "heroes," considered that killing a peaceful population was exactly what was needed. How could they do less than their brothers in Northern Transylvania, who had sent more than one-hundred-fifty thousand Jews to the concentration camps that spring in order to be killed? On September 8, 1944, the Jews were obliged to mark their houses with a yellow star, and the so-called National Guards, made up of Hungarian peasants from the village, pulled all the Jews, 126 in number, in the place out of their houses. Among them there were children, women, old people, and men of all ages. The camp was organized in the courtyard of Ion Pop, the Romanian construction foreman. There they were beaten dreadfully and later forced to work.

While they were imprisoned, Alexandru Szallay, the mayor of the commune, and Iosif Szyraky, the deputy mayor, "distributed" the residences of the Jews to the peasants in the commune. Everything was plundered, even the windows in the houses. When a person to whom a house was "distributed" in order to be pillaged found that this plundering had been done by others earlier, he would rush back to beat up the Jew who owned it in order to assuage his anger and frustration.[111]

On September 16, 1944, a Saturday morning, the Jews were interrupted at their prayers. The gendarmes burst into the camp, picked out twenty strong young men, gave them sledgehammers and spades, and sent them out of the village towards Sarmasel.

That evening fourteen carts drawn by oxen gathered in front of the camp, and the 126 Jews were loaded into them. They were taken to Suscut Hill, to the place called Scaldatoarea Bivolilor (Buffle-Cow Hot Springs), and there they were killed! In connection with this crime, Dumitru Misina, a sergeant in the gendarmes, made the following statement:

On September 5, 1944, the Hungarian troops occupied the commune of Sarmas. I disguised myself by dressing in peasant clothing, and followed the course of events in the commune from close by. I stayed that way for five weeks until the sector was occupied by the Romanian troops. . . . Alexandru Pall and Ioan Panczel, soldiers who lived in the commune of Sincai in Mures County, were members of the company of Hungarian gendarmes, and they actively participated in the execution of the Jews of Sarmas, and they were later seen in civilian clothing in their native commune that I have just named.[112]

Ion Moceanu, a peasant, completed the picture as follows:

At 2:00 A.M. I saw how the Jews had been hauled out and taken up the slope of the hill towards a lantern. Then I heard a great deal of noise and wailing among the Jews. About half an hour after the Jews had arrived up there, I heard machine gun fire. I believe there were three machine guns because they were firing the whole time between 2:00 A.M. and daybreak. . . . The howling of some young boys was heard much longer than anything else. After that too had ceased, the shooting stopped.[113]

Matatias Carp, the industrious and untiring chronicler of the Jewish tragedy in Romania, wrote another book after the war entitled *Sarmas*, subtitled "One of the Most Horrible Fascist Crimes."[114] In the preface to the book, the late B. Branisteanu, the prestigious journalist, writes as follows: "A book like this is written with a pen dipped in blood, with eyes blinded with tears, and a heart choked with pain and throbbing with indignation."[115]

From the middle of October 1944 to the end of the month, after the last remnants of the Hungarian troops were pushed out of the Cluj-Turda area, frightening details were found out about the crime at Sarmas. Some Jews from that commune who were at work in other camps succeeded in escaping with their lives. They informed the Magistrate of the Court Martial of the 2nd Territorial Corps at Sibiu, who ordered an investigation. Being superficial and wrongly intentioned, the investigation led to nothing. Those Hungarians who had participated in the crime and the pillaging were freed after being held under arrest for a few days. There was insufficient evidence!

Later, the Ministry of Justice ordered a new investigation. Matatias Carp participated in it as a delegate of the Federation of Jewish Congregations. He wrote, "Nothing that I experienced, saw, felt, or heard in those four years of fury can surpass what I saw at Sarmas."[116] To describe it is apocalyptic. Anger puts a lump in your throat, so that you can no longer either shriek or weep.

I have touched those 126 bodies. I have seen some holes where the murderous bullets penetrated, and I have seen skulls shattered because the bullets did not kill. . . . I have seen children of five, of three, and even of less than one year of age who were not struck by the bullets and were thrown in and buried alive. I have seen husbands and wives in one final embrace, and I have seen a father with clenched hands hugging a year-old boy in his arms.[117]

The peasants who assisted in this operation bowed in shame when they found the body of the man who had been Arthur Hasz, the miller at Sarmas, among the corpses that were dug up. On the way to the Hill of Death, he had hidden in the stable of a well-wisher. When the drama took place, he could stay there no longer and followed the column, which was climbing towards the place where the end awaited all of them. Together with him were his wife Elisabeta and Veronica, their beautiful daughter, who had been barbarously raped before she was killed.

For Ignatiu Hönig, the old rabbi, who was present when the common grave where the martyrs of Sarmas were killed was uncovered, it was as if he too had died the same day this was done.

The corpses were buried according to custom. Rabbi Hönig felt himself buried with the others, beside his wife and three daughters. He was never again able to say the prayers after silence had spread over the hill bearing the name of Suscut and the place called Scaldatoarea Bivolilor. Iosif Varga, the druggist, in whose house they had decided on the crime, committed suicide, together with his wife, on November 5, 1944. Pavel Kiss, a resident of the village, hung himself from the ridgepole of his house when he was called before the investigating commission. Those who were guilty had disappeared or fled with the Hungarian troops. Those who had been freed by the Magistrate of the Court Martial at Sibiu had also disappeared. Their complicity in the crime was evident!

In his preface to Matatias Carp's book *Sarmas*, Branisteanu writes, quoting a great author:

You have robbed me of all my innocent games of childhood. You have poured salt into the sweet cup of youth and you have set malicious calumny and stupid mockery in my way as a man. Nevertheless you have not cut [me] off from my path, for I have reached my goal. But I have reached it bitterly and without joy. . . . In the end, no renewal of good is left for me, because it has come to the point where I no longer have the power of forgiving, nor the weakness of punishing. . . . Where I see a prison, I recognize my homeland. . . . Where I see persecution, I breathe the air of my childhood.[118]

Ion Antonescu and Adolf Hitler: A solid alliance.

Ion Antonescu and Horia Sima: The Legionary National State in full swing.

Bucharest: The Morgue. Looking for the loved ones.

Bucharest: The Great Sephardic Synagogue plundered, destroyed and burned.

Bucharest: A shop, plundered, destroyed and burned.

Bucharest: The Legionary National State ceased to exist.

Bucharest: The Jewish Cemetery. The silent tombs accuse.

Iasi: Jews rounded up on the street and watched by Romanian soldiers and an armed civilian.

Iasi: An entire family was killed.

Iasi: German soldiers taking pictures of the Jews killed on the street.

Iasi: The Police Headquarters. People beaten up and killed.

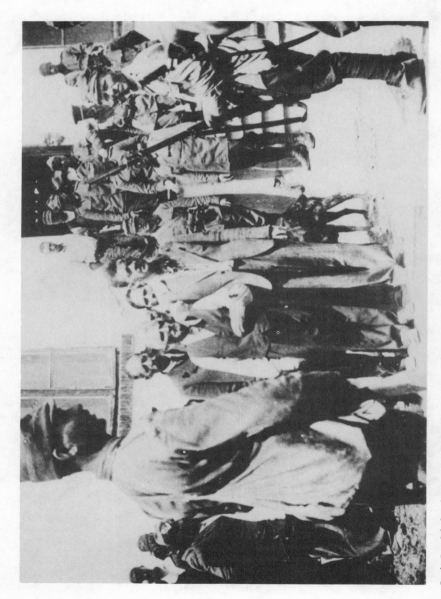

Iasi: Jewish leaders rounded up by dogs and beaten by Romanian soldiers.

Iasi: The Police Headquarters. The Jews were obliged to clean the pavement stained with blood.

Iasi: In front of the railroad station. Jews facing the pavement for hours were sent one by one on the death trains.

Corpses thrown away from the death train under the watchful eyes of Romanian officers.

Corpses from the train loaded onto trucks, in order to be sent to the Jewish cemetery.

Pillaging the corpses from the death train.

Peasants from the nearby villages, pillaging the corpses.

Călăraşi: The death trains arrived at the destination. The survivors.

Călăraşi: The courtyard of the camp. The survivors of the death train from Iasi.

MORTI TIMPUL POGROMULUI
LA
29 IUNIE 1941

Tata   ...
Mama   Sima Waisman
Fratele Itic Waisman
Sora.   Mali Bergher
Cumnat. Zalman Bergher
Nepot. Avram Bergher

Iasi: A tombstone in memory of a whole family killed in the pogrom.

Bălţi: The leaders of the Jewish community before being executed. The only survivor who told the story was the man in the white suit.

Thousands of deportees waiting to cross the River Dnester.

Waiting for the barge. In front, Romanian officers. On the hill, gendarmes watching.

The barge arrives. Jews from Bukovina ready to cross the river.

The barge arriving on the Eastern bank of the river.

The gates are sealed. Nobody can go back!

Transnistria: Taking care of the orphans.

Orphans in Transnistria.

Dr. W. Filderman (first row, center) deported to Moghilev, together with the leaders of the camp.

Young man from Transnistria.

Bershad-Transnistria: A drawing of a memorial monument erected in the memory of the 20,000 Jews who perished there.

Sărmaş-Transylvania: After the war. A governmental commission participating at the exhumation of the Jews of Sărmaş killed by the Hungarians.

Building a dam on the river Siret.

Digging trenches along the highways.

Jewish slaves from the labor camp Baldovineşti-Brăila.

4

Behind the Rainbow

1

In Romania, in the years after World War II, the Jews were no longer killed and beaten, their houses no longer plundered or burned, their synagogues devastated, their cemeteries desecrated. They enjoyed the rights of citizens, which they had never had under past political regimes, and their access to education, the governmental administration, justice, and the army was no longer limited.

Those who returned from the concentration camps, from the ghettoes in Transnistria, or from the forced labor camps were naked, poor, and without shelter, but they carried in their hearts the star of hope and unshaken faith in the new world in which they would find the place they deserved, the place which suited them.

In September 1944, the Jewish population of Romania that had survived the Holocaust was estimated at approximately 300,000 persons. According to data furnished by the Jewish World Congress of 1947 (the only such data available), the Jewish population of Romania in 1945 was 428,312 people.

This discrepancy between the figures given in 1944 and 1947 does not actually point to a real increase in the Jewish population. The number of Jews in Romania immediately after the war was augmented by an appreciable number of displaced persons who had escaped from concentration camps in Hungary and Poland, and those that had come from Transnistria in the wake of the Soviet armies, many of whom were Bessarabian, Ukrainian, or Russian Jews.

The return of the deported Jews to the localities from whence they had come was not desired, and their presence was looked upon with reserve, and even enmity by the Romanian population. They wanted—as was natural and legitimate—to go back to their houses, and that they couldn't do! They wanted to resume their small businesses, and they did not have the right to engage in them. Many handicraft shops did not function because they did not have the raw material or any place where they could carry on such activity. The homes of the Jews were occupied by new owners, who considered themselves the rightful heirs and legal beneficiaries of Romanization and did not want to renounce their benefits at any price.

Personal possessions, furniture, clothing, and everything that once had made up their households had long since been stolen or "bought up" at the so-called auctions organized to turn the property of the Jews into cash. The new owners, those who had come from various regions of the country during the war years and had become established in those respective localities, considered the demands of the Jews to be absurd.

Restitution could not be taken up for consideration, and those who tried to reclaim what had belonged to them were seen as displaying a new and inadmissible form of Yiddish chutzpa.

Having been dispossessed of their property, and lacking any possibility of resuming their occupations or exercising their professions, the majority of the Jews found themselves completely dependent on social welfare from the very first days of their "liberation." The problem of sheltering, feeding, and clothing them, and especially providing them with medical help, became acute. An immense number of them were seriously ill because of the work and food regimens in the camps. The truly disastrous effects of the stress of the camps and ghettoes in which they had lived began to be felt.

To all these were added the approximately two hundred thousand Jews whose rights of citizenship had been withdrawn under the Goga-Cuza government. As noncitizens they did not have the right to work or to exercise their professions, and they constituted a burden on the Jewish congregations in the country, which had been at the limit of their economic capabilities for a long time.

This state of affairs led to the need for a long and painful series of discussions and negotiations between the representatives of the Ministry of Justice, headed by Lucretiu Patrascanu, and the leaders of the Federation of the Unions of Jewish Congregations in Romania, led by Dr. W. Filderman in 1945.

What was extremely painful was that the same leaders who had appeared before the Antonescu government to solicit a remedy for the desperate situation of the Jews were now appearing before the Communist authorities, seeking rights which were, or which should be, accepted as inalienable.

   This situation proved to be extremely delicate for the Romanian government and especially for the Communist representatives in the first coalition government.

   The situation of the Communist party after the liberation was extremely precarious. Since they had no mass base, the Communists, with a membership numbering about one thousand, had to solve the problem of gaining power and holding it. To do so they needed the masses, but the masses looked rather suspiciously on the new Communist leaders in the coalition government that had been set up after the overthrow of the Antonescu government.

   To return directly all the property that had been seized by Romanians during the war years would have led to an extremely delicate situation for the Communist party, which had the primary problem of gaining adherents and identifying itself with the pressing needs of the masses. A measure for moral and material reparations to the Jewish population would have led to a very real explosion by those affected by this measure in one way or another and would have driven them directly into the arms of the "historic" political parties, which had resumed their activity and were seeking support for their traditional policies.

   The decree of December 14, 1944, which was issued to resolve this situation, failed because of the very letter and spirit with which it was issued.[1] This decree contained so many paragraphs of special provisions drawn up under the slogan "Justice, not Revenge," that the results were few and insignificant. Thousands of claims by Jews piled up in the files of the courts and high government officials and remained unanswered.

   Some of the Jews employed by various firms before the war succeeded in regaining their old jobs. Many of these enterprises had ceased activity, however, for various reasons, and when the Jews formerly on the payroll sought their jobs, the firms had disappeared or were operating under a different name or different management.

   Some of the handicraft workshops resumed activity. During the period 1944–1946 and even through the middle of 1947, when business was still free, a series of stores were opened, and commercial life began to take shape.

   This situation did not affect the mass of refugees and those whose citizenship status had not been settled. They continued to lead an existence at the edge of Jewish social life, without any income, and, more important, without the right to work. They had to leave the localities they had come from, or where they had settled after returning from the camps to which they had been deported to seek work in Bucharest.[2]

   From among them a considerable number of persons were recruited who occupied themselves with trading on the black market, risking their lives and liberty in order to earn a living.

   Facing a situation from which they could see no way out because of an acute lack of material resources, the leaders of the Jewish community made a new appeal to the same Jewish organization that had helped them during the years of Antonescu's dictatorship. In 1946 alone the American Jewish Joint Distribution Committee (JDC) guaranteed assistance to more than 200,000 people.[3]

An inquiry undertaken to determine the status of the health of this population gave results that were truly catastrophic. Diseases arising from malnutrition, with all their train of complications, stirred deep concern. Endemic diseases of the limbs, generalized troubles, gastroenteritis, and states of exhaustion had to be treated with urgency.

About 60 percent of the women were suffering from serious menstrual disturbances; this alarming proportion led to an unusual decline in the birth rate. Many people were living in a permanent state of nervous tension, which led to furious outbursts or states of depression, sometimes ending in suicide. Cases of paralysis caused by the notorious fodder beans were unusually numerous, and their treatment raised difficult problems.

Inflation gripped the entire economy of the country, and in 1947 a decree authorized owners of industrial and commercial enterprises to lay off office workers and laborers. The Jews, being considered the latest arrivals, were the first laid off.

An immense number of Jews again found themselves out of work, swelling the ranks of those seeking social assistance. In spite of these hard times, or perhaps more precisely, on account of them, a veritable network of institutions of social and medical assistance was opened in 1947: twenty-two hospitals, forty-four dispensaries, and eighty-one dental clinics went into operation, staffed with skilled and dedicated personnel.

During this period, the cooperative banks, the so-called Small Loan Banks, which had been operating before the war, played an exceptionally important role in the life of the Jewish community. They lent money in various amounts to small businessmen and artisans at a low rate of interest, thus giving these people the possibility of reactivating their businesses or handicraft shops.

It is significant that in this whole complex political and economic situation, the representatives of the various political parties opened a campaign to attract various unsettled political elements that had been compromised during the war years, but which because of their numbers constituted an important political force.

Special attention was given to the former members of the Iron Guard; although this organization was outlawed, and some of its leaders were in exile and others imprisoned, it made up a force which every party was seeking to attract to itself.

Moreover, violent anti-Semitic demonstrations occurred as early as the first days after the political changes, defying the new regime. In the first days of September 1944 a group of Jewish students who had been taking courses at Onescu College appeared at the University of Bucharest to get information about the new academic year, which was soon to begin. They were beaten by a group of hooligans who opposed admitting Jews to university courses.[4]

When a group of Jews appeared for an audience with Iuliu Maniu at the beginning of September 1944, wishing to discuss current problems for the Jewish people, he told them:

In the present situation there are more important problems to solve than the Jewish problem. If nothing has been done up to now, you must remember that it was generals who were in charge [Maniu had participated in the government] and they stopped work. What other problem do you have? You have always solved them with your money and your intelligence.[5]

This attitude was further demonstrated publicly. In some commentaries made in the same newspaper (*Dreptatea*), Iuliu Maniu wrote as follows:

Horia Sima's unsuccessful attempt to govern has created a political atmosphere around your Legionary party which makes it impossible to take off and fly with [the] enthusiasm which is demanded at the current time.... We have every reason to believe that the gates of the parties engaged in the National Democratic Bloc are open to all who are not guilty of crimes or dishonorable activities.[6]

This inclination of the leaders of the PNT, National Peasant Party, to attract and court Legionary elements continued, and on November 12, 1944, in an article entitled "Maniu and the Legionaries," the following statement was made:

After the prodigal son returned home, he was accepted by his father after striking his head against the lintel and bowing down to the doorsill, and that is the way we will proceed with the young Legionary who recognizes that he has sinned and repents and asks to be accepted into the regular parties; he will be accepted.[7]

Many outstanding figures in the National Peasant party were not in agreement with Iuliu Maniu's attitude toward the Legionaries.[8] What is more, the Communists had the same attitude towards this political movement and its members when they thought that it was necessary to collaborate with it.

One should recall that Corneliu Zelea Codreanu, when invited to a secret meeting with King Carol II, refused to go, saying that he would make his own way to the Palace with a sword. Until the Legionaries gained power, and even after that, the behavior of some people in the leadership of the movement showed a spineless attitude, plunging into the crassest kind of opportunism and careerism. In the summer of 1940 they collaborated with Carol's government; they collaborated with Antonescu; they collaborated with the Peasant party and especially with the Communists, when they understood that power was on the side of those groups. In this case, they felt "sheltered," with the assurance of a guaranteed existence, enjoying all the advantages of their total subservience.

Nicolae Patrascu had a meeting on November 4, 1944, with Teohari Georgescu, the Minister of the Interior, who together with Ana Pauker held a discussion with this Legionary leader, who agreed to collaborate with the Communists. Following this "understanding" a large number of Legionaries, even including entire organizations of them, enrolled in the Communist party. It appears that the verse once attributed to Pastorel Teodoreanu was written at that time, reflecting perfectly the current situation: "Comrade, don't be sad / the Guard is marching forward / through the Communist Party!"[9]

As a consequence of this state of affairs, the problems of the Jews were looked upon as quite secondary, and the actions directed against those who had played an active role in planning and perpetrating crimes against Jews during the Legionary and Antonescu eras and even earlier under the Groga-Cuza government were buried in the court record books.

It is significant that General Corneliu Calotescu, the governor of Bucovina, and the sinister Colonel Modest Isopescu, both of whom had been sentenced to death for crimes they committed directly or through orders they gave, had their sentences commuted by the Groza government in 1946 to forced labor for life. Afterwards, nothing more was ever heard of them!

It was necessary to wait nearly four years to bring the case of the Iasi criminals to trial. The reasons for this attitude must be sought in the general orientation of the Communists towards the masses, they did not wish to create misunderstandings or to lose the popularity for which they had worked so hard and with great compromises.

The political trials that were organized, beginning with the case brought in 1945 against Ion Antonescu and his collaborators, Iuliu Maniu and Ion Mihalache and seventeen partisan politicians, which took place in 1947, were great public political spectacles organized by the Communist party.

In May 1945 it was already too late for the Communists to try to appear in a more favorable light than Marshal Antonescu. For even then the Groza government and the Romanian Communists themselves seemed to be more submissive to Moscow than Antonescu had ever been to Berlin.[10]

A. C. Cuza died comfortably in his bed and was never judged for his misdeeds. Not a line has been written to condemn his long period of political activity in which anti-Semitism was the predominant ideology, nor the hatred, contempt, and incitement to crime, the means he considered to be natural, right, and perfectly moral for solving the "Jewish problem." Cuza was brought before the tribunal to defend his doctoral thesis after being accused of plagiarism, and he won. He was not tried for his criminal acts, and so he won a second time! He was an old man in the years of the trials of the war criminals. "Moralists" and promoters of "socialist humanism" could not conceive of bringing a man of his age before a court.

Corneliu Zelea Codreanu entered the political arena with a pistol in his hand, killing a high government official and seriously wounding two other civil servants. He was tried, and there on the defendant's bench, where he pleaded not guilty, he was rewarded with the title of national hero. No one ever reopened his case, either to condemn posthumously a man who killed consciously and deliberately, or to vindicate the memory of the man who was killed, if not for his sake, at least for his descendents.

For the Jewish population, in that period of worry and confusion, the problem of going ahead into the next phase of their struggle to organize their lives had arisen.

When social assistance was somehow assured, a sufficient number of Jews began to practice their professions or crafts. The need to educate their young people and give them professional training arose, particularly for those who had not had the opportunity to learn anything productive because they were living in the camps, and who, after the liberation, did not have any material resources with which to begin serious study. A group of Zionist organizations took over part of these burdens and a considerable number of young people received serious preparation, with the intention of emigrating to Palestine.[11]

Throughout this time, attention was given to reorganizing traditional life in the Jewish communities in the country. In 1947, 252 new congregations of this kind were organized over the ruins of the old Jewish institutions in Romania. The Talmud-Torah schools carried on regular activity, ritual baths began to be put into operation, and homes for old people, orphanages, and other kinds of social assistance were now administered by local congregations. Living in the midst of the Jewish population, they knew its needs best and were able to act, within the limits of their capability, to alleviate current needs.

2

The people, tired of war and worried about the presence of Soviet troops and the idea that Romania might become a country ruled by the

Communists, were in a permanent state of agitation. Opening the gates of the party was an important step in attracting the masses in greater numbers. It is worth mentioning that at the National Conference of the Communist Party on November 16, 1945, it was reported that the number of members was about eight hundred thousand. This exceptional growth in the number of party members was not understandable to many.

This great human kaleidoscope made its presence felt in the ranks of the party in various ways. Legionaries could be found among the party members. They had begun to carry on activity under another form, but with the same purpose, either as individuals or as part of the entire organization, especially after the "cartel" agreement between Nicolae Patrascu and Teohari Georgescu. There were elements that came out of that lumpenproletariat, people with no profession who in those postwar years were at a loss as to what to do with themselves and had no definite direction in life, and elements recruited from the domestic workers in the so-called bourgeois families, whose presence in the party was desired in order to have ears ready to listen in those circles of society, as well as mouths ready to denounce. There were individuals who had gone through all the political parties and who, with the flair developed through long practice, considered the Communist party an ideal place where they could find a comfortable bed; they were ready to serve whoever held power without murmuring and without hesitation.

At first the working masses looked on the actions of the Communists with reserve. About one hundred thousand peasants who had been allocated land received a party membership card and were added to the number of party members. Privileged members were recruited from the soldiers and officers of the Tudor Vladimirescu and Horia, Closca, and Crisan divisions, both of which had been formed from among the prisoners of war in the Soviet Union.

The party had a desperate need for people with prestigious names. They needed to demonstrate, both within the country and especially abroad, that the intellectuals of Romania had rallied around the party from conviction and especially from a sincere desire to bring ideals into existence. There was a need for people who could infiltrate into the government machinery, the army, and the courts; there was a need to present to the people a party with deep roots in the masses and with mighty political power.

It is unquestionable that a considerable number of party members were recruited from among the Jews—people who saw, like so many others, a way to solve their economic problems or fulfill their aspirations to power. But the immense majority of Jewish party members, especially young people and intellectuals, entered the ranks of the party with the firm conviction that it was the place where they really ought to be!

On the other hand, the Communist party saw in the presence of Jews in the party and governmental machinery a guarantee that these people were not, and had never been, fascist! In a country in which the most aberrant crimes had been made during the years of fascist regime, the very existence of the Jews in the Communist party stood as a guarantee that at least that part of its members could be considered road companions.

This state of affairs led to a reawakening of anti-Semitism in a new form. Significant impetus in shaping this postwar anti-Semitism can be attributed to the political parties, which sought to capture the interest and the votes of certain parts of the population that were opposed to the Communists. Public anti-Semitic demonstrations, like those in Transylvania in 1946, were not a reason for concern to the Groza government. That this government, on which the Jews had placed so many hopes, by hiding behind obscure bureaucratic procedures deliberately delayed the adoption of measures affecting the pressing problems of the Jewish population—especially those of citizenship, restitution of stolen property, trial of war criminals guilty of crimes against the Jews, and many others like them—was a direct incitement to those who were discreetly and persistently disseminating anti-Semitic ideas.[12]

The fact that there were Jews in the higher party leadership apparatus who held positions of importance had no effect on the mass of the Jewish people. These Communists of Jewish origin never considered themselves as Jews, never took any action in favor of the Jews, and did not hold themselves responsible to the population from which they came.

In order to show their "principles," the Jewish Communists, in forming an attitude on what was really a Jewish problem, would treat it in the best of cases with indifference. Most of the time, in order not to be accused or suspected of pro-Jewish attitudes, they took positions unfavorable to the Jews, which they used every means to publicize. These opportunists intentionally ignored problems affecting the Jewish congregations, or allowed them to be resolved by Romanian Communists, for fear that they would be accused of feelings for the Jews, when in fact they had none.[13]

This quiet anti-Semitic attitude persisted both in the upper echelons of the party apparatus and in the more obscure mass organizations. Anti-Semitism was sometimes practiced discreetly, and at other times directly and bluntly. It was reflected in the measures directed against the Jews, which, as has been pointed out, were always interrelated with certain internal situations or interests in the international arena, and were especially taken to follow directives received from Moscow.

With an eye towards carrying out party directives in the Jewish community without hesitation and particularly without opposition, and in order to take direct action without the party appearing to exert pressure or to give directives contrary to the interests of the Jewish community, a political organization was set up which had serious consequences for the life of the Jews of Romania.

The Jewish Democratic Committee (Comitetul Democrat Evreisc, or CDE), known as the "transmission belt" between the party and the Jewish masses, was created by the Communist Party in 1945 by an alliance between this committee, the so-called Working Palestine organization (Mishmar and Ichud), as well as some members of the Union of Romanian Jews.

On creating the CDE, the Communist party clearly expressed its program of action in matters affecting the Jewish population. *Unirea*, the official newspaper of this organization, wrote that the purpose of creating the CDE was to give "the Jewish community an organization which would orient Jewish political life in the spirit of the National Democratic Front which is governing the country."[14]

While the Federation of the Unions of Jewish Communities, led by Dr. W. Filderman, and the Jewish party enjoyed respect in Bucharest and in other large cities, its influence over the masses in the towns of Moldavia and Transylvania or Bucovina had begun to decline, because direct, effective actions aimed at solving the pressing problems of the people there had not been taken.

The appearance of the CDE, with its democratic slogans about a struggle against anti-Semitism and its support for immediately beginning trials of war criminals and especially for restitution of property confiscated under the racial laws, attracted the attention of a populace that felt itself thoroughly abandoned. In order for these efforts to have even greater weight, especially among the ranks of the youth, the CDE activists, who were usually party members, infiltrated the Zionist organizations, carrying on activity to undermine them from within.

This gave the activists in the CDE the opportunity to appear before the masses as true, honest fighters, and when there were not sufficient means for convincing people, an appeal was made to government authorities, and the results were immediate.

As a result, the traditional Jewish newspapers, the *Curierul Israelit* and *Minturea* (Redemption), were suspended. Synagogues were transformed into political forums. The rabbis were forced to give sermons that condemned the attitude of the Anglo-American imperialists and "inciters to war," while other speakers tried to prove to the silent Jewish masses the advantages of total integration into the party's struggles.

As has been pointed out, the 1946 elections had broad support among the Jewish population, who came to the polls to vote for the first time in years, voting for the Bloc of Democratic Parties. The promises made by preeminent members of the Groza government during the election campaign that the problems of the Jews would be solved after the elections were received with confidence, and indeed with hope.

The Jewish National Bloc, which appeared in these elections, was from its first day a homogeneous organization determined to take direct actions to solve Jewish problems. The activity of this organization, before and during the elections, was a determining factor in getting the Jewish masses to come to the polling places.

What was not known, or was not understood in its true magnitude, was that while the Communist party was conducting a hard fight in those years to push aside and later to dissolve the political parties that might have damaged it in its struggle to gain power, the same game would later be played with the Jewish organizations.

The Communist party had no need of political organizations that brought up questions or raised problems. The CDE, an organization set up by the party, was considered sufficient for putting into effect the program drawn up by the party with regard to Jewish society in Romania.

During the sessions of its 1947 National Conference, the CDE demanded the dissolution of the Jewish political organizations, accusing their leaders of opposing the spirit of democracy in matters affecting the Jewish population. It was necessary that those "rotten, bourgeois, exploiting" elements be excluded from membership in the Jewish congregations. This action, which began in the fall of 1947, was charged with unusual significance.

Beginning in 1945, economic conditions in Romania had been continuously deteriorating, leading to a truly dramatic situation. Collaboration with Hitler's Germany, which had drained the country's reserves; the continuation of the war on the Allied side, which constituted a new and massive burden on the Romanian economy; and the observation of the terms of the armistice with the Soviet Union had all left traces that were felt in daily life. Besides all these factors, the so-called Sovormuri played a sinister part in the economy of the country. These were Soviet-Romanian enterprises which had appeared in the most important and vital sectors of the economy.[15]

In organizing production in the enterprises that still continued to carry on their activities, the interference by the so-called Workers' Committees led to great disturbances in production and the spoilage of manufactured products. Most of the time, because of denunciations by these committees, the owners of enterprises and highly qualified technicians were accused of sabotage, arrested, and sentenced to many years of imprisonment.

Small businessmen had no means of supplying their stores with goods by using the traditional channels for replenishing stocks. The great wholesale supplies of goods disappeared, and the only source of supply was the black market. When they could no longer get goods even through that channel, or they could not pay the prices demanded, the stores continued to "operate" with empty shelves. When their proprietors wanted to stop business activity, either because of lack of goods or out of fear of years of imprisonment if they continued to supply themselves with goods from the black market, their request was considered to be sabotage, and their arrest was imminent. People were forced to sell household goods or other articles of value in order to be able to pay the taxes on a bankrupt business.

The result of this state of affairs, which had been aggravated to a point of desperation during 1946 and 1947. Those two years of horrible drought, led to inflation and a devaluation of the leu, which had never been known in Romanian history.[16]

The monetary reform in August 1947 was a mortal blow to small businessmen and artisans, and also to the more well-to-do Jewish people. Regardless of how many lei a person possessed, he had the right to exchange only the sum of 3 million (devaluated) lei. The equivalent established by the government was 150 lei!

In the midst of this whole complex situation, which broke the Jewish population economically while they were desperately trying to recover from the blows they had received and to earn a living for themselves and their families, the CDE tossed out a new theory, that is, that of "two blocs on the Jewish street."

This was hoisted like a flag at the 1947 National Conference, in an attempt to destroy not only the unity of the Jewish population but also its morale.

Precisely because of the economic situation just described, this "theory" proved false, diversionist, and extremely dangerous.

On November 17, 1947, while the National Conference of the CDE was still conducting its business, Dr. W. Filderman "resigned" from the leadership of the UER. After a short time, he succeeded in leaving the country clandestinely. It was found that they were "preparing" a plot in which he would be accused of being a spy for Great Britain!

A few weeks later, on December 22, 1947, the new leader of the Federation of Jewish Congregations appeared at the residence of the Chief Rabbi, Dr. Alexandru Safran, bearing word from the government that he had to leave Romania within two hours! The expulsion of Dr. Safran from the country and his replacement by Rabbi Moses Rosen represented a turning point in the life of the Jewish community in Romania.

3

Under the new conditions created by social and political changes after the war, the Zionist movement regained legal activity, which under a variety of organizational forms involved more than one hundred thirty thousand Jews, especially young people.

The traditional Jewish publications reappeared. Between 1944 and 1948 publishing houses such as Bicurim (First Fruits) published more than eighty titles covering belles lettres, translations from the Hebrew, poetry, history, and the history of Zionism.

These publications had a powerful resonance in the social and cultural life of the Jewish people, who had been profoundly disoriented after years of terror and imprisonment. In these pages, they found answers to the problems that were worrying them, and in particular a direction to follow in a world tormented by different currents and political tendencies. The powerful attraction of the masses to Zionist ideas caused the CDE, from its beginning, to have ties with these Zionist organizations, with the intention of undermining and liquidating them.

The "two bloc" theory, which had been destined to split the mass of Jewish society, proved to be nonviable. These blocs in fact did not exist, and the desire to present them as a sort of class struggle proved false and so had no practical consequences. It is an indisputable fact that in the ranks of the Jewish population there were rich men and people with influence on the economy of the country. But these represented an infinitesimal percentage, and because of their social position they were set apart from the Jews and their problems. In general, the so-called Jewish bourgeoisie had been destroyed by the pressures of the government in power and particularly by the so-called economic stabilization of 1947.

The great mass of the Jewish population was made up of small merchants, artisans, intellectuals who were either unemployed or had modest incomes, a younger generation seeking a path to a successful future for itself, and people who were leading a marginal existence, seeking their income through speculation and operations on the black market. All these people did not consider the class struggle to be something real for which they had to fight. Therefore they remained passive towards the demagogic assaults of the CDE leaders and activists.

This total bankruptcy in ideas and the direct and uncompromising rejection of the Communist ideology which pretended to protect the interests of the "Jewish working class" led to the creation of a powerful wave of emigration. Between 1948 and 1949 about 200,000 requests to emigrate were filed for approval with the Embassy of the State of Israel in Bucharest.

The cause of this new wave of emigration—in addition to the social and economic factors that have been pointed out, the political conditions, and an anti-Semitism which persisted in the consciousness of some and manifested itself every time it had a chance—lay in a series of subjective factors which were not lacking in importance.

One of the most powerful losses suffered by the Jewish population in the period of the Holocaust had been the destruction of what had been the very nucleus of society: the family.

The Jewish population had been caught up in that jumble of facts and events while it was still organized as a homogeneous, viable unit. Whole families had been hauled out of their places of residence, and those that succeeded in surviving were merely isolated individuals, lone people, desperately trying to reconstitute from the fragments a mosaic which had many painful gaps.

In Jewish society in Romania, the family had played an extraordinarily important role throughout its whole existence. Individuals in a profoundly hostile environment, living—or to put it better, trying to slip unscathed—through cyclic periods of violent anti-Semitic demonstrations, found in the midst of the family moral and material support, shelter, kindness, and consolation. In his family a Jew had a feeling of certitude and assurance which mobilized his inner strength and gave meaning to his existence whenever it was threatened or when he was brutally struck.

In the crimes committed in the Holocaust in Romania it was not only individuals that were killed or destroyed. In that nightmare which darkened humanity, the Jewish family—with all of its moral system—was destroyed! Feeling acutely the lack of the family, the Jews who survived strove and invested gigantic efforts in readapting, in order to rebuild from the ashes, from the ruins, from the rubble, the certainty they needed so desperately.

From somewhere afar, calls reached them from people who had long been settled in other parts of the world. Feeble traces were sought out; sorrows long since forgotten were revived. Those bitterly tragic advertisements began to appear in the newspapers—"relatives are seeking relatives!" Using unseen bridges, people were sought, and some were found.

In those moments, sorrowfully evaluating the conditions and the hostile atmosphere, and living through their own disappointments, they believed that going away could be a solution! The idea of Jewish emigration from Romania took on new dimensions.

In seeking a haven where they could make a new home, the new families turned to those who had left long before, and yet seemed to them a hope of rebuilding the new moral unity they needed so badly.

Emigration of Jews from Romania in the 1960s was a demonstrated proof of this state of affairs, and those governing the country understood the phenomenon exactly; they encouraged it, and some even deliberately forced decisions to be taken.

The mass of the Jewish population did not leave out of the desire to make a success or to have an adventure. Plenty of attempts were made to reconcile certain concepts with Communist ideology, if it had remained compatible with their principles!

People felt deeply bound to the country to which they belonged, but the blows they had received, the uncertainty about the days ahead, and the anti-Semitism they encountered, which stirred up painful fears in their scarred souls, dominated their thinking and determined their actions. The process was slow, and in all of its complexity one can distinguish two basic phases. The first phase continued the illegal activity led by the Zionist organizations and lasted into 1946; the second phase began almost at that point and continued to the end of 1947, coinciding with the seizure of governmental power by the Communist party.

The first category, numbering about sixty thousand persons, was made up of those liberated from the concentration camps, especially those in Transnistria, who had no possibility of returning to their devastated or pillaged homes, or who came from Bessarabia or Bucovina, now reoccupied by the Soviet Union. Without any material support, without any prospects, these people saw in emigration their only possibility for survival.

Another category, similar in number, was made up of those Jews who because of the racial laws, and afterwards because of the conditions under which they were obliged to carry on their professions in Romania, had been brought to an extremely serious economic and financial situation; the majority of them, as has been pointed out, had become dependent on social welfare. These persons sought to use every possible means of leaving the country, especially to go to Palestine, although the difficulties in getting there were immense, because of the prohibitions set up by the British authorities.[17]

This mass of Jews, whose economic condition was getting worse from day to day, found an escape route by clandestinely crossing the border into Hungary and moving from there to Austria and Italy.

Again the Jews, this time having a new status of liberty and legal equality, were forced to take with them whatever they could carry on their backs, and were piling up in the border cities in western Romania, seeking to escape.

Certainly this exodus was not hidden or unknown to the Romanian authorities. It was impossible for this mass of "clandestine" travelers to assemble in those towns, get in touch with a veritable network of smugglers, perfectly organized, who would get them across the border, and still not be observed by the border guards who were patrolling the frontier.

Everything was known and had tacit approval. It would have been impossible otherwise! For those governing Romania it was a perfectly suitable formula, because from their point of view, it solved part of the

"Jewish problem," which they could not or would not solve in a natural manner or in conformity with the most elementary principles of morality and law.

This massive movement of people, facing new risks of clandestine journeys and an uncertain future, caused the unleashing of a violent campaign against the Zionist organizations, which was directed by the Communist party and carried out by the CDE with its well-known loyalty.

Articles in newspapers and other publications urging employment in production, professional reeducation, and the advantages of continuing to live under the Communist regime had no effect! So again the CDE requested the "principled" and totally disinterested help of the government authorities.

Severe orders were issued, and a savage hunt began in the forests through which the Jews were slipping during the night. They were caught and beaten; many were even killed, and the rest were arrested. Towards the end of 1947, on the basis of Communist solidarity, the Hungarian authorities began the same kind of hunt on their territory, returning to Romania those who had been trying out of desperation for better luck!

The jails again began to be populated by Jews. Along with those charged with "sabotage of the national economy" were Jews who, after being dispossessed of everything they still had, were condemned to hard years in prison.

4

The Romanian intelligentsia, with rightist nationalist training and education, looked upon the Communist regime with hostility and, at best, with suspicion. This attitude towards the Communist party was to be expected, and the intelligentsia moved towards an actual noncollaboration. The fall of Lucretiu Patrascanu, a Romanian with an intellectual background, led to sharper differences between the intelligentsia in general and the party and its surrogates.[18]

The Jewish intelligentsia, of different ages and backgrounds, either attached to the party since the years of illegal struggle or joining after it came to power, formed a serious force, and many of them considered themselves deeply engaged in the work of shaping a Communist Romania.

One could fit the presence of some of them in the party, especially after the monetary reform and the closure of the borders, and hence fewer possibilities for emigration, into the limits of open opportunism or an attitude of renouncing other ideals and seeking to accommodate themselves to the existing situation. To all these factors must be added the fact that the appearance of one-year, two-year, and five-year economic plans after 1949 raised before the party the necessity of attracting cadres of intellectuals, specialists, and technicians for the gigantic work of putting these ambitious projects into effect.

An immense contingent of architects, engineers, doctors, and others were attracted by substantial advantages. Many who were in jail because of various political activities during the fascist era were freed and put into leadership jobs.

The establishment of the so-called Workers' Universities gave a new lift to higher education. In that period the first graduates of these "short courses" and of "night universities" began to appear. Many of them had a superficial theoretical education and most lacked any practical training. The situation was not viewed with concern, since the best qualified did the work, and the state began to harvest the advantages of a "new" intelligentsia, which "came out of the people and was working for the people," as the party propaganda slogans proclaimed. Because of their "sound" origin and the qualifications they pretended to possess, they began to make a place for themselves by force, in a world they wanted exclusively for themselves.

Just then a galaxy of writers, newspapermen, men of letters, painters, composers, and others, all those who had formed the "silent Jewish intelligentsia" in the years of persecution, began to write, compose, paint, and publish, at first with some freedom of movement and thought, but later becoming more and more subservient to the directives given by the party.

The attitude of the party towards the intelligentsia sometimes vacillated, but the position with regard to those who expressed disagreement with its so-called directives was clear and unequivocal. Intellectuals who, if they were not "with" the regime, were considered against it, began to appear in the jails, alongside various politicians and former Legionaries.

So on the one hand, certain advantages "convinced" some intellectuals to rally to the party and to support it in accordance with their training, and on the other hand, certain measures restricted the freedom to express other options. The problem of attracting intellectuals with an earlier type of schooling was a difficult, delicate problem, but due to the factors just mentioned, some results were positive. Many of them were old men; they could no longer risk the road to jail!

The younger generation of writers, poets, and playwrights was more practical. Because they wrote as they were asked to, they could claim villas, material advantages, substantial author's rights, and privileged jobs in publishing houses. A remark made in this connection seems significant: "The Communist government of the Romanian People's Republic is feeding its writers better, but the Communists in Poland allow their writers to 'bark' freely."[19]

To the same extent that Romanian intellectuals trained either in the new school or the older school were attracted to the party, Jewish intellectuals were pushed aside, by the use of different means. Everything was done slowly and cautiously, finding the most apt occasions, but tenaciously and without renouncing any "principles."

In this climate, the decision to emigrate and renounce Communist ideas was usually a subjective one, determined by internal and external factors that affected tangentially the life of some of these intellectuals. They began very slowly to decipher not only reality, but their own position in Communist society. Others, in order to demonstrate their total loyalty to the party, began a bizarre game of denigrating their own origin. The condition of being a Jew was considered humiliating, Jewish names were "camouflaged," and denials of being Jewish were made publicly and brazenly. Departure from Judaism, denial, contempt, or, in the best case, disinterest in everything connected with it, were carried like a banner of total alignment with the ideology of the party by people who belonged to a group that had barely come out of the death grip of fascism. This led some Jews, who often became "more Marxist than Marx himself," to earn not the esteem and appreciation for which they hoped, but contempt both from other Jews and from the Romanian population.

5

One cannot assert that the Jews in the higher leadership levels in the party organized and initiated the measures that led to the revival of anti-Semitism. However, it can be asserted that they knew of everything that was happening, everything that was decided on and put into effect, without taking stands, and most of the time these actions had their complete approval. The fear that they could be accused of pro-Zionist attitudes, or of subjective support of the Jews in actions which could be interpreted as sympathy for them, paralyzed their wills, and a crass opportunism destroyed their personalities.[20]

This operation to "purge" the party and the later removal of the group led by Ana Pauker, who was made responsible—it was said—for recruiting party members, put the situation of Jews in the party and the governmental machinery in general in a new perspective.

In the party elections that took place on March 13, 1951, stress was placed on having a preponderance of workers in the organization, and their leaders would be Romanians. "Romanization" of the party machinery was an important objective in that year and in those that followed, and moreover, it was permanent in nature. These actions had a powerful impact, especially on those that had wished to align themselves with and integrate themselves into the life of the party, acting directly, with enthusiasm and sincerity, in all its activities. The consequences of the rightist or leftist deviations in the party were deeply felt by the Jews.

Those who had the mission of pulling out by the roots the negative activities and influences of those in the party who had promoted these "lines" had a perfect opportunity for exercising anti-Semitic influence and pressure, politely camouflaged under the lily-white banner of class principles.

The methods used to hit at the Jews were varied and readily available. A Jewish member of the party who had relatives "abroad," that is, in Israel, was looked upon as a potential enemy, capable of having liaison with imperialist agents. The fact that a Jew received letters from abroad, or sent letters abroad, although these were opened and the contents known, proved his "cosmopolitan" character and so awakened suspicions with regard to his sincere acceptance of party ideology. A shirt received from abroad and worn in the sight of all was a manifestation of liberalism, contempt for the working class, and so on.

The Jewish young people who entered the party had parents who had been completely or almost completely pauperized, especially after the nationalizations in 1948 and 1950. The old people, who had been artisans, small merchants, or commercial salesmen, were of course not of working-class origin! That was the social structure of the Jewish community in Romania. That was the result of the conditions under which the Jews lived in Romania. The descendents of those who had lived through those times and suffered so severely were made to pay for events for which they were not guilty, much less responsible.

As a direct consequence, and in order to eliminate the "poisonous roots" of all kinds of deviations, for the sake of and under the banner of class purity (this time not race purity!), an immense number of Jews were removed from the party and government machinery. Later, when others had been found guilty of these unspeakable abuses, the Jews, and others, of course, were again given jobs. Management was needed, and they were a labor force for which there was a terrible need. But never were they given back the positions they had once held. Those had long been occupied by native bearers of the seal of class purity. This scar was never erased from the souls of those who were so brutally thrown out into the street, not because they had been reproached for something, but because they had nothing to be reproached for.

The establishment of the State of Israel was a powerful stimulant to the desire of the Jewish population of Romania to emigrate. Unquestionably these motivations had a strong economic basis.

Israel, which was throwing wide its gates to those who wanted to come and settle there, constituted a powerful, attractive force, in spite of all the difficulties at the outset, which were only too well known. The CDE, then the only Jewish organization in Romania after it had eliminated the Zionist organizations by means of practices borrowed from its Communist mentors, directed its attention to the mass of the Jewish population, which was disoriented and deeply worried about the future.

When the campaign against emigration in the 1944–1947 period proved bankrupt, the CDE vigorously turned the focus of its propaganda against the State of Israel. Jewish nationalism was denounced as an enemy of the people's cause, and damaging to a state where Jews were living. The fight waged both within the CDE and outside it led to various "purges," and people who were perfectly molded in accordance with the desires and interests of the party were installed in the leadership of that organization.

In order to provide an ideological basis and "legal" cover for the actions that were to be taken, the need for purging the party of certain Jewish members who had slid down the slope of nationalism was sketched out in a resolution of December 1948 regarding the minorities in Romania.

The resolution concluded that such actions had to be taken even in the framework of reorganizing the CDE, which was to be purged of Zionist elements and strengthened by taking in "sound" elements who would be capable of getting the support of the Jewish masses.

This resolution opened the way to direct and ruthless action against the Zionist organizations, which led to their "voluntary" disbandment. A number of party activists were named as leaders of the Jewish community. They were people who were totally unknown to the Jewish masses, who looked on them with suspicion and indifference.

The Jewish deputies, elected on the party electoral list, never raised any of the acute problems affecting the Jewish population from the platform of the Great National Assembly. They were remarkable for total silence, and for votes given in total obedience which could not be discussed. Things that constituted fundamental problems for this upset population represented no problem at all for the deputies who were elected by Jewish voters, too.

The mere idea of raising a question from that platform—from which genuine representatives of the Jewish people had in the past raised their voices with courage and dignity in defense of the Jews of Romania, even in extremely difficult and critical conditions—was rejected as absurd.

Beginning in November 1948, the Romanian police wrecked the offices of the Jewish National Fund Organization, and so-called indignant young workers broke into the buildings they occupied, vandalizing the offices, destroying the files, trampling underfoot the pictures of the leaders of the State of Israel. When young Zionists tried to defend the offices of their organizations, they were beaten and arrested by police units sent there to "maintain order."

The leaders of the Jewish community and the Zionist organizations, people who had fought in the clandestine resistance movement against fascism, were arrested again!

Newspapers, special exhibits pointing out the serious economic situation in Israel, and word of mouth propaganda were used to persuade the Jewish population of Romania to take an antagonistic or at least indifferent attitude towards the State of Israel. The attachment of the Jews to the State of Israel and their idea of emigrating there were presented to the Romanian population as equivalent to an attitude of enmity. The same anti-Semitic slogans, dusted off but clothed in old clothing, and with the same content and intention, were used with great success.

Eugen Cristescu, the hangman of Iasi, "starred" again in the inquiries and investigations against the Zionists organized by the police and security forces, this time as a tool of the Communist authorities.

A new wave of arrests followed in 1951 and was extended into 1952. In the jails and in the work camps, especially those along the Danube-Black Sea Canal, alongside Legionaries and war criminals of all categories, one could find Jews, those Jews who had only wanted to leave Romania.

To these had been added an impressive number of Jews who had been fired from their jobs and who had been unable to get jobs because they had been classified as "inadequate." Thus characterized as "parasites" in the socialist society, they were sent to forced labor camps, especially the sinister yards on the Danube-Black Sea Canal. The theaters, Jewish schools, and even the synagogues were forced to develop broad anti-Zionist activity and to combat so-called Jewish nationalism. On Yom Kippur and Rosh Hashanah the rabbis were obliged to give sermons against Israel and the Zionist movement. Any resistance was punished with imprisonment. The same actions were aimed against the Orthodox Jews, who were persecuted and mocked because of their style of clothing.

Unirea (Unity), the organ of the CDE, was abolished and reappeared under the title *Viata Noua* (New Life). *Unirea* had not succeeded in uniting the Jewish population, because this platform and the ideas it propagated were not their own. *Viata Noua* never reflected "life," the real life of those people, and became what *Unirea* had also really been, a servile propaganda organ, working against the vital interests of the Jewish population.

6

After the inner life of the Jewish communities was smashed, and especially after the campaign to arrest the Zionist leaders, Jewish society entered a more and more pronounced decline. The tragedy of this situation lay in the fact that discriminatory measures of such a destructive nature were not only taken by Romanians, but to a large extent put into effect by Jews. The operations were developed systematically, on many fronts, according to a perfectly studied plan that was applied with the meticulousness that only opportunism could achieve.

Tramping brutally over the basic nature of a population, its characteristics, education, spiritual background, and then even its aspirations, a series of plans to "restructure" and to "educate" the masses of Jewish citizens began to be applied.

A Department of Restratification was established, which the Jews had to enter just as they were. They were expected to come out as if from a perfectly synchronized automatic machine or from the effect of a magic wand, perfectly indoctrinated and prepared to live in the new society, the Communist society.

One-year, two-year, and five-year plans were drawn up to educate and prepare them; appeals were made to Jewish wives to leave their occupations and "requalify" themselves. It was decided to gather small handicraftsmen into cooperatives in order to teach them the great advantages of collective labor, under the attentive supervision of the police and the party.

For the most part these plans simply remained on paper. The necessary funds were lacking, and international Jewish organizations were no longer sending the money requested of them through intermediaries. Once the Zionist movements were disbanded and their leaders thrown into jail, the new leaders of Jewish social life decided arbitrarily, ignoring realities, to abolish the traditional institutions for medical and material assistance. Hospitals, asylums, schools for religious study, and institutions for professional training were removed from the life of the Jewish community. "Aid to those in need must cease to be an encouragement for the lazy and indolent"[21] was the emphatic declaration of an unknown member of the Jewish apparatus who had just been enthroned as president of the Federation of Jewish Communities by the Communists.

As a consequence of this state of affairs, the Hebrew schools were closed and integrated into the general educational system. Fighting against Zionism, the new Jewish leaders waged a bitter battle against the Hebrew language, promoting Yiddish as the proper language for the people. In reality, Yiddish was no longer taught in the schools, and generations grew up without the traditions of their culture and education in Judaism.

In those Hebrew schools that continued to exist, an open campaign of propaganda was waged to indoctrinate the young against Zionism and traditional Jewish life. The Jewish theater in Romania, which has its origins in the theater of Avram Goldfaden and troubadours like Brodski,

Zbarjer, and others, attempted to return to its traditional sources, but it was impossible!

As in the Romanian theater, the party propaganda line made itself more and more felt, and opening the doors, turning on the lights, and paying the artists and theater staff had to be "paid for"!

When the place of classic plays and even some contemporary themes was usurped by party propaganda, when the sufferings of the Jews were brutally depicted in plays in which "speculators," "the rotten and corrupt bourgeoisie," and "the Anglo-American imperialists" were violently denounced, Jews began to leave the theater, which had ceased to be "their own"!

Socialist realism in art and literature was felt to be painful and violent in the Jewish community, too. The authors had to write on themes that were commanded, and the party line had to appear in the foreground as a messianic factor in saving, educating, and creating a "new" life for the Jews in Romania.

7

Waiting before the closed doors of the institutions in charge of issuing exit visas, the Jews began to understand that this opportunity, at least in the period between 1950 and 1960, was becoming more and more precarious. After the wave of emigration that took place mainly between 1944 and 1947, the obstacles put in the way became harder to overcome, and a silent and bitter resignation spread in their hearts.

This led to real tragedies in Jewish families, many of which found themselves separated in an arbitrary manner when the wife would get a passport and the husband would not, or when parents got passports, but they were denied to the children. All these things and many others led to a true state of desperation.

The exclusion from the party leadership of some Jewish Communists accused of either rightist or leftist deviations and the negative repercussions on Jews, even down to the most obscure party organizations, were perfect responses to latent dissatisfactions in the masses brought about by various causes, which could easily be attributed, as always, to the Jews!

Purging the government and party machinery, removing the Jews from the army, the courts, and the press, which was a prolonged process with permanent effects, took on new dimensions.

In those years there began to appear from the halls of the universities the first classes of graduates who made up a new Romanian intelligentsia. They came from the working class, from the poor peasantry; they had been educated by the party and were eager to take administrative positions in the state and party machinery which they had coveted during their years as students. But the number of jobs was limited. There were not enough places to live. There was only one solution in sight: get rid of the Jews! Allow them to emigrate!

In the fall of 1958, on the occasion of the Jewish high holidays, the rabbis and the leaders of the Jewish congregations announced from the pulpit that whoever wished to could file a request to emigrate! The news ran like an electric current through the whole Jewish community, which made up its mind with a spirit of deep responsibility for the action it was taking, and then calmly made its position known, publicly and without reticence!

A silent multitude gathered in front of police headquarters in Bucharest and throughout the country, beginning during the late hours of the night. That mass of people waited for hours for the moment when they could put their signature on the paper requesting the right to leave. A great amount of disillusionment had collected in their hearts, but they never hesitated.

In the first years after the war, there were those who desperately sought to slip across the border into Hungary; others left, paying large sums, on the ship *Transylvania*; and many left knowing that they risked being imprisoned in the British concentration camps on the island of Cyprus. As regards social structure and spiritual background, they belonged to the same category as the people about whom we have been speaking.

Those who were asking to leave on those unforgettable fall nights in 1958 were exactly the same Jews, the majority of whom had joined the party as soon as it began its legal activity, either with sincerity or through opportunism, and through it all they had struggled to apply the party line in everyday life.

The lesson of those years had been so harsh, so bitter, so painful, and the awakening of the Jews to the reality of life under Communism so amazing, that their decision was beyond appeal!

According to the official statistics, there were 146,264 Jews living in Romania in 1956. In the fall of 1958 more than 100,000 Jews requested exit visas! This mass movement in a populace that had expressed its position so clearly amounted to a plebiscite, and the Romanian authorities reacted harshly to it.

It is obvious that what led the Romanian government to approve Jewish emigration in those years was the acute economic situation, brought about by the government. Moreover, in those years, the party wanted to avoid as much as possible exacerbating the dissatisfaction of the masses, who were already frustrated enough by so many failures.

The departure of the Jews from the country and the arrival in the cities of a stratum of workers and peasants with a new cultural background had radically changed the class structure of the population of those localities and transformed their political physiognomy. Houses were vacated, jobs so much desired became open, property which the Jews had possessed and which they could not take with them could be bought at ridiculous prices, and the money obtained from all these things was being spent on things that were really useless, but the money stayed in the country!

The emigration of the Jews was a solution for which the government had considered the moment propitious. But the massive demand for exit visas took everyone by surprise; steps had to be taken at once! To all of these factors was added pressure from Moscow, which looked with disapproving eyes on this emigration, and even more, that from the Arab states, which protested to Romanian representatives. Since Romania was interested in those years in competing in the markets of the Near East, it could not allow itself to have the Arabs as real opponents. This set of circumstances led to an abrupt change in direction with regard to Jewish emigration. What had appeared at the outset to be a beneficial move for the economy of the country turned out to be fraught with problems.

The measure was followed by a series of coercive dispositions with severe effects on the Jewish community. As soon as the requests to emigrate were filed, they were communicated to the enterprises where those Jews were working. Those who had requested exit visas were fired or given positions below their qualifications. If there was no one qualified to replace them, they continued to hold their old positions, but were paid a lower salary.

These measures were considered "humane" because by requesting to leave the Jews had proved their lack of "loyalty" to the regime. When those who asked to leave were members of the Communist party, a furious avalanche of incriminating words was unleashed at party meetings against those who were considered traitors because they wanted to leave. The most insulting epithets were hurled in the faces of those who were so incriminated. Resentments that had been kept hidden for a long time surfaced.

Jews who received approval to leave during this period and had liquidated all their property woke up to find their passports confiscated. Then followed weeks and months of waiting in front of the offices of the proper authorities with requests for a favorable reply that would resolve the desperate situation in which they found themselves. At the same time, a new campaign was opened against the State of Israel, which was accused of having misled the Jewish masses of Romania. This campaign to intimidate those who wanted to leave was followed by a mass arrest of part of the Jewish population on charges of "espionage" and "treason," and Israeli diplomats were expelled under various pretexts.

In view of this state of affairs, as well as the subtle pressures exerted on families whose children were expelled from schools and universities, many Jews were forced to submit affidavits "renouncing" their emigration. This did not basically alter things. They never regained the jobs they had held, since they continued to be considered second-class citizens. Following these mass actions to request exit visas, Jews were never again promoted to positions of leadership. In a well-planned and organized operation, even the Jews who had not requested approval to leave were gradually replaced or were offered the possibility of retirement.

All kinds of means by which the Jewish element could be made to disappear from public life were constantly being sought and found. In civil administrative jobs, a Jew could aspire in the most fortunate case only to a position of "assistant." In the army and the courts, Jews were replaced almost entirely, and they had long since disappeared from the police and security organizations. In the media they held only minor positions, while in the literary field they could get their books published only with difficulty, and Jewish topics were prohibited.

Growing tension in the relations between Romania and Moscow implicitly led to a change in attitude towards the State of Israel.

Beginning in 1961 the government began to approve some departures, and between 1960 and 1965 about thirty-five thousand Jews left Romania. In order not to stir up the Arab countries again, the departures were generally made through Vienna, so it appeared that the Jews who were leaving were not going only to Israel, which was to a large extent the truth of the matter. Inside the country, the Jews arrested in 1959 were released, and by the end of 1960 departures had been approved for most of them.

In the sixties some aspects of life in the Jewish communities began to improve. When approval was again given to some international Jewish organizations to help members of their faith in Romania, canteens began to function again, clothing was distributed, and old people's homes were opened. Jews were permitted to go to the synagogue!

Some steps were taken and then given a distorted significance, in an attempt to hide the sad reality. In 1966 the Romanian government authorized sending about two thousand Torahs to Israel. The gesture was supposed to demonstrate a change in attitude, and perhaps that is what it was![22]

Inside the shattered windows of the synagogues that had been wrecked, burned, and pillaged, there was emptiness! Their communities had died in the concentration camps or had emigrated. There, in those synagogues, there was no one any more. The Torahs were standing mute and sad, awaiting their times of glory. And finally they too emigrated!

For the Jews who had filed their emigration papers many years before, the situation had not changed significantly, and as for those who would have liked to leave, their requests for approval to leave had not been accepted.

Discreet liaison offices began to function in some European capitals. Various intermediaries sought hard currency from Jews who wished to bring their relatives out of Romania. The prices varied by profession and degree of relationship and lacked any criteria at all, or else had just one single criterion—the country would sell its Jews as dearly as possible!

A bizarre situation would arise when someone who had relatives willing to pay for his jump from one world to other *disappeared*! Such persons were called to the office of some authority; they were made to see that they should file the necessary documents, and they left, quietly, with no fuss.

After the Helsinki Conference, when Romania was eager to be seen in the eyes of the world as a country where human rights were respected, "invitations" of this sort were made on a grand scale. Discreet transactions in anonymous offices were replaced by public discussion in the offices of diplomats. Romania badly needed most favored nation trade status!

8

Years have passed, many years, since everything happened that caused and made up the drama included in these pages. Those who were hangmen or victims have passed and are passing, quietly, into the land of shadows. The descendents of those who put the scythe in the hands of Death had received hatred and contempt for the Jews since their tender childhood like a nobleman's inheritance. They kept these feelings of resentment in the depth of their souls for their entire life, devaluating grudgingly only those at the surface. The "spirit" lived, even though they were conscious that the "time" had not yet come.

Their children, the present generation, have grown up in a country where there are Jews only in reduced numbers, sadly reduced! After a while, when the new century rises to face the sun, Romania will be "purged" of Jews, exactly as those who shaped anti-Semitic thinking foresaw and desired so hotly.

They practice it in a strange, bizarre, perverse form: anti-Semitism without Jews! If they don't have them at hand any more, as they had them for so many long years, they will persecute those who have left and mock them with hatred attuned to the new realities.

A long road has been traveled, with all its ups and downs—a road splattered, as someone said, with blood and tears, with tears and blood, a road which generations of Jews have trod, seeking a home in the hospitable land of Romania, making the place flourish, blessing bed and board.

They built and erected, they taught and spread light. They were born on that soil and took their first steps to decipher the secrets of their Scriptures; they sang to their first loves, seeking to look with faith, calmly and serenely, for the victory which unfortunately never came to them.

They identified themselves with the aspirations of the people in whose midst they lived, although they were challenged for this; through their deeds they demonstrated their profound attachment to the places where they saw the light of day and where they buried grandparents and great-grandparents, but their sincerity was denied to their faces. They were beaten, humiliated, and plundered, but as long as the lamp of life still flickered in their souls, they remained in or returned to the places to which they felt themselves indissolubly bound, whence they had been dispersed.

They were moved out of their tents brutally and mercilessly. But they fought, as much as they were able, to stay alive, telling themselves that all the calamities that befell them were temporary and that one day, however distant and hypothetical it might seem, the sun would shine on them again and warm their souls.

But they were killed! Killed brutally by means which only persons with perverted hearts hardened by hatred could have used. They were killed and plundered, plundered and then killed!

A black cloud hung over the Jewish congregations in Romania. The Jewish community mourned. The yellow star identified them; black clothing marked them out. When they returned—those who could return—to their emptied homes, they tried to shape a new life for themselves in the bleeding, pitiful ruins.

It was a stopping place on a journey without a final refuge! They believed that they were considered equal to the others, and set themselves to work with rolled-up sleeves, every one at what he knew. They did so with verve, unstintingly, with enthusiasm and unlimited faith.

But the poisonous vapor of anti-Semitism arose from somewhere. It could not be ignored. In Romania there is silence! Everything that happened "in those years" has been left to be covered up with the blackness of oblivion. A gag has been put on speaking the truth, and what is told seems distorted, interpreted according to "directives" and presented in a truncated form.

But you cannot pass by the cemeteries without baring your head! You cannot move towards "tomorrow" without feeling yourself at one with and responsible for "yesterday," even though what was done then by others has not stained your hands or darkened your conscience.

This book is not a history of Jews in Romania; it is not a history of Romania or a history of Romanian political life. This book wishes only to be a cry to strip away the layers of indifference and guilty silence.

No, the problem has not been, nor can it be, exhausted in these pages. It is much more vast, much more complex!

The study of anti-Semitism in Romania—particularly during the period of the Holocaust and the years that followed—looms as an imperative necessity. This "subject" was avoided in Romania! There can exist only one explanation: writing the truth about that tragedy would have meant writing the truth about those who brought it about in all its complexity.

And this could not be done!

Ashes of oblivion have been spread over the years. In the souls of sorrowing people there is a turn towards remembering, seeking to understand the meaning, to decipher the causes, and to give themselves their own answers to questions that have no answer!

You can forgive, but you cannot forget!

Appendix

A.1
Some Statistics
On the Jewish Population in Romania

Up to World War I	Population	Percentage
1899	266,652[1]	4.5%
1912	241,588[2]	3.3%
In Greater Romania		
1922	708,230	4.4%
1930	756,930[3]	4.2%
(1939)	(765,218)	3.8%
1942	292,149[4]	1.7%

1. The census of 1892.
2. Census of 1912. The decrease of the number of Jews is due to emigration, due to the increase of anti-Semitism.
3. The census of 1930. Although the Jewish population increased in the period from 1930 to 1939, the official figures used are those of the 1930 census. In those figures the natural increase of Jewish population is not included.
4. In those figures of this census known as "Census of the population of Jewish blood" the Jews from the labor camps and from political concentration camps are included.

Jews in the Seized Territories in 1940

Bukovina	93,101
Bessarabia	202,958
Herta district	1,940

Northern Transylvania   148,172

Southern Dobrogia   846

                                                             447,017

Deportation	Transnistria	Remaining Jews
Bucovina	75,580	17,521
Bessarabia	202,731	227
Herta district	1,940	—
Dorohoi	12,558[1]	2,316
	292,809	20,064

Northern Transylvania   148,172
deported by Hungarians and
Germans to Auschwitz

1. The city and county of Dorohoi of Moldavia and the cities of Radauti (11,578) and
   Suceava (6,697) Jews were not occupied by the Russians in 1940, but the Jewish
   population was deported from those cities too.

Jews in Transnistria

German sources   185,000[1]

Romanian sources   185,000[2]

Unaccounted   107,809[3]

1. According to the newspaper "Bucharester Tageblatt" of August 8, 1942.

2. Report of the Minister of Internal Affairs number 13530 of October 16, 1943 stated
   that to the 185,000 Jews deported in Transnistria should be added 10,000 to 20,000
   Jews deported after those figures were published in the German newspaper. The
   total deported Jews should be around 200,000. The official figures remained
   185,000.

3. The difference between the figures of those deported Jews and those who arrived in
   Transnistria represent Jews deported in Siberia by the Russians in the year 1940,
   some conscribed in the Russian Army and most of them died of starvation, sickness
   or were shot on their way to Transnistria. In those figures there are not included
   around 150,000 Ukrainian Jews from the city of Odessa, those of Transnistria killed
   by Romanians, Ukrainean militia and German colonists (Folkdeutsche), or those
   from this area deported over the river Bug and killed by the Germans.

Survivors

Transnistria   50,741[1]

Northern Transylvania   29,405

1. Not all of those survivors succeeded in returning to Romania. The natives from
   Bucovina and Bessarabia who settled in Romania after the war, were obliged to
   return to the Soviet Union.

The City and the County of Iasi up to World War II   Population

1930   41,120[1]

1942   32,369[2]

Unaccounted   8,751[3]

1. In those figures are included the Jews from towns and villages from the county of Iasi and the city of Iasi.

2. The figures represent the Jews from Iasi. There were no Jews living there in the county.

3. This figure represents the Jews killed in the pogrom in Iasi. According to other sources the figure is 12,000. We consider that the figure of 8,751 is more appropriate.

Bucharest

1941   129[1]

1. Jews killed in the pogrom in Bucharest. Jews killed in other cities are not included.

After the War

In Romania after the war, there remained approximately 350,000 Jews.

Today there are around 15,000 to 18,000 Jews.

The data used in this chapter is from "Breviarul Statistical Populatiei evreiesti din Romania" (1943, Summary of the statistic of the Jewish population). Published by Centrala Evreilor din Romania (The Jewish Center of Romania) which was in charge of the organization of this census.

A.2
Anti-Semitic Legislation in Romania, 1800–1944 (an incomplete list)

1803	Prince Alexandru Moruzzi prohibits Jews from renting agricultural lands.
May 18, 1804	Prince Alexandru Moruzzi prohibits Jews from buying farm produce.
1817	The Calimach Code, Section 1430, prohibits Jews from buying property.
1818	The Ioan Caragea Code reconfirms the old Ecclesiastical Code, which prohibited Jews from being witnesses against Christians in their cases before the courts.
1831	Chapter 3, Section 4 of the Organic Regulations obliges all Jews to be registered by the local authorities, specifying the profession of each. Jews who could not prove useful employment had to be removed from their respective localities. Other Jews in the same situation had no right to settle in those localities.
March 11, 1839	An obligatory levy of 60 piastres per year is placed on every Jew living in Moldavia.
December 12, 1850	No Jew is allowed to enter Romania unless he possesses the amount of 5,000 piastres and has a well-established profession.

May 15, 1851   A Commission against Vagabondage is established in
                        Iasi to determine the right of Jews to enter and settle
                        in Moldavia.

June 17, 1861   An order by the Ministry of the Interior prohibits
                        Jews from being innkeepers in rural areas.

April 12, 1864   The Municipalities Act grants the right to vote to Jews
                        who have:

                            1. obtained the rank of an officer in the army;

                            2. received a university degree in Romania;

                            3. received a degree at a foreign university recog-
                            nized by the Romanian government; or

                            4. established an industrial enterprise.

December 4, 1864   Jews are prohibited from being lawyers.

April 14, 1866   The Ministry of the Interior permits Jews settled in
                        villages as of this date to continue to hold rented land
                        until the expiration date of the lease. The contract
                        cannot be renewed.

March 1868   A bill is introduced in the Chamber of Deputies to
                        prohibit Jews from the following:

                            —holding farm land;

                            —settling in villages;

                            —selling foodstuffs;

                            —doing business without special authorization.

                        Jews settled in villages as of this date are to be re-
                        moved. The bill was withdrawn and was not voted on
                        because of external pressures.

June 23, 1868   Military service is compulsory, but not for "foreign-
                        ers."

December 27, 1868   Jews are excluded from the medical profession.

January 15, 1869   Jews are prohibited from being village tax collectors.

July 1869   Replying to a protest by the French government about
                        the condition of Jews in Romania, Mihail Kogalni-
                        ceanu sends a note refusing to consider Romanian
                        civil rights for Jews.

October 1869   A supplementary levy is laid on kosher meat in the
                        cities of Focsani and Roman.

October 25, 1869   Jews are prohibited from being proprietors of phar-
                        macies.

February 15, 1872   Everyone who sells tobacco products must be a Ro-
                        manian.

April 1, 1873   A law is passed prohibiting Jews from selling alcoholic
                        beverages in the villages. Jews with Romanian citizen-
                        ship will receive a special authorization.

August 4 and September 5, 1873	An initial order and a second supplementary order are issued establishing that the chief medical officers of counties must be Romanians.
January 8–20, 1874	The Health Code establishes that chief medical officers of counties and hospital chiefs must be Romanians. Pharmacists may work on the basis of special authorization. New pharmacies may be opened only by Romanians.
1876	The revised Military Code establishes that "foreigners" are to perform military service. They can be excused if they prove that they are citizens of a foreign country.
October 21, 1879	Article VII of the Constitution, which limited the rights of Jews to be citizens contrary to the provisions of the Treaty of Berlin, is amended.
June 6, 1880	The "Aliens Act" gives the Ministry of the Interior the right to extradite or to move from one place to another any foreigner who disturbs the public order, without giving any explanation.
July 16, 1881	A law establishes that stockbrokers must be Romanians or naturalized Jews.
October 21, 1881	The cabinet issues a decree extending the prohibition of the sale of alcoholic beverages by Jews in the villages, market towns, and cities.
November 11, 1881	Any "foreigner" living in Romania must have special authorization to move from one locality to another.
February 26, 1882	Jews are prohibited from being customs officers.
November 3, 1883	A law establishes that all residents of the country must perform military service, with the exception of aliens who are subjects of a foreign power.
January 31, 1884	A law prohibits "foreigners" from submitting petitions directly to Parliament.
March 19, 1884	A law prohibits itinerant peddlers from doing business in the villages.
April 15, 1885	The Pharmacy Act gives the Ministry of the Interior the right to close any pharmacy run by an unauthorized person; pharmacies may be owned only by Romanians and naturalized Jews.
March 13, 1886	Those making statements before the Chamber of Commerce must only be persons who hold Romanian citizenship.
June 15, 1886	Only Romanians and naturalized Jews may be owners of drug stores.
December 7, 1886	Bank accounts must be kept in the Romanian language or in a modern European language.

February 28, 1887   All employees of the state monopoly for the sale of
                      salt and tobacco must be Romanians or naturalized
                      citizens.

April 28, 1887   Only persons who have the right to hold public jobs
                      may be tax collectors.

May 22, 1887   The majority of the members of the Administrative
                      Councils must be Romanians.

May 24, 1887   Five years after an enterprise is established, two-thirds
                      of its workers must be Romanians.

August 4, 1887   A ministerial order establishes that preference must
                      be given to children of Romanians for admission to
                      the public schools.

1889   Of 1,307 licenses to do itinerant peddling, 126 have
                      been given to Jews.

August 31, 1892   Retired Jewish soldiers do not have the right to serve
                      in the rural gendarmerie.

April 21, 1893   "Foreigners" can be admitted to schools only if there
                      are vacant spaces and after payment of a tax. The
                      number of "foreigners" accepted cannot exceed one-
                      fifth of the total number of pupils. "Foreigners" are
                      not to be admitted to agricultural schools.

May 20, 1893   The Senate votes in favor of a bill regarding the right
                      of preference for Romanian children in the primary
                      schools, and levying a tax on "foreign" children.

June 26, 1893   A royal decree establishes that all hospital employees
                      must be Romanians. Jewish patients are to be admit-
                      ted to hospitals only after paying a tax, and cannot
                      occupy more than 10 percent of the beds.

January 26, 1894   Peasants may be represented in lower courts by their
                      servants, provided these are not Jews.

May 22, 1895   Students in military hospitals must be Romanians or
                      naturalized Jews.

April 13, 1896   Jews do not have the right to be brokers in Romanian
                      customs houses.

June 1896   A ministerial order establishes that letters from par-
                      ents conducting private schools, excusing the absence
                      of their children from public schools, are not to carry
                      a tax stamp, except for those written by "foreign"
                      parents, who must also pay a tax for giving exami-
                      nations.

June 26, 1896   A ministerial order gives the right to municipal coun-
                      cils of villages to establish whether Jews in their lo-
                      calities may remain permanently. The authorization
                      may be revoked at any time.

April 4, 1898	A law establishes that "foreign" children can be admitted to secondary schools if there are vacant spaces and on payment of a tax. (Education is free in Romania.)
October 1898	Twelve thousand Jewish children have not been admitted to state schools.
February 18, 1899	Only Romanians have the right to be employees of the railroads.
1900	The quota for Jewish children in the primary schools is reduced to 5.5 percent; in the secondary schools it is reduced from 10.5 percent (the level in 1895) to 7.5 percent.
February 27, 1900	A ministerial order obliges Jewish school children to attend classes bareheaded.
March 28, 1900	Sixty percent of the paid employees of privately owned railroads must be Romanians.
April 17, 1900	A ministerial order requires Jewish schools to be open on Saturday.
March 16, 1902	The Trades Act requires Jews to have special authorizations, referring to a list of discriminatory laws and orders imposing a series of obstacles that are impossible to overcome.
August 9, 1940	A Judicial Statute for Jews in Romania is instituted, citing a list of discriminatory laws and orders regulating the conditions of existence of the Jews in Romania.
September 6, 1940	At Bucharest, the leading bar association of the country, without having any orders from above, bars 1,479 lawyers from professional duties from this date until (at least) September 13, 1940. Only 177 Jews continue to exercise their profession.
September 11, 1940	By Decree No. 42352, the Mosaic religion is eliminated from the historic religions.
	By Decree No. 42354, houses of worship that do not have enough members are closed. Where there are not enough synagogues, the community will also be dissolved.
	By Decree No. 42181, actors of Jewish origin are barred from Romanian theaters, as well as persons working together to put on a show.
	By Decree No. 42180, it is prohibited for all Christian services to be supplied directly or indirectly by any Jewish enterprise.

September 13, 1940   The General Association of Romanian Engineers (AGIR) expels Jewish engineers from the association, withdrawing their right to practice their profession. By October 10, 1940, all Jewish engineers have no possibility of working.

September 14, 1940   By Decree No. 3151, a new title for the Romanian state is ordained: the National Legionary State.

September 20, 1940   The Sports Federation cancels the passes for Jewish journalists.

September 21, 1940   The Social Security Office eliminates Jewish suppliers.

     The Romanian Opera fires all Jewish employees.

September 22, 1940   By Decree No. 44400, Jewish artists can perform in theaters that carry the label "Jewish Theater," but all personnel must be Jewish. The shows are henceforth to be presented only in the Romanian language.

September 25, 1940   The Journalists' Union expels its Jewish members.

September 29, 1940   The Council of the Union of Commercial Advisers expels Jews from that organization, replacing them with Romanians.

October 3, 1940   By Decree No. 3294, rental of pharmacies and drug stores to Jews is prohibited.

October 4, 1940   The Romanian Writers' Society expels Jewish writers, poets, playwrights, literary critics, literary historians, and others from its ranks.

October 5, 1940   By Decree No. 3347, Jews are no longer to hold any type of farmland, either as proprietors, beneficial users, or administrators. All affected properties pass into the hands of the state.

     By Decree No. 2261, the Romanization Commissions Act, Romanization Commissions are named for all Jewish enterprises, with the intention of taking them over.

October 6, 1940   The Journalists' Union of Bucovina expels its Jewish members.

October 7, 1940   The Association of Licensed Electricians withdraws the right to practice their trade from its Jewish members.

October 10, 1940   The General Association of Stomatologists expunges its Jewish members from its ranks and establishes standards for their activities.

     The Association of Public Works Contractors forbids Jews from engaging in or taking over activities of such nature.

The Society of Architects expels its Jewish members from its ranks, on the occasion of celebrating fifty years of activity.

The Fine Arts Union expels from its ranks painters, sculptors, graphic artists, set painters, and others who are Jewish.

October 12, 1940   The Romanian Society of Otorhinolaryngology forbids its Jewish members to practice their profession any longer, as they have been excluded from the ranks of this association.

By Decree No. 49782, Jewish firms are prohibited from participating in public auctions.

The General Association of Chemists expels Jews from its ranks.

October 14, 1940   By Decree No. 3438, Jews can organize their own schools, which are to operate only for Jews and with Jewish personnel. Romanian teachers are prohibited from teaching in Jewish schools.

October 16, 1940   By Decree No. 191730, teaching personnel of ethnic Romanian origin are not to publish their educational and scientific works through publishing houses belonging to Jews.

October 17, 1940   The "Picturesque Romania" Tourist Association expels its Jewish members.

The Jewish lawyers who have remained in the bar association can practice their profession only for other members of their own religion.

The Cimpina Council of Commerce expels the Jewish merchants among its members.

The Endocrinology Society expels its Jewish members.

October 30, 1940   The Butchers' Guild at the Bucharest abattoir expels its Jewish members.

November 7, 1940   By Decree No. 2713, the members of the Bar Councils must not be Jews. Those still in these positions are expelled.

November 9, 1940   By Decree No. 151696, Jews are expunged from the list of tax assessors.

November 10, 1940   Licenses to distribute and sell products treated as state monopolies of the C.A.M. (salt, tobacco, matches), to which disabled, orphaned, and war-widowed Jews had been entitled, are cancelled.

The General Assembly of the General Association of University Teachers excludes its Jewish members from its ranks.

The Romanian Deaf and Dumb Association expels its Jewish members.

November 13, 1940   By Decree No. 3801, persons who participate in illegal gatherings will be punished in accordance with the law. Jews will receive double penalties.

By Decree No. 3802, when it is determined that those who take part in a meeting of a political nature are Jews, they will be given double penalties.

By Decree No. 3804, employees of public offices or of institutions having such a nature are prohibited from marrying persons of Jewish origin.

November 15, 1940   By decree No. 3789, Jewish doctors, those that have become Christians, and Jewish women married to Christians are expelled from the Medical School. In order to be able to practice, Jewish doctors are obliged to wear a special insignia with the inscription "Jewish Doctor." They can give medical assistance only to Jews.

November 16, 1940   By Decree No. 3825, all commercial and civil enterprises of whatever nature must fire all the Jews on their payroll by December 31, 1940.

By Decree No. 218585, Jewish students are excluded from drawing the foreign exchange necessary to continue their studies abroad.

November 17, 1940   By Decree No. 3810, the following items are expropriated from Jews: woodlots, mills, country oil presses, distilleries, lumber plants, stocks of grain, crops made on Jewish properties, and the entire inventory of stock living or dead.

November 18, 1940   By Decree No. 551117, Jews are prohibited from being members of labor unions.

November 19, 1940   By Decree No. 3850, licenses giving the right of ownership or administration of moving picture houses, film offices, travel agencies, etc., are withdrawn.

November 28, 1940   Food stores are to be closed on Sundays and legal holidays.

December 4, 1940   By Decree No. 2968, ships and every type of vessel flying the Romanian flag belonging to Jews are expropriated.

December 5, 1940	By Decree No. 3984, Jews are excluded from military service without any distinction. They must pay a military tax.
December 6, 1940	By Decree No. 924, twenty-seven barges and five tugs expropriated from Jews are placed at the disposal of a German shipping company.
December 9, 1940	By Decree No. 246961, diplomas obtained by Jewish students in Germany and Italy or any other country cannot be made equally valid in Romania.
December 24, 1940	By Decree No. 67794, apprenticeship contracts for Jewish apprentices are suspended.
	By Decree No. 64054, the issuance and exchange of certificates of professional capability for Jewish workers and craftsmen are suspended.
January 10, 1941	The Stock Exchange Act is amended; only Romanians may be official brokers.
January 15, 1941	By Decree No. 34, a special census of Jews is organized under the supervision of the Legionaries.
January 19, 1941	By Decree No. 121, the Romanization Commissions are abolished, and enterprises where these commissions were functioning are forbidden to make any move for disposal of property such as sale, purchase of real estate, dissolution of the enterprise, etc.
January 21, 1941	By Decree No. 132, the obligation for military and premilitary service for Jews is transformed into fiscal obligations and obligations for forced labor.
September 4, 1941	By Decree No. 2507, all expropriation laws are extended to cover the provinces reconquered from the Soviets. All real and personal property of the Jews passes into state ownership.
	By Decree No. 2509, Romanian nationality is maintained for all residents of the liberated territories, with the exception of Jews.
November 11, 1941	By Ordinance No. 23 of the Government of Transnistria, regulations are set for the living conditions of Jews, who are obliged to live in ghettoes, provide labor to whoever demands it, etc.
November 12, 1941	By Decree No. 3118, Jewish lawyers in Northern Bucovina and Bessarabia are suspended from the bar associations and have no right to practice their profession.
November 17, 1941	By Decree No. 3208, credit is granted to set up new enterprises in the liberated territories. Jews are excluded from these benefits.

December 22, 1941	Jewish real properties expropriated in Bessarabia encumbered by mortgage burdens owed to the Urban Credit Company in Bucharest and Iasi are given as payment of these debts.
January 12, 1942	By Decree No. 51, the National Bank of Romania is authorized to sell rubles to Jews that will be valued at a rate set by the Ministry of Finance.
March 30, 1942	By Decree No. 252, exchange of correspondence between Transnistria and families which have remained inside the country is prohibited.
May 20, 1942	The Reintegration Loan. Jews are ordered to subscribe at a rate four times greater than the rest of the population (by this date, Jews had subscribed 1,994,209,141 lei).

—By Order No. 3450, the Jews in Bucharest were obligated to turn over to the army the following items: 4,000 beds, 4,000 mattresses, 8,000 sheets, 8,000 pillowcases, 4,000 light iron bedsteads, 4,000 pillows, and 1,200 complete beds for the hospitals in the inner area of Bucharest. The order had to be executed within twenty-four hours. The value of all these things amounted to 500,000,000 lei.

—For the Home for the Disabled: the Jews subscribed 100,000,000 lei.

—Articles of clothing valued at 1,800,135,000 lei were turned in.

—Jews who could not turn in articles of clothing were sentenced to imprisonment for terms varying between five and ten years. In January 1943 amnesty was granted for these persons, after which a sum of 100,000,000 lei was deposited.

—An exceptional contribution of 4 billion lei: by April 1943 a sum of 734,156,308 lei had been paid.

—Taxes for release from snow removal work amounted to 144,024,375 lei.

—Taxes for release from work in concentration camps. Between April 1, 1943, and August 23, 1944, 3,034,148,141 lei were paid.

September 22, 1942   By Decree No. 698, the death penalty is instituted for Jews of both sexes over fifteen years of age who had been transported to Transnistria and who reentered the country illegally. Those who abet the crime are to be punished with forced labor for five to twenty-five years. The same punishment is reserved for instigators, accomplices, and those who conceal the crime.

December 7, 1942   By Decree No. 2927 of the Government of Transnistria, regulations are set for the conditions for work by Jews in the concentration camps, ghettoes, and other centers where they are living.

Notes

PREFACE

1. Robert St. John, *Foreign Correspondent* New York: Doubleday, 1957, 217.
2. Ibid, 215.
3. M. Pelin, "Saptamana" *The Almanac of 1986*.
4. Henry Kamm, "Rising Verbal Attacks Strike Romania's Jews." *The New York Times* July 1, 1991, A10.
5. Henry Kamm "Romanian are Told of Nation's Role in the Mass Killing of Jews," *The New York Times*, July 2, 1991.
6. Henry Kamm, "Anti-Semitic Taunt at Wiesel Talk in Romania" *The New York Times*, July 3, 1991, A.8.
7. *Micro-Magazine* New York, July 12, 1991, 9.
8. Editorial, "Romania's Dirty Secrets," *The New York Times*, July 5, 1991, A20.

CHAPTER 1

1. The Jewish Museum, Bucharest.
2. Ibid.
3. J. B. Brociner, *Chestiunea Israeliților Români* (The Issue of the Romanian Israelîtes) vol. (Bucharest: Horia Carp & Co., 1910), 1:p.99.
4. The Jewish Museum, Bucharest.
5. Brociner, 1:106. The explanation given to the citizens of Lemberg, Poland, by the Voievod of Moldavia was as follows: "It was not a whim. It was due to the despair of our merchants who spent their time waiting at the border for cattle buyers. In the meantime, the Jews crossed [the border] elsewhere and brought Polish cloth into the country, which they would then sell and purchase cattle, leaving our merchants at the border 'holding the bag.' We would allow

them to buy cattle inside one country, if those of the border were not in sufficient numbers but we could not allow them to ruin the trade of our merchants."

6. Ibid.

7. Ibid., 1:139–40. The attitude of the Moldavian Voievod was strongly criticized by the diplomatic representative to his court. In a letter written on June 22, 1726, d'Usson d'Allion says: "Monsignor, the ministers of the Porte are busy these days because of the complaints about leaders of the Jewish community. Mihai Racovitza, the Prince of Moldavia, who re-attempted to exhort the Jews, had accused those who lived in the Principality of having killed a Greek child in order to mix his blood with their unleavened bread and, under this pretext—like a new Attila—destroyed their synagogues, burned their books and beat the alleged criminals; he made them all contribute. This Prince should not ignore the fact that this idea has became ridiculous in civilized countries."

8. Ibid., 1:137, 138.

9. Ibid., 1:20–21. Brociner gives the following explanation for the word *raia*: "The Muslims vow to recognize two categories of subjects of the Sultan: the Mohammedan who is *acha* or *agha* and the non-Mohammedan who is *raia* (i.e., friend). Given the significance of the word *raia*, if the Jews had been called *raiali* in the old legislation, they could not have been taken as foreigners.... All Romanians were *raia*, and so were all the Jews who had not been under foreign protection."

10. Ibid., 1:27. After the war of 1761, when the town of Suceava was destroyed by Polish troops, the Jews were urged to come and settle in that town and rebuild it. In another instance, when the expansion of the town of Focsani was decided upon in 1796, the City Council took a similar attitude towards the Jews. In 1798 Chief Simion issued a charter to bring sixty families to that town.

11. Ibid., 1:196. Among other sanctions that regulated the life of the Jews is a decree issued by Voievod Ioan George Caragea on April 17, 1813, which banned Jews from hiring girls or Christian children as servants. However, the decree mentions that this measure is only to prevent any charges which may be brought against the Jews.

12. Ibid., 1:224.

13. David Mitrani, *The Land and the Peasant in Romania: The War and Agrarian Reform (1917–1921)* (London: Oxford University Press, H. Milford 1930), 16, 38.

14. J. B. Brociner, 1:33.

15. Ibid., 1:257.

16. Ibid., 1:225.

17. Ibid., 1:51, 52. The document was never taken into consideration because "the proper time" had not come, as recommended by Th. Bals, a typical retrograde, reactionary representative of the great landowners. The document was later found in the personal archives of Mihail Kogalniceanu.

18. Ibid.

19. Ibid., 78. A great number of deputies with anti-Semitic views tried to undermine this generous initiative. The debates that took place in the General Assembly of Romania on March 4 and 5, 1864, were significant. At those meetings, the assembly discussed the Communal Law. The government submitted a bill that included the right of Jews to participate as voters in local elections. The

bill stipulated the right to take part in the elections but limited this right only to those who (a) served in the armed forces and achieved officer rank; (b) completed college or university studies in Romania; (c) after attending regular courses earned a Ph.D. or master's degree in any field from a foreign university; or (d) founded in Romania a factory or useful manufacturing plant with at least fifty craftsmen.

20. E. Schwartzfeld, *Adevărul asupra revoltei de la Brusturoasa* (The Truth Regarding the Uprising at Brusturoasa) (Bucharest: Stefan Mihailescu Publishing House, 1885), 32, 38. The newspaper *Lupta* (The Fight), on August 1, 1885, analyzed the causes of the unrest: "The peasants in Brusturoasa had been freeholders for years and became 'socmen' following an agreement with Mr. Ghica-Comanesti Senior, only to pay back a debt of 16,000 ducats to a Greek Cantopol. Once becoming socmen, a new rural law in 1864 gave them title to land which they owned twenty years earlier. Consequently they had to pay for it again. Here comes a capitalist, a tenant called Grumberg who closes their small sawmills, replacing them with others systematized and larger. After taking away their trade tools, the tenant offered them a job on their land and forests."

21. E. Sincerus [E. Schwartzfeld], *Les Juifs dans la Roumanie* (London: Macmillan, 1901), 18. The idea of reaching out and knowing the population from the first day of school concerned the country's leaders in different periods of time. Thus, the Decree of May 24, 1803, issued by Voievod Constantin Alexandru Moruzzi, clearly provided: "In every school we shall accept students from our country and others because, by spreading the knowledge of books, we shall ensure that no one abuses it." Later, Voievod Alexandru Ghica in Moldavia, in the Public Education Regulations of 1851, stipulated in Article I: "Public Education is free and open to all inhabitants of Moldavia." In 1865 the Department of Public Education, in a circular addressed to the Jewish communities, insisted that all Jewish children attend classes at state schools: "Nobody wants to separate schools because the separation of schools perpetuates the separation of the nation; they will not accustom themselves to life among Romanians, and will form the idea from childhood of separation between Christian and Jews."

22. Ibid., 122.

23. Ibid., 5.

24. (Radu Rosetti) Verax, *Roumania and the Jews* (Bucharest: I. V. Socecu, 1904), 82, 83.

25. Ibid., 49.

26. William O. Oldson, "The Historic and Nationalistic thought of Nicolae Iorga," *East European Quarterly* (1973): 79. In a speech delivered on the occasion of the reform of the judiciary on January 26, 1884, Ion Bratianu stated: "We must work twice as hard or as much as the foreigners whom we are competing with. Do you know why everyone here wants a job with the government? Instead of working or managing our land well, we prefer to leave it in charge of representatives, so we can have fun abroad. Look to our cafés, our casinos. They are always full of landlords without occupation and particularly with office clerks."

27. Ibid., 84.

28. Mitrani, 85.

CHAPTER 2

1. A. C. Cuza, *Jidanii în Război* (The Kikes in the War) (Bucharest: Steaua Graphic Institute, 1923), 20.

2. In his speech during the session of Parliament on July 18, 1918, Cuza said: "As a matter of fact, I would like to dispel from the very beginning the theory whereby if they [the Jews] participated in the war, they should have political rights.... Why did the Kikes have to participate in defending our country? They had to because they were fed from the country's soil, because they benefitted and prospered from this soil; should we be bound to let them prosper and defend them at the same time, along with their fat wives and children? It does not sound logical to me."

3. *The Jewish Minority in Romania* (London: Joint Foreign Committee, 1927), 32. Here is a significant note in the media of the time: "On June 24, 1927, a group of students walking through the Cismigiu Gardens attacked a Jewish passer-by.... First they attacked a group of three young Jews and beat them with clubs. The hooligans stopped two Jewish passers-by accompanying a lady. Eventually the gang was stopped by police officers and two agents who managed to arrest two of the attackers. Their names were: Ion Cristescu and Ion Manciulescu; the rest managed to escape."

4. Here is an excerpt from a memorandum presented on September 17, 1925, to the Romanian Minister of Foreign Affairs in Geneva. Jewish international bodies aware of the anti-Semitic movements in Romania "In the past four years an intense anti-Semitic campaign has exploded in Romania. Thousands of manifestos, newspapers, and magazines are circulating in the country. As a result, demonstrations were [held] in several towns and properties were destroyed. Damages amounted to more than 20 million [lei]. Jewish travelers were attacked in trains; Jews were chased out of cafés, restaurants, and theaters, and followed through the streets; Jewish students were attacked in schools, undergraduates were attacked in universities, synagogues were profaned." *Jewish Minority in Romania*, 5.

5. Ibid., 1927, 12, 14.

6. Eugen Weber, *Varieties of Fascism* (New York: Van Nostrand Reinhold), 517.

7. Nicholas M. Nagy-Talavera, "The Green Shirts and Others," *East European Quarterly* (1973): 253.

8. The newspaper *Carpati*, the official organ of Cuza's party, wrote on January 24, 1927: "Kill! The Jews had taken the offensive all over the country, destroying its riches and undermining the state. The government remained silent!... Our national prestige is urgently calling on us to deal a mortal blow against anybody trying to destroy our people and our country.... I repeat: to kill the enemy of our country is not a crime! It is the greatest honour of a Romanian. Kill them!" In the city of Buzeu, in a manifesto circulated in January 1927, one read: "Christian brothers. The country is in danger! The Christians are threatened to be under the control of the Kikes.... What are you waiting for? Until further instructions we must start the economic boycott today.... Remember: all of those who buy from or sell to the Jews will be declared enemies of the Romanian nation" *Jewish Minority in Romania*, 28, 29.

9. W. Filderman, *Adevărul asupra problemei evreieşti în România* (Bucharest: Triumful Printing Co., 1925), 2. In connection with these events, Filderman wrote: "Two years have passed since their organizations were founded by the same few people: 'The National Christian Union,' 'The League of the Christian National Defense,' 'The Christian Democratic National Party'...for three organizations that had the same objectives, and the legal means were: denying the Jews any equality, denying them any rights as human beings or as people; and the para-legal means were: insults, beatings, destroying the Jews and causing bloodshed." In 1925, other less important rightist groups, such as Fascia Nationala Romana and Actiunea Romaneasca, were organized in Cluj by students and professors who joined Cuza's party. Within the organization in Cluj, Ion Mota carried out his activity, later becoming the closest collaborator of Corneliu Zelea Codreanu.

10. Ibid., 11.

11. *Jewish Minority in Romania*, 42.

12. Ibid., 43.

13. Ibid., 42.

14. Ibid., 44.

15. Ibid.

16. Ibid., 46.

17. Ibid., 42: "On Yom Kippur in 1927 the Jews in a synagogue in Piatra Neamt were surprised in the midst of the prayers by the breaking of windows. One of them went out and found a group of three students who were continuing to throw stones at the windows of the synagogue. A clash took place, and eighteen Jews, merchants and prominent community leaders, were arrested. [Despite] statements by eye-witnesses in favor of the defendants, the judge rejected the evidence from the files and sentenced two of the Jews arrested to six months in jail, three of them to one year in jail, and the other twelve Jews to two years in jail. One was acquitted. Besides this, they were sentenced jointly to pay the three hooligans damages to the amount of 4 million lei."

18. Ibid., 55.

19. Ibid., 53.

20. Ibid., 14.

21. Henry L. Roberts, *Romania: Political Problems of an Agrarian State* (New Haven: Yale University Press, 1951), 292.

22. Ibid., Nagy-Talavera, 273.

23. Ibid., 282.

24. Ibid., 285.

25. Horia Sima, *Histoire du mouvement légionaire* (Rio de Janeiro: Dacia, 1967), 276.

26. Dinu Zamfirescu, *Punte de vedere* (Paris, 1980), 4.

27. Ibid.

28. Ibid., 1.

29. Ibid., 2.

30. Gala Galaction, a prestigious Romanian writer, was known for deep humanism, because of which he was a constant friend of the Jews of Romania. An admirer of Theodor Herzl, whom he compared to a biblical prophet, he wrote pro-Zionist articles that gave witness not only of his high moral rectitude but

also his great courage and civic dignity. His translation of the Bible, made jointly with Vasile Radu, had extraordinary influence on Romanian readers. Throughout the period of the Legionaries and Antonescu's dictatorship, Galaction constantly maintained a warm relationship with the Jews.

31. Zamfirescu, 2.

32. Bela Vago, *In the Shadow of the Swastika* (Saxon House), 218.

33. Ibid., 27.

34. Ibid., 37.

35. *Pe Marginea Prăpastiei*, (On the Brink of the Precipice [or Abyss]) 2 vols. (Bucharest, 1942), 1:34.

36. Vago, 272.

37. Ibid.

38. Grigore Gafencu, *Prelude to the Russian Campaign* (London: Frederik Muller, 1943), 228: "The Iron Guard intends to base its policy on that of the Axis, and as soon as it reaches power it will change Romanian foreign policy and will create a tight alliance with Germany and Italy. By this declaration, Codreanu becomes Hitler's associate inside Romania. Berlin knew that it could count on him. Codreanu, on his part, has learned for sure that he can count on Berlin."

39. Nagy-Talavera, 298.

40. Ibid. The accusation led to no convincing proof of Codreanu's direct responsibility. There is no evidence at all of any links with a "foreign power." The liaison with the Nazis appears to have been made by Goga-Cuza's party, and even Gheorghe Bratianu's fascist and neo-liberal wing, rather than by the Legion.

41. Zamfirescu, 4. In spite of all this there is something significant in a telegram sent to the Ministry of Foreign Affairs in Berlin by Fabricius, the German Ambassador in Romania: "The prosecutor has let it be known that he will use against Codreanu a document which is the rough draft of a letter which the accused Codreanu addressed to the [Führer] office at the begining of 1935, in which he announced that he was going to bring about a revolution in Romania, on the National-Socialist model, and that he was asking for help from Germany. ... Codreanu asked for help and instructions from Germany and proposed a political and economical alliance with Germany."

42. Raoul Hilberg, *The Destruction of the European Jews* (Chicago: Quadrangle Books, 1961), 270.

43. Nagy-Talavera, 300. The representative of the Reich in charge of the economic problems between these countries explained very clearly Germany's point of view regarding the very volatile situation in Romania: "We have one single purpose, and that is to maintain order in the region where there are raw materials. We don't want to Germanize Romania or to make it fascist. Any government that will have the power and authority to maintain such order in this region of raw materials can do so (counting on Germany's support)."

44. Hilberg, 301.

45. Gafencu, 228: Carol ordered the assassination of Codreanu in line with a method belonging to the New Order. "He [Codreanu] was executed just as Roehm was done away with in Germany, and he himself [Codreanu] would have

done the same, without doubt, to suppress his adversaries if he had the time and capability for doing so."

46. Ibid., 229.

47. Weber, 556.

48. Gafencu, 195.

CHAPTER 3

1. In the elections for which the best data are available, that is, among the few in which legality was observed, due to a coalition between the Peasant party and the Legionaries, the voters gave the Legionary movement 478,378 votes; Goga-Cuza's National Christian Party received 281,617; and the Neo-Liberal party led by Gheorghe Bratianu got 119,361 votes. Their total vote was 879,906, with 121 deputies elected in Parliament.

2. *Pe Marginea Prăpastiei*, 1:111.

3. Ibid., 1:82: "Even the Army was not spared. Using nationalist ideas as an incentive, it recruited sympathizers, either by direct contact, or indirectly (through wives, children, or relatives). Attention was directed particularly to young officers and students in the military schools. The presence of Legionaries in the ranks of the Army as reserve officers and troops made it easy to convert many young officers and NCO's on active duty and get them to join the Legionary movement. There were also some confused senior officers who went so far [as] to ask for the dismissal from the Army of those who held to the strict line of military training and did not sympathize with the Legion."

4. Ibid., 1:5: "The approval given by Horia Sima for reorganization of the Legionary Workers' Corps to be accomplished under the command of Groza, a notoriously militant communist, is a symptomatic thing. The enlistments in the Corps are massive. Workers that have been adherents to the Socialist or democratic parties are being received, organized into cells, and given instruction and training."

5. Minister of the Interior in the Groza-Cuza government.

6. Vago, 288.

7. Ibid., 299.

8. *Pe Marginea Prăpastiei*, 1:63.

9. On September 13, 1940, the General Association of Romanian Engineers (AGIR) expelled all Jewish engineers from its ranks, denying them the right to practice their profession. Journalists, writers, architects, and sporting personalities followed them as in a dark chain. Even the butchers in the capital decided that Jewish butchers could no longer slaughter cattle at the abattoir or sell meat in the nearby market squares. These were just a few steps taken under so-called laws to "purge" the nation.

10. Matatias Carp, *Cartea Neagră. Suferinţele Evreilor din România. 1940–1944*, Vol. 1, *Legionarii şi Rebeliune* a (Bucharest: Atelierele Grafice Socec & Co., 1946), 59.

11. After I. G. Duca was assassinated, the presiding judge of the full court that tried and acquitted Corneliu Zelea Codreanu was General Petrovicescu. In the first government formed by Antonescu, he was named Minister of the Interior.

12. The following properties were confiscated without any compensation: 42,320 hectares of prime land; 68,644 hectares of forest; 2,062 hectares of vineyards; 78 lakes and ponds; 265 mills; 115 timber industry plants; 152 shipping vessels; 40,758 pieces of real estate. All these properties were confiscated complete with their entire inventory and personal property, including the entire standing crop. The properties that were plundered in Bucovina and Bessarabia are not included in these figures; in those areas, in addition to these categories, all commercial and industrial enterprises were confiscated. The value of these properties has never been estimated exactly, but a statistical analysis published in *Commerce and Industry* in October 1943 speaks of a figure of 70,687,849,734 lei. To this should be added the fact that in the governmental budget for the years 1941–1944, the income alone obtained from these expropriated properties amounted to 10,525,000,000 lei. All of this was further increased by a series of "contributions" that the Jewish population was obliged to make: the Reintegration Loan, the Sanitary Equipment Fund, the Veterans Home, clothing taxes for exemption from forced labor, military taxes, and others, amounting to 21,258,073,565 lei in the years 1941–1944. In April 1943 a special "contribution" of 4 billion lei was imposed on the Jews, of which 734,156,308 lei was collected.

13. Carp, *Cartea Neagrǎ*, 1:150.

14. Nagy-Talavera, 32.

15. *Pe Marginea Prǎpastiei*, 1:139.

16. Ibid., 1:140.

17. Ibid., 1:142. In the months after the Legionaries came to power, some 1,109 professors were absent from their classrooms, missing 2,130 hours of classes; 8,976 students in the advanced courses missed 97,902 hours. This came as a result of taking part in various Legionary activities.

18. Nagy-Talavera, 323.

19. Ibid., 323, 324.

20. Ibid., 325.

21. *Pe Marginea Prǎpastiei*, 1:17.

22. Ibid., 1:21.

23. Ibid., 1:17.

24. Nagy-Talavera, 326.

25. Carp, *Cartea Neagrǎ*, 1:229, 230.

26. Ibid., 1:232.

27. Nagy-Talavera, 327.

28. Matatias Carp, *Cartea Neagrǎ*, Vol. 2, *Pogromul de la Iasi* (Bucharest: Societatea Naţionalǎ de Editurǎ Dacia-Traianǎ, 1946), 24.

29. Ibid., 2:39.

30. Ibid., 2:20.

31. Ibid., 2:9.

32. At this time, Curzio Malaparte, an Italian journalist, was in Iasi as correspondent of *Corriere della Sera* of Milan. In a volume of memoirs entitled *Kaput* (Florence: Valleccki Editore, 1966), he gave an evocative description of Iasi before the pogrom and the atmosphere of terror and panic that enveloped the Jewish population. What he saw later during the pogrom constitutes unusually valuable testimony for evaluating the crimes that were perpetrated: "There were groups of Jews in the streets followed by soldiers and inhabitants of the city

armed with sticks and iron bars, and groups of gendarmes were firing weapons into the doors and windows of the Jewish houses." Continuing the description of the horrors he saw, the Italian journalist relates the following: "I looked out of the window [of the Italian Consulate] on Lapusneanu street. The street was covered with human bodies. . . . Packs of dogs ran up to the cadavres, and were feeding on the meat, and groups of Jews guarded by gendarmes and soldiers armed with guns were watching over them, seeking to separate the corpses and put them at the edge of the streets so that the German soldiers marching on foot and motorized vehicles could move about without hindrance" (128, 129).

33. Ibid., 30.

34. Ibid., 140. When the Death Train reached the station at Calarasi, its destination, it was stated in a protocol drawn between Aurel Triandaf, the train commander, and the local authorities, that "of the Jews coming from Iasi, 1,011 (one thousand eleven) living Jews; 69 (sixty-nine) moribund Jews, and 25 (twenty-five) dead were unloaded from the train."

35. Marius Mircu, *Pogromul de la Iaşi* (Bucharest: Editura Glob, 1947), 84 (hereafter cited as *Iasi*).

36. Ibid., 98.

37. Ibid., 99.

38. Malaparte, 133, 134.

39. Carp, :43. By a decree issued on August 1, 1941, labor camps were organized on a strictly military pattern. Even before this date, General Ion Antonescu had given direct orders in this sense which had a special character. Thus it was clearly specified by Order No. 5811 of July 18, 1941, that "General Ion Antonescu, the Leader of the State, has formally ordered that all Jews that are in the labor camps and all prisoners be put to hard labor. If anyone escapes, one in every ten will be shot. If anyone does not work when asked, he will [not be] given anything to eat, nor will [he be] allowed to obtain or buy anything. Take measures to enforce this. (Signed) The Minister and Under Secretary of State, Division General, I. Popescu."

40. Ibid., 2:44.

41. Paul Lendvai, *Anti-Semitism Without Jews: Communists in Eastern Europe* (New York: Doubleday, 1971), 74.

42. Matatias Carp, *Cartea Neagră*, Vol. 3, *Transnistria* (Bucharest: Societatea Nationalā de Editurā Dacia-Traianā, 1947), 92.

43. Ibid., 3:91.

44. Ibid., 3:93.

45. Mircu, *Iasi*, 47.

46. Carp, :49. In Report No. 1055 of August 14, 1941, forwarded by the Balti Legion of Gendarmes, the Inspector of the Chisinau Gendarmerie remarked, among other things, that "it has not been proved that Romanian soldiers have pillaged and killed Jews." This fact is significant: the Report of the German XI Army addressed to the Romanian General Staff, entitled "With reference to the excesses of Romanian soldiers and civilians in the occupied territories," states that "in order to avoid similar incidents we request to send strong police forces into the occupied territories."

47. Ibid., 3:55.

48. Ibid., 3:69–71.

49. Malaparte, 285.

50. Ibid., 289.

51. Marius Mircu, *Pogromurile din Basarabia* (Bucharest: Editura Glob, 1947), 16, 17 (hereafter cited as *Basarabia*).

52. Carp, 3:66. The following decision is found in Report No. 121239, dated September 17, 1941, from the Provost Marshal Service to the Commander of the 3rd Army: "September 22, 1941. The question with regard to the shooting of those 200 Jews at the Dniester, which was investigated by General Topor, has been classed as to be filed."

53. Ibid., 3:153. Order No. 219 of that date issued by General C. Calotescu, the governor of Bucovina, states, among other things, that "it has been decided to evacuate the Jewish population of Bucovina (all of Bucovina, not just the liberated territory). For this purpose the Jewish population of the Municipality of Cernauti will first [be] confined to the Ghetto established by the Mayor, and later it will gradually be transferred out of there by rail. The enclosure operation, guarding the Ghetto, and embarkation and transportation to the border points will be the responsibility of this Command and the Cernauti Inspectorate of Geandarmerie."

54. Ibid., 3:158. In order for affairs to be given the best "organization," a regulation was drawn up for the functionaries of the ghetto, which specified, among other things: "(point 4) No one, regardless of title, may enter the Ghetto unless he has written authorization from the Governor.... (point 5) It is forbidden for business to be done in the Ghetto between Jews and Christians, or between Jews and Jews, whoever they be, including exchange or sale of currency, gold or silver coins, objects of precious metals, precious stones, or other articles of value. Those who violate these provisions will be shot."

55. Ibid., 3:172, 173.

56. Marius Mircu, *Pogromurile din Bucovina şi Basarabia* (Bucharest: Editura Glob, 1945) 85 (hereafter cited as *Bucovina*): "Peasant women from the surrounding areas, Romanians from the city and genteel ladies would come into the Ghetto, every kind of intermediaries and 'benefactors' who speculated on the misfortune of the Jews. An overcoat would be given for a salami, silk shirts would be given for a few eggs. The ladies would come into the Ghetto wearing plain used coats and would go out in Astrakhan furs."

57. Carp, :90. The Federation of the Union of Jewish Congregations sent Musat, a Romanian lawyer, to Chisinau with the mission of doing everything within his power to save all those he could from the ghetto and from deportation. On October 30, 1941, he telegraphed in despair to Bucharest: "The case is lost ... Musat, Attorney."

58. Ibid., 3:128.

59. Ibid., 3:180, 181.

60. Ibid., 3:110. One early memorandum, dated August 19, 1941, was forwarded by the leaders of the Jewish community to the Ministry of the Interior, which was informed among other things that "the misery which prevails among them [the Jews interned in the camps in Bucovina and Bessarabia] is destined to kill them all. But it can also become a danger threatening the entire population, insasmuch as such a massing of people can become a focus for generating and

propagating infectious diseases and epidemics. I beg you, please look into sending aid."

61. Ibid.

62. Ibid., 3:112. Colonel Agapie, the commander of the Vertujeni camp, sent to Iasi Petre Gr. Nicolau, a magistrate who had been mobilized into the military unit under his command. At Colonel Agapie's trial, his emissary declared: "At the moment I turned the sum of 300,000 lei over to Lt. Colonel Petrescu, the cashier of the camp, the sum of 50,000 lei was turned over to Lt. Iufu Cretu in the form of a loan, by order of Colonel Agapie. If Colonel Agapie had good intentions with regard to the internees, he would surely have turned this sum over to the Jewish committee which existed in the camp, a committee which was, moreover, the only organization with the right to collect funds from the communities of the country for the deported Jews."

63. Ibid., 3:143.

64. Ibid.

65. Ibid., 3:150.

66. Ibid., 3:152.

67. Ibid., 3:175.

68. Ibid., 3:176.

69. Ibid., 3:178.

70. Ibid., 3:183: "Today I received a desperate appeal from the leaders of the Chisinau Ghetto. On the morning of October 8, 1941, 1,500 people departed, mostly on foot, taking with them only what they could carry in their hands, and consequently exposed to death, since they were cold, naked and hungry, without the slightest possibility of getting food. They set out on foot on a trip at least eight days long, through rain, cold, and snow. . . . It is death, death, death without guilt, without any guilt other than that of being Jews. I once [again] implore you, Marshal, not to allow such a tragedy to be consummated."

71. Ibid., 3:184.

72. Ibid., 3:183, 185.

73. Ibid., 3:199.

74. Ibid.

75. Ibid., 3:210, 211.

76. On March 21, 1942, the epidemic of exanthematic typhus reached its peak. Jewish doctors who themselves had been deported tried to put an end to the illness, without any material resources and under unimaginably difficult conditions. They too fell prey to the epidemic: in the month of February alone, twenty-five doctors died in Mogilev, and in Shargorod twenty-three of the twenty-eight doctors who fell sick died. Along the banks of the Bug ravages of exanthematic typhus took unbelievable dimensions. At the town of Bershad 20,000 people died. In the city of Ustea, located five kilometers from the Bug River, 1,600 of the 2,500 deportees died.

77. In the summer of 1942, Order No. 5295 of April 21, 1942, and later Law No. 503 and Instruction No. 55500 of June 27, 1942, which was developed in the spirit of the law, providing for regulation and especially the punishments to be applied to Jews who might infringe the provisions of the law, made a framework within which Jewish slave labor was organized and used. These regulations provided for a whole variety of punishments, beginning with beating,

years of imprisonment, or deportation of the guilty person and his whole family to camps in Transnistria or beyond the Bug.

78. Carp, 3:341. Engineer S. Jaegendorf wrote in a report addressed to the Jewish Centrale in Bucharest, requesting various kinds of material help: "Absolutely nothing was left undamaged, not even a desk, not even a sheet of paper, with which to begin the work required by the circumstances. Moreover, our improvised offices in an empty warehouse have been stormed by a crowd of desperate people who have been asking for moral and material help."

79. Ibid., 3:346. In a report forwarded by S. Jaegendorf to Gingold: "A famished and desperate crowd appears at our windows with their hands outstretched and their last hope is for us to grant some aid. We cannot satisfy them and we must refuse these people who are already beaten down enough.... Mr. President, in the name of life, send us the help we ask, and we can rescue and sustain these young lives. Bear in mind that without this help, these people who have not had the opportunity to live will fall prey to hunger and all the diseases that result from it."

80. Ibid., 3:247. One youth who escaped from the grip of winter saw the sun and wrote: "I am young / and so is May / Outside the sky is calm / warm. / O sun, / the grass sparkled with emeralds / and perfume of lily of the valley." Dora Litani, the Israeli writer, in a sober and interesting work entitled *Transnistria*, noting these verses on May, wrote: "Unfortunately their author, the young poet Isidor Karmil, was shot a month later when he tried to escape from the labor camp."

81. Carp, 3:248, 249.

82. Ibid., 3:251, 252.

83. Ibid., 3:252, 253.

84. Ibid.

85. Ibid., 3:242.

86. Ibid., 3:413.

87. Ibid., 3:415.

88. Ibid., 3:417.

89. Ira Hirshmann, *Life Line to a Promised Land* (New York: Vanguard Press), 55.

90. Ibid., 57.

91. Ibid.

92. Ibid., 58.

93. Ibid.

94. Ibid.

95. In the report concerning the repatriation of the Jews from Transnistria prepared by Dr. W. Filderman and forwarded to the government, a statistical summary was presented based on clear and precise data furnished by the Jewish organizations in Transnistria. "The Bukarester Tageblatt of August 1942 asserts that 185,000 Jews were deported; adding those deported after 8 August 1942 [there] were about 190,000–200,000 deportees.... Today there are only about 78,000 deportees living in Transnistria, so that 122,000 or 61 percent died in the course of two years. (This number of dead in Transnistria does not include

the Jews in that region and the city of Odessa who were killed by the Romanian army and civil administration under well-known circumstances.)

96. Carp, 3:457.
97. Ibid., 3:459.
98. Ibid., 3:307.
99. Ibid., 3:310.
100. Ibid., 3:66.
101. Mircu, 5.
102. Ibid., 10.
103. Ibid., 31, 36.
104. Ibid., 69.
105. Carp, 2:96.
106. Ibid.
107. Ibid., 3:148.
108. Ibid., 3:128.
109. Ibid.
110. Matatias Carp, *Sărmas—una din cele mai oribile crime fasciste* (Sarmas—One of the Most Horrible Fascist Crimes) (Bucharest: Atelierele Grafice Socec & Co., 1945), 32 (hereafter cited as *Sarmas*).
111. Ibid., 38. The statement by Dr. Emil Mora, the Romanian doctor, is significant: "On September 8, 1944, I was arrested by the National Guard of Hungarian Gendarmes and afterwards I was taken to the concentration camp which was at the house of Ion Pop, the construction foreman in the commune of Sarmas. In the camp I found, among others, Sirbu, the police inspector, Mornaila, the notary, Vasile Ban the lawyer, Persa the health worker, Dogaru, the landowner and many other Romanian prisoners of war, among them a lieutenant. Two days later all Jews in Sarmas, 126 in number, were brought into the camp.... The Jewish internees to whom food was brought were treated better at the beginning, but then, like us, they were stripped of all their money and articles of value. After some days the men were put to work at forced labor (digging graves, trenches, hauling war materials). In the morning we were made to dance the hora, and hop like frogs, and other such mockeries. On the night of September 12–13, two girls, Baira Vais (Weiss) and Vera Hasz, were forcibly hauled away from their parents by four Gendarmes [and] were taken out into the garden of the camp and were raped all night long by four Hungarian guards on duty at that particular camp. In the morning the Gendarmes came in to see us, to provoke us, mocking us by saying we should come and rape the girls."
112. Ibid., 41.
113. Ibid.
114. This book was published on the initiative of Dr. Alexander Safran, the Chief Rabbi, supported by the energetic efforts of Dr. W. Filderman and the spirit of understanding of human pain of Lucretiu Patrascanu, the Minster of Justice, and Attorney I. Staier, the General Secretary of the Ministry of the Interior.
115. Carp, *Sarmas*, 18.
116. Ibid., 19.

117. Ibid., 7.
118. Ibid.

CHAPTER 4

1. For example, paragraph 5 of this decree established some rights, while another passage in the same paragraph limited them or plainly annulled them. After providing that all properties formerly belonging to Jews which at that date were the property of the state or a private individual were to be restored to their old owners, without any other legal disposition being necessary, farther on it stipulated that Jews could not reenter into possession of their properties if these were now occupied by new owners on the date of Romanization. War orphans, war widows, civil servants, and people without any income were exempted from making total restitution of these properties.

2. This state of affairs meant that the city of Bucharest in the years after the war had a population of one hundred fifty thousand as against approximately eighty-five thousand before the war.

3. Of the more than four hundred thousand Jews in Romania, more than sixty thousand were children; among these, according to the estimates and findings of the JDC, about forty thousand were in urgent need of help. Up to the end of 1947, 164 homes for old people and orphanages for twenty-one thousand children were opened, among other institutions. Some three thousand two hundred of the children were in need of special medical care due to the living conditions in the camps from which they came. At the end of 1947, according to data from the Medical Department of the JDC, three hundred forty thousand people among the entire Jewish population of Romania needed public assistance, and medical attention in particular. Among these, 60 percent had been in labor camps and ghettoes, especially in Transnistria. When they returned they were suffering from a number of diseases and had no ability to pay for medical care. Because they lacked shelter and the right to work, many were suffering from tuberculosis or serious nervous depression.

4. Zamfirescu, 8. Furthermore, the activity of the Legionaries after the war was public and visible. On August 31, that is, only a week after the overthrow of the Antonescu government, *Dreptatea* (Justice), the official newspaper of the National Peasant party (PNT), published an appeal, dated August 26, 1944, by Horatiu Comaniciu, the commander of the Legionary movement, which stated, among other things: "We recognize the changes that have taken place, and we are aware that in view of the changes we cannot remain indifferent. Therefore, we are responding to the call of the king and the government by saying: to our post of duty!" In the same issue of the paper, Iuliu Maniu, the president of the PNT, wrote: "To my great joy, your statement gave proof that you feel determined to participate with complete sincerity in the constructive effort to which the nation has been called."

5. Emil Dorian, *The Quality of Witness: A Romanian Diary 1937–1944* (Jewish Publication Society of America, 1982), 349.

6. Zamfirescu, 32.

7. Ibid.

8. Ibid.: Nicolae Penescu, the nominee for General-Secretary of the party

(PNT), wrote in his work entitled *The Will of Iuliu Maniu*: "On December 4, 1944 [the actual date was November 4, 1944] the second Sanatescu government was formed, in which I was Minister of Interior. One of the first measures that I took was to free the Legionaries.... I ordered the freeing of the Legionaries throughout the country.... Within a day, Manu, a university professor, asked for a meeting with me at which Nicolae Patrascu, the Secretary General of the Legionary movement, would be present. He had clandestinely returned to the country (although he had been condemned to death for failing to appear in court after being charged with organizing the Legionary rebellion in 1941). I saw these two Legionaries.... Patrascu asked for a collaboration between the Legionary movement and the PNT.... I told him that this collaboration already existed.... I communicated this proposal to Maniu. He replied to me: "We have collaborated with the Legionary movement since 1942, but we will not collaborate with those Legionaries responsible for what occurred in 1941–1942 and those who participated in the so-called Vienna government."

9. *Pe Marginea Prăpastiei*, 2: 113–14. These ties were older. In this connection, the remarks in this work are significant: "On December 16, 1940, the former prefect of Romanati County, Liber Tirnoveanu, accompanied by the Press and Propaganda Director of the Legion, a young fellow named Stroe, visited the Caracal internment camp, with the approval of the Ministry of the Interior. There, the Communist leaders, Constantinescu-Iasi, Mihai Bujor, and Ilie Cristea, were introduced to them, and they talked in the presence of Captain Iordachescu, the deputy commander of the camp. The discussion which followed principally led by young Stroe, was on Legionary and Communist ideology. It was pointed out that both were similar, the unique difference being that the Communist movement was based on atheism. There would be a time when the Communist movement would change views, because [Stroe understood] the Legionaries would mobilize their whole intellectual capacities and unite, especially since more than twenty thousand workers in the Grivita, STB, and Malaxa plants had gone over to their side."

10. Gita Ionescu, *Communism in Romania* (London: G. P. Putnam's Sons, 1985), 114.

11. In 1947 more than eight thousand persons received such training, especially in agriculture, and more than one thousand young students participated in ORT (organization for youngster qualification schools). Likewise, more than seven thousand well-prepared young people able to begin a new life in Palestine came, of those one hundred thirty hakhsharot (training place for agricultural skills).

12. Nicolas Sylvain, "Romania," Chap. 5 in *The Jews in the Soviet Satellites*, 526. Such ideas were also expressed plainly by Ion Mihalache (a leader of the PNT), who stated in a tendentious, aggressive manner, in a meeting about the presence of Jews in the governmental apparatus, as equivalent to a way to eliminate Romanians, that he considered their presence a "direct provocation."

13. Ana Pauker's brother, who had settled in Israel, spoke, in an interview granted to a British newspaper, about his sister's attitude and her persecutions of the Jews.

14. Sylvain, 527.

15. The great majority of these enterprises were in reality the property of

Jews, which the Germans had seized from them during the Legionary and Antonescu leadership.

16. Ionescu, 138: "While the amount of money in circulation at the end of 1938 was 43.9 billion lei, it was 211.8 billion in June 1944, and on August 14, 1944, it was 48,451 billion. While the cost of living index in August 1944 was 944 (against 100 in 1939), in April 1947 it was 440,869, and in July 1947 it was 525,688. Gross industrial production had fallen to one-third of what it was in 1944."

17. In the summer of 1947, the Jewish Telegraph Agency in Bucharest announced that in that period 150,000 persons had been registered and were ready to leave for Palestine, in comparison with 75,000 persons in the year 1944.

18. The general attitude of the party towards the intellectuals was one of rejection and lack of interest. Gheorghe Gheorghiu-Dej himself looked on them as so many luxury "objects," which the party could use but did not consider necessary. The presence of some intellectuals from the older generation in the party, or as fellow travelers with it, was not enough to demonstrate the attachment of the Romanian intelligentsia to the regime.

19. Ionescu, 180.

20. In the great operation of checking up on the members of the party, which took place in 1949, about 192,000 members were expelled. They were considered "elements foreign to the working class, people who were corrupt from the moral point of view, fascists . . . careerists, bourgeois nationalists, exploiters."

21. Sylvain, 543.

22. In the town of Radauti, for example, there were twenty-three synagogues at the beginning of the war, which later were converted into stores and warehouses; there were no longer any Jews! From the 157 holy scrolls left in the keeping of a man named Kuczinsky, regiments in transit made drums, and shoemakers made lining for light shoes. In the village of Turcoaia in Macin County, the fishermen wrapped their legs in the parchment of Torahs before going into the waters of the Danube.

Bibliography

REFERENCES

Breviarul Statistic al Populaţiei Evreiesti din România. Bucharest: Centrala Evreilor din România, 1943.

Encyclopedia Judaica. Jerusalem: Keter Publishing House, 1971.

The Jewish Encyclopedia. London: Funk and Wagnalls, 1905.

The Jewish Minority in Romania. Correspondence with the Romanian Government. London: Joint Foreign Committee, 1927.

Limite. Paris, September 24–25, 1977.

Notice sur la Roumanie en 1900. Paris: L'Agence Officielle Roumanie, 1900.

Pe Marginea Prăpastiei. 2 vols. Bucharest, 1942.

Arendt, Hannah. *Eichmann in Jerusalem.* New York: Viking Press, 1963.

————. *The Origins of Totalitarianism.* New York: Harcourt, Brace and World, 1966.

Bernstein, Perez F. *Jews: Hate as a Sociological Problem.* New York: Philosophical Library, 1951.

Bluntschli, Johan Kaspar. *Roumania and the Legal Status of Jews in Roumania.* Anglo-Jewish Assn. London, 1879.

Bobango, Gerald J. "The Emergence of the Roumanian National State." *East European Quarterly,* 1979.

Brănişteanu, B. "Prefaţă" (Preface) to Matatias Carp, *Sărmaş—una din cele mai oribile crime fasciste.* Bucharest: Atelierele Grafice Socec & Co., 1945.

Brociner, Andrei. *File Culese, 1876–1930.* Bucharest: Atelierele Grafice Răsăritul, 1930.

Brociner, J. B. *Die Judenfrage in Rumanien, und iher Lösung.* Vienna: Buchdruckerei von Georg Brög, 1879.

————. *Chestiunea Israeliţilor Români.* Bucharest: Tipografia Horia Carp & Marinescu, 1910.

Călinescu, George. *Istoria Literaturii Române de la Origini pînă în Prezent*. Bucharest: Editura Minerva, 1982.

Caraion, Ion. *Insectele Tovarăşului Hitler*. Ion Dumitru-Verlag, 1982.

Carp, Matatias. *Sărmaş—una din cele mai oribile crime fasciste*. Bucharest: Atelierele Grafice Socec & Co., 1945.

———. *Cartea Neagră. Suferinţele Evreilor din România. 1940–1944*. Vol. 1, *Legionarii şi Rebeliunea*. Bucharest: Atelierele Grafice Socec & Co., 1946.

———. *Cartea Neagră*. Vol. 2, *Pogromul de la Iasi*. Bucharest: Societatea Naţională de Editură Dacia-Traiană, 1946.

———. *Cartea Neagră*. Vol. 3, *Transnistria*. Bucharest: Societatea Naţională de Editură Dacia-Traiană, 1947.

Cuza, A. C. *Jidanii în Război*. Bucharest: Institutul Grafic Steaua, 1923.

Dorian, Emil. *The Quality of Witness: A Romanian Diary 1937–1944*. Philadelphia Jewish Publication Society of America, 1982.

Eidelberg, Philip Gabriel. *The Great Rumanian Revolt of 1907*. Leiden: E. J. Brill, 1974.

Eminescu, Mihai. *Articole de Politică Românească*. Iaşi: Editura Athanase Gheorghiu, 1941.

Fătu, Mihai, and Ion Spălăţelu. "Garda de Fier-organizaţie teroristă de tip fascist." Editura Politică, ed. II-a 1980.

Filderman, W. *Adevărul asupra problemei evreieşti în România*. Bucharest: Tipografia Triumful, 1925.

Fischer, I. *Transnistria: The Forgotten Cemetery*. 1969.

Gafencu, Grigore. *Prelude to the Russian Campaign*. London: Frederick Muller, 1943.

Hâciu, Anastasie. *Evreii în Tările Româneşti*. Bucharest: Editura Cartea Românească, 1943.

Hilberg, Raoul. *The Destruction of the European Jews*. Chicago: Quadrangle Books, 1961.

Hilgruber, Andreas. *Hitler, Köning Carol und Marshal Antonescu. Die Deutsch-Romanischen Beziehungen, 1938–1944*. Mainz: Institute für Europäische Gesichte.

Hirschmann, Ira A. *Life Line to a Promised Land*. New York: Vanguard Press.

Ionescu, Ghţă. *Communism in Rumania*. London: G. P. Putnam's Sons, 1985.

Lendvai, Paul. *Eagles in Cobwebs*. New York: Doubleday, 1969.

———. *Anti-Semitism Without Jews: Communists in Eastern Europe*. New York: Doubleday, 1971.

Levai, Eugene. *Black Book of Martyrdom of Hungarian Jewry*. Zurich: Central European Times, 1948.

Litani, Dora. *Transnistria*. Jaffa: Typo-Studio Ijak, 1981.

Malaparte, Curzio. *Kaput*. Florence: Valleccki Editore, 1966.

Marcus, Israel. *Sapte Momente*. Editura Glob, 1945.

Mircu, Marius. *Pogromurile din Bucovina şi Dorohoi*. Bucharest: Editura Glob, 1945.

———. *Pogromurile din Basarabia*. Bucharest: Editura Glob, 1947.

———. *Pogromul de la Iaşi*. Bucharest: Editura Glob, 1947.

Mitrani, David. *The Land and the Peasant in Romania: The war and Agrarian Reform (1917–1921)*. London: Oxford University Press, 1930.

Nagy-Talavera, Nicholas M. *The Green Shirts and the Others: A History of Fascism in Hungary and Romania*. Stanford: Hoover Institution Press, 1970.

Oldson, William O. "The Historic and Nationalistic Thought of Nicolae Iorga." *East European Quarterly* (1973).

Patai, Raphael. *The Vanished Worlds of Jewry*. New York: Macmillan, 1980.

Pavel, Pavel. *Why Rumania Failed*. London: Alliance Press.

Preda, Marin. *Delirul*. Bucharest: Cartea Românească, 1975.

Reitlinger, Gerald. *The Final Solution*. New York: A. S. Barnes, 1968.

Roberts, Henry L. *Rumania: Political Problems of an Agrarian State*. New Haven: Yale University Press, 1951.

Rogers, Hans, and Eugen Weber. *The European Right*. Stanford: University of California Press, 1965.

Safran, Alexandru. "Prefață" (Preface) to Matatias Carp, *Cartea Neagra*, Vol. 1 (Bucharest: Atelierele Grafice Socec & Co., 1946).

———. "Religious Persecution in Romania," *Jewish Monthly* 2, no. 8 (November 1948).

———. "L'Oeuvre de sauvetage de la population juive...en Roumanie. "Les Juifs en Roumanie", "Les Juifs en Europe" 1939–1945, Paris: Edition du Centre, 1949.

———. *Resisting the Storm: Romania 1940–1945*. Jerusalem: Paris Yad Vashem, 1987.

St. John, Robert. *Foreign Correspondent*. Garden City, N.Y.: Doubleday, 1957.

Sartre, Jean-Paul. *Réflexions sur la question Juive*. Paris: Gallimard, 1954.

Schwartzfeld, E. *Adevărul asupra revoltei de la Brusturoasa*. Bucharest: Tipografia Stefan Mihailescu, 1885.

Seicaru, Pamfil. *Un Junimist Antisemit: A. C. Cuza*. Madrid: Editura Carpați, 1956.

Seton-Watson, Hugh. *The East European Revolution*. New York: Praeger, 1945.

———. *Eastern Europe Between the Wars, 1918–1941*. Hamden, Conn.: Archon Books, 1962.

Sima, Horia. *Histoire du mouvement légionaire*. Rio de Janeiro: Editura Dacia, 1967.

Sincerus, E. *Les Juifs dans la Roumanie*. London: Macmillan, 1901.

Stavrianos, L. S. *The Balkans since 1453*. New York: Holt, Rinehart and Winston, 1958.

Steuerman-Rodion, A. *Frontul Roșu: sonete postume*. Iași: Institutul de Arte Grafice Cartea Românească, 1920.

Ussoskin, Moshe. *Struggle for Survival: A History of Jewish Credit Cooperatives*. Jerusalem: Academic Press, 1975.

Vago, Bela. *In the Shadow of the Swastika: The Rise of Fascism and Anti-Semitism in the Danubian Basin, 1936–1939*. Saxon House, 1975.

Verax. *Roumania and the Jews*. Bucharest: I. V. Socecu, 1904.

Vago, Bela, and George L. Mosse. *Jews and Non-Jews in Eastern Europe, 1918–1945*. Jerusalem: Israel University Press, 1975.

Voledi-Vardi, I. *Baricade: Cei de la Onescu*. Tel Aviv: 1984.

Weber, Eugen. *Varieties of Fascism*. New York: Van Nostrand Reinhold, 1964.

Zamfirescu, Dinu. *Puncte de reper*. Paris: 1980.

Name Index

Place Index

ABOUT THE AUTHOR

ION C. BUTNARU was in a Romanian labor camp during the Holocaust. After the war, he was a writer and a member of the Society of Romanian Writers. Forbidden to write freely on political issues, he immigrated to the United States in 1976. He lectured on the Holocaust and the arts at Boston University. He is the author of five earlier books.